Michigan

ADVENTURES IN TIME AND PLACE

OUR STATE SEAL IS IN THE CENTER OF OUR STATE FLAG. THE MOTTO AND BALD EAGLE AT THE TOP OF THE SEAL REPRESENT THE UNITED STATES. THE ELK, MOOSE, AND SHIELD IN THE CENTER STAND FOR MICHIGAN AND ITS ABUNDANCE. THE LATIN WORD ON THE SHIELD PROUDLY ANNOUNCES "I WILL DEFEND." THE TWO LINES IN THE LATIN BELOW THE SHIELD MEAN "IF YOU ARE SEEKING A PLEASANT PENINSULA, LOOK AROUND YOU."

Author
Dr. Joellen McNergney Vinyard
Professor of History
Eastern Michigan University

Senior Consultants
Dr. Norman McRae
Former Director of Fine Arts and Social Studies
Detroit Public Schools

Mel Miller
Social Studies Consultant
Macomb Intermediate School District

NATIONAL GEOGRAPHIC SOCIETY

THE PRINCETON REVIEW

 McGraw-Hill School Division

New York · · · Farmington

AUTHOR

JoEllen McNergney Vinyard is a Professor of History at Eastern Michigan University, where she teaches courses in Michigan History and United States History. Dr. Vinyard is also a member of the board of the Historical Society of Michigan and has written many articles about the state. She lives with her family near Detroit, Michigan.

SENIOR CONSULTANT

Norman McRae is the author of numerous books and articles including "Negroes in Michigan During the Civil War" and "Early Blacks in Michigan 1743-1800." He has served as an elementary school teacher, social studies supervisor, and more recently as Director of Fine Arts and Social Studies for the Detroit Public Schools.

Mel Miller is the Social Studies Consultant for the Macomb Intermediate School District. He also teaches at Wayne State and Saginaw Valley State universities. In 1980-1981 he was Michigan Teacher of the year. He is a member of the Michigan Council for the Social Studies Executive Board and is a past president of the National Social Studies Supervisors Association.

PROGRAM AUTHORS

Dr. James A. Banks
Professor of Education and
  Director of the Center for
  Multicultural Education
University of Washington,
Seattle, Washington

Dr. Barry K. Beyer
Professor Emeritus, Graduate
  School of Education
George Mason University
Fairfax, Virginia

Dr. Gloria Contreras
Professor of Education
University of North Texas
Denton, Texas

Jean Craven
District Coordinator of Curriculum
  Development
Albuquerque Public Schools
Albuquerque, New Mexico

Dr. Gloria Ladson-Billings
Professor of Education
University of Wisconsin
Madison, Wisconsin

Dr. Mary A. McFarland
Instructional Coordinator of Social
  Studies, K-12, and Director of
  Staff Development
Parkway School District
Chesterfield, Missouri

Dr. Walter C. Parker
Professor and Program Chair for
  Social Studies Education
University of Washington
Seattle, Washington

NATIONAL
GEOGRAPHIC
SOCIETY
Washington, D.C.

CONTENT CONSULTANTS

Francis X. Blouin, Jr.
Professor of History
University of Michigan
Ann Arbor, Michigan

Dr. Philip P. Mason
Professor of History
Wayne State University
Detroit, Michigan

Dr. Roger L. Rosentreter
Bureau of History
Michigan Department of State
Lansing, Michigan

GRADE-LEVEL CONSULTANTS

Christina Campbell
Fourth Grade Teacher
Onekama Consolidated School
Onekama, Michigan

Yvonne Cofer
Fourth Grade Teacher
Brewer Elementary School
Detroit, Michigan

Mary Dunn
Fourth Grade Teacher
Franks Elementary School
Lansing, Michigan

JoAnn Potvin
Fourth Grade Teacher
Fisher Elementary School
Marquette, Michigan

Lucy Suchecki
Fourth/Fifth Grade Teacher
Graham Elementary School
Mt. Clemens, Michigan

CONTRIBUTING WRITERS

Joan W. Blos
Dr. Norman McRae
Tom Pohrt

CONSULTANTS FOR TEST PREPARATION

THE PRINCETON REVIEW
The Princeton Review is not affiliated with Princeton University or ETS.

ACKNOWLEDGMENTS

The publisher gratefully acknowledges permission to reprint the following copyrighted material: "Michigan, My Michigan," by W. Otto Miessner and Douglas Malloch. Copyright © 1911 by W. Otto Miessner. Excerpts from MICHIGAN VOICES, compiled and edited by Joe Grimm. Copyright © 1987 by Wayne State University Press. Lines from "Big Two-Hearted River" are reprinted by permission of Charles Scribner's Sons, an imprint of Macmillan Publishing Company from IN OUR TIME by Ernest Hemingway. Copyright 1925 by Charles Scribner's Sons; copyright renewal 1953 by Ernest Hemingway. Excerpt from SLEEPING BEAR, by George Weeks. Copyright 1988 by George Weeks. Excerpt from BOOM COPPER, by Angus Murdoch. Copyright © 1964 by Dier and Koepel. Excerpt from the Orlando Carpenter Diary. University of Michigan Library. Excerpts from WORKING DETROIT, by Steve Babson et al. Copyright © 1986 by Wayne State University Press. Excerpts from UP COUNTRY, compiled and edited by William Joseph Seno. Copyright © 1989 by William Joseph Seno. Excerpt from "Follow the Drinkin' Gourd," words and music by Paul Campbell. Copyright © 1951 by Folkways Music Publishers, Inc. Excerpts from the *Detroit Free Press*, January 4, 1988 and October 1979. Excerpt from *Jewish News*, August 25, 1989. Excerpt from MINNIE'S IN THE MONEY by Leo Robbin and Harry Warren. © 1943 WB Music Corp. (Renewed) All Rights Reserved. Used by permission. Excerpt from THE TRUMPET OF CONSCIENCE, by Martin Luther King, Jr. Copyright © 1978 by Harper and Row. Excerpt from RESPECT Words and Music by Otis Redding. © 1963 and 1967 Irving Music, Inc. (BMI) All Rights Reserved International Copyright secured. Other sources consulted: MICHIGAN A HISTORY OF THE WOLVERINE STATE, by Willis F. Dunbar and George S. May. Copyright © 1980 by William D. Eerdmans Publishing Company. FORGING THE PENINSULAS, by David B. McConnell. Copyright © 1989 Hillsdale Educational Publishers, Inc.

McGraw-Hill School Division

A Division of The McGraw·Hill Companies

McGraw-Hill School Division
Two Penn Plaza
New York, New York 10121

Printed in the United States of America

ISBN 0-02-149196-8

1 2 3 4 5 6 7 8 9 027 04 03 02 01 00

Handbook for Reading Social Studies

One important thing you will do this year is to read this textbook. In order to understand important facts and ideas it is necessary to read in a certain way. This Reading Handbook will show you some helpful ways to read Social Studies.

Main Idea and Supporting Details

As you read, look for the **main idea** and **supporting details**. The main idea is what a paragraph or section is mostly about. The details support or expand the main idea. Keeping track of the main idea and details will help you remember what you read.

- The first sentence or two of a paragraph often—but not always—contains the main idea.

- Use titles and sub-heads in your book as a guide in identifying the main idea.

- Make an outline of the main ideas and supporting details of a lesson to help you review.

To Find the Main Idea
Ask yourself:

• What is this paragraph or section mostly about?

To Find the Supporting Details
Ask yourself:

• What words give more information about the main idea?

On page 33 of your book, you will read about Michigan's minerals. Minerals are natural substances beneath the earth's surface. Note the main idea.

One such mineral resource is iron. Many millions of years ago, volcanoes in what is now northern Michigan formed deep beds of this valuable metal. These beds of iron ore remained undiscovered until about 150 years ago. Then, many people rushed to our state to mine the ore. Today we use iron to make steel for cars, railroads, bridges, and hundreds of other products.

Main Idea:
Iron is a valuable mineral resource of Michigan.

Details: people rushed to mine the ore; used to make cars, railroads, bridges, and other products

TRY IT!

Read the passage below from page 62 about the work of archaeologists. Then copy and complete the main idea and details chart below.

> Archaeologists study the way people lived a long time ago. They do this by digging up the remains of ancient villages and tombs, or burial sites. They study the tools, weapons, pottery, and other objects that earlier people left behind. These objects are called artifacts.

Archaeologists study the way people lived a long time ago.

dig up remains of ancient villages, tombs, and burial sites	They study tools, weapons, pottery, and other objects.

• **How did you find the main idea and details?**

Practice Activities

1 **READ** Read the first paragraph under "Life in Wartime Michigan" on page 171. Identify the main idea and details.

2 **WRITE** Write a paragraph describing your neighborhood or school. Be sure to include a main idea and supporting details.

Keep in Mind...

For more help in reading social studies, try these strategies:

☑ **Reread**
Review each sentence carefully. Make sure you understand what each sentence means.

☑ **Form the big picture**
As you read, think about the topic and the most important information in each paragraph or section.

☑ **Look up unknown words**
Use a dictionary or the glossary in your book to find the meanings of any words or terms you do not know.

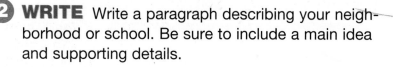

Context Clues

As you read from your book, you may find words or terms you do not know. One way to find the meaning of a new word or term is to look for context clues. **Context clues** are the words and sentences around the unfamiliar term. Using context clues helps you become a better reader.

To Use Context Clues

Ask yourself:

- What word is new to me?
- What might the word mean?
- What other words, phrases, and sentences in this paragraph help me figure out the meaning of the word? What information do these other words provide?

On page 68 of your book, you will read about Native Americans that made Michigan their home. What context clues would you use to identify the meaning of the word *migrated*?

- Have you heard this word before? How was it used?

- Write down the context clues you used to find the meaning of the new word.

- Use the new word in a sentence of your own to help you remember it.

Around 1,000 years ago, several Native American groups left their homes along the eastern coast of North America and migrated westward. They may have been looking for new hunting grounds. Perhaps they were forced off their lands by other Indian groups. Whatever the reason, they began a long, slow journey toward the Great Lakes.

Context Clue:
forced off their land

Context Clue:
left their homes; westward

Context Clue:
they began a long, slow journey

Context Clue:
looking for new hunting grounds

TRY IT!

Read the passage below from page 91 about the expedition of Robert Lasalle, a French explorer, in 1679. Copy and complete the chart below to find context clues for the word *bluff*.

La Salle sailed down the western coast of Lake Michigan. On November 1, 1679, the expedition arrived at what is now St. Joseph. High on a bluff overlooking the lake, La Salle and his men built Fort Miami, the first fort in the Lower Peninsula.

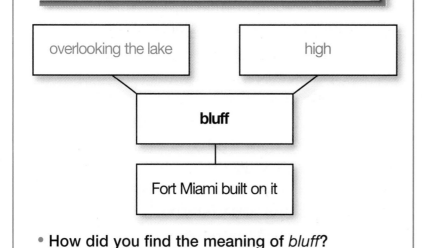

overlooking the lake	high

bluff

Fort Miami built on it

• How did you find the meaning of *bluff*?

Keep in Mind...

For more help in reading social studies, try these strategies:

☑ **Reread**
Review each sentence carefully. Make sure you understand what each sentence means.

☑ **Form the big picture**
As you read, think about the topic and the most important information in each paragraph or section.

☑ **Summarize**
In your own words, briefly describe what you are reading about.

Practice Activities

1 READ Read the second paragraph under "The Rebellion Ends" on pages 101-102 of your book. What context clues helped you discover the meaning of the phrase *bury their hatchets*?

2 WRITE Look in the dictionary for the definition of the word *sagacious*. Write a paragraph using this word. Include context clues.

Sequencing

As you read, look for the order in which things happen. **Sequencing** events is listing them in the order in which they happen. Sequencing events helps you understand and remember what you read.

■ Look for clue words such as *first*, *next*, *then*, *finally*, *until*, *last*, *before*, and *after* to identify the sequence of events.

■ Look for dates—years, months, or centuries—that tell when events happened.

■ Use chapter time lines to help you remember the sequence of events.

To Find the Sequence of Events
Ask yourself:

• Which events happened first?

• Which events happened next?

• Which order of events makes sense?

On page 153 of your book, you will read about the beginning of iron and copper mining in Michigan. Read the paragraph below about iron mining and note the sequence of events.

Iron mining was hard work. Miners cleared the trees and bushes off the land. Then they used picks and hammers to dig out the ore. Later on they dug deep shafts into the earth to recover still more iron.

Third event:
They dug deep shafts to recover more iron.

First event:
Miners cleared the trees and bushes off the land.

Second event:
They used picks and hammers to dig out the iron.

TRY IT!

Read the text below from page 153 about copper mining. The chart below shows the first three steps. Complete the chart by adding the next four.

Miners first had to sink a shaft beside a deposit of copper. From the shaft, men dug tunnels out at different levels.

Working within the tunnels, the miners drilled holes in the rock. Then they set off explosions in each hole that blew out chunks of rock and copper. These big chunks were then raised to the surface by a bucket. A mill near the shaft crushed the rock to free the copper chunks. The copper was then shipped to Detroit and other factory towns.

Miners sank a shaft beside a deposit of copper.
⬇
Men dug tunnels out at different levels.
⬇
Men drilled holes in the rock.
⬇

• How did you determine the sequence of events?

Keep in Mind...

For more help in reading social studies, try these strategies:

☑ **Look up unknown words**
Use a dictionary of the glossary in your book to find the meanings of any unfamiliar words.

☑ **Form the big picture**
As you read, think about the topic and the most important information in each paragraph or section.

☑ **Summarize**
In your own words, briefly describe what your reading is about.

Practice Activities

1️⃣ **READ** Read the section titled "Building a Fort" on pages 92-93. List the sequence of events.

2️⃣ **WRITE** Write about the events of your day. Include words such as *first*, *then*, *next*, and *finally*.

Make Predictions

As you read your book, think about what might come next. This is your **prediction**. A prediction does not have a correct or incorrect answer. Making predictions helps you to carefully consider what you are reading.

To Make a Prediction
Ask yourself:

• **What happened in this section?**

• **What background knowledge do I already have?**

• **What do I think might happen next?**

On pages 99-100 of your book, you will read about the French and British settlers of North America and their relations with the Native Americans. Read these paragraphs below. Do you agree with this prediction?

TIP!

■ Think about other things you know that will help you make an "educated guess."

■ Test your prediction: read further to see if you were correct.

■ Revise your prediction: read further to see if more information changes your prediction.

The Indians had lost many men during the French and Indian War. Many Indian villages had been destroyed. These Native Americans needed British goods to rebuild their communities.

The Indians also needed to hunt, fish, and farm the land in order to live. When the French lost the war, however, British colonists began pushing westward onto Indian land. The Indians knew that there were many more British colonists than there were French. Indian leaders grew worried and angry.

Background Knowledge:
Today many Native Americans live on reservations.

Text Information:
After the war the British began moving into Indian land. Indian leaders grew angry.

Prediction:
Native Americans and British will fight over land. The British win but agree to give Native Americans land.

TRY IT!

Read below about acid rain from page 249. Then complete the chart below.

Acid rain has become one of the most serious environmental problems facing the United States and Canada today.... [M]any power companies burn coal to produce energy. The burning of coal, however, causes an especially harmful kind of air pollution.... When the pollution from burning coal combines with moisture, the result is acid rain.

Acid rain badly damages trees, lakes, and streams. It can even kill ... wildlife that live in a lake or stream. Canadians and Americans are working hard to end acid rain, but it remains a difficult problem today.

Text Information

Acid rain damages our environment.

Background Information

Solar energy is another source of energy.

Prediction

Some day we will use a cleaner and cheaper form of energy.

• How did you make your prediction?

Keep in Mind...

For more help in reading social studies, try these strategies:

☑ **Sequencing**
As you read, think about the order in which things happened.

☑ **Form the big picture**
As you read, think about the topic and the most important information in each paragraph or section.

☑ **Relate to personal experience**
Think about how what you are reading about relates to your own life.

Practice Activities

1 **READ** Read "The Legislative Branch" on pages 254-255. Predict whether the governor was convinced.

2 **WRITE** Write a paragraph predicting what you will do after high school. Give reasons why.

Compare and Contrast

This book often **compares** and **contrasts** people or events. To compare things is to show how they are alike. To contrast things is to show how they are different. Comparing and contrasting helps you understand the relationship between things.

To Compare
Ask yourself:

• What are the things being compared?

• How are they alike?

To Contrast
Ask yourself:

• What are the things being compared?

• How are they different?

On page 180 of your book, you will read about the changes that occurred in Michigan in the late 1800s. The paragraph below talks about one of these changes. Read this paragraph to compare and contrast African American men, African American women, and white Americans.

■ To compare, look for clue words such as: *like, similar, in common, both, same,* and *resemble.*

■ To contrast, look for clue words such as: *before, after, different from, unlike, however,* and *by contrast.*

In 1870, the state constitution was changed to allow African American men to vote. However, both black women and white women were still not permitted to vote. And all of Michigan's African Americans, both men and women, were still denied many of the rights that white Americans had.

Compare:
All African Americans were denied many rights that white Americans had.

Contrast:
African American men could vote; African American women and white women could not.

TRY IT!

Read the paragraph below from page 178 about changes in farming since the Civil War. Copy and complete the Venn diagram below to compare and contrast the changes.

Many farmers had stopped cutting grain by hand. Instead, horse drawn reapers and mowers now moved through fields with remarkable speed. Rather than planting kernels of corn in little hills by hand, farmers now used "seed-drill" machines to plant the seeds. These new kinds of equipment made farm work easier and faster.

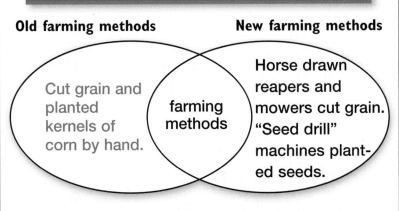

Old farming methods   **New farming methods**

Cut grain and planted kernels of corn by hand.

farming methods

Horse drawn reapers and mowers cut grain. "Seed drill" machines planted seeds.

• What steps did you take to compare and contrast?

Keep in Mind...

For more help in reading social studies, try these strategies:

☑ **Sequencing**
As you read, think about the order in which things happened.

☑ **Summarize**
In your own words, briefly describe what your reading is about.

☑ **Form the big picture**
As you read, think about the topic and the most important information in each paragraph or section.

☑ **Look up unknown words**
Use a dictionary or the glossary in your book to find the meanings of any words or terms you do not know.

Practice Activities

1 **READ** Read the section titled "The Soo Canal" on page 154. Compare and contrast the transportation of iron and copper before and after the opening of the Soo Canal.

2 **WRITE** On a separate sheet of paper, compare and contrast two of your favorite books.

Summarize

After you read a paragraph or section of this book, you can **summarize** what you have read. In a **summary**, you briefly tell in your own words about the most important information in that section. Summarizing is one way to help you understand what you read.

To Summarize

Ask yourself:

- **What is this paragraph or section about?**

- **What information is most important?**

- **How can I say this in my own words?**

On page 227 of your book, you will read about the struggle for equal rights in Michigan. One of the people who made a difference in this struggle was Coleman Young. Read the paragraph and summary below.

- Look for titles, headings, and key words that identify important information.

- Keep your summary brief, and organize the information in a clear way.

- Don't include information and facts that are not important.

In 1973 <u>Coleman Young</u> was elected as Detroit's first African American mayor. As a union member and state senator, he had <u>worked to bring integration and equality to Michigan.</u> While he was mayor he <u>increased the number of African American city workers.</u> Young helped African American Detroiters to feel that they were a part of their city at last.

Important information is underlined.

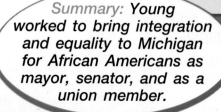

Summary: **Young worked to bring integration and equality to Michigan for African Americans as mayor, senator, and as a union member.**

TRY IT!

Read the paragraph below from page 272 about Native Americans in Michigan. Copy and complete the chart below to summarize.

Today there are 56,000 Native Americans living in Michigan. Most belong to the groups of the Three Fires—the Chippewa, Ottawa, and Potawatomi. Thousands of Native Americans in Michigan live on reservations, or land set aside by the government. Many Chippewa live on the state's largest reservations near Sault Ste. Marie. Not all of Michigan's Native Americans live on reservations, however. Most live in the cities of Michigan.

Important Ideas

There are 56,000 Native Americans in Michigan today.

many live on reservations; most live in the cities of Michigan

Summary

Most of Michigan's Native Americans live in cities, but many live on reservations.

• How did you choose what to include in your summary?

Practice Activities

1 **READ** Read the two paragraphs under "An Indian Leader" on page 100. Then write a summary.

2 **WRITE** Write a summary of a book you have recently read.

Keep in Mind...

For more help in reading social studies, try these strategies:

✔ **Reread**
Review each sentence carefully. Make sure you understand what each sentence means.

✔ **Form the big picture**
As you read, think about the topic and the most important information in each paragraph or section.

✔ **Make an outline**
As you read, write an outline of the topic and the main ideas of the reading.

Use Visuals

One way to learn from your reading is to use visuals. Visuals are the graphs, charts, pictures, and maps in your book. Visuals provide useful information in a clear, easy-to-study form.

To Use Visuals

Look closely at the visual. Ask yourself:

- What does the graph, chart, picture, or map show?

- How does it help me to understand what I have read?

- How does it add to the information I have read?

- What information does the visual's caption provide?

On pages 152-153 of your book, you will read about the "green gold rush" of the 1830s. During this time people came to Michigan to cut timber for homes, stores, and roads.

TiP!

- Read the caption and labels for information they provide.

- Look for objects in the picture that might give additional information.

- When looking at graphs, maps, or charts, be sure to read the legend or key to find the meanings of special symbols.

Lumberjacks worked in teams to put towering piles of logs onto horse-drawn sleds. They used hammers like this to stamp the ends of each log.

The caption tells us that lumberjacks stamped their logs and worked together to put them onto sleds.

Two horses are attached to a harness; appears to be summer; black and white lumberjacks work together.

The logs were piled very high onto horse-drawn sleds in the winter.

TRY IT!

In your book you will read about the African American struggle for equal rights in the 1960s. Study the pictures and complete the chart below.

In the summer of 1963, Martin Luther King, Jr. led a march for **civil rights** through downtown Detroit.

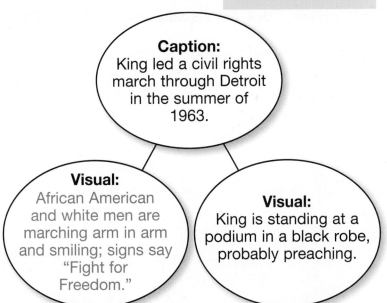

Caption:
King led a civil rights march through Detroit in the summer of 1963.

Visual:
African American and white men are marching arm in arm and smiling; signs say "Fight for Freedom."

Visual:
King is standing at a podium in a black robe, probably preaching.

- **What steps did you take to use the visuals?**

Keep in Mind...

For more help in reading social studies, try these strategies:

☑ **Reread**
Review each sentence carefully. Make sure you understand what each sentence means.

☑ **Sequencing**
As you read, think about the order in which events happened.

☑ **Look up unknown words**
Use a dictionary or the glossary in your book to find the meanings of any words or terms you do not know.

Practice Activities

1 **USE VISUALS** Copy an outline of the chart above. Use information from the visuals on page 212 to complete the chart.

2 **CREATE A VISUAL** Create a visual illustrating something you like. Write a caption for it.

REFERENCE SECTION

Building Citizenship

Building Skills

THE PRINCETON REVIEW HANDBOOK OF TEST-TAKING STRATEGIES   TP1

Charts, Graphs, Diagrams, and Time Lines

Maps

Krystal Gordon With Dad

Steve Alberts

Alexandra Sophiea

Joey Hatton

Darrin Voskuhl

Renee Fornes

Alexandra Felski

Nyamekeye Smith

Luke Parker

Jaleasha Minor

Lyndsay Dusek

WHAT IS A *Michiganian*?

Dear Student,

Look at the photographs on these pages. Krystal Gordon is from Mount Clemens. Renee Fornes lives in Mackinaw City. Luke Parker lives in Schoolcraft. They all go to different schools, but they are all Michiganians.

What does it mean to you to be a Michiganian? As we wrote the book some answers to this question seemed especially important to us.

A Michiganian...

- can visit four of the five Great Lakes without ever leaving our state.
- watches the seasons change from fall to winter, from spring to summer.
- is learning how important it is to protect our land and water.
- is proud of living in the state that has given the world lumber, automobiles, furniture, copper, iron ore, and many other goods.
- might live in a city, in a town, or on a houseboat.
- often has a parent or a grandparent who was born in a different state or country.
- lives among and learns from people of different groups and nationalities.

Most of all, a Michiganian is an American who lives in Michigan.

As you read this book and study about our state, we hope you will have some new ideas of your own about what it means to be a Michiganian.

Sincerely,

Le Ellen McNergney Vinyard

Norman McRae

Demar Cranford With Friend

Michigan, My Michigan

Douglas Malloch

W. Otto Meissner

A song to thee, fair State of mine, Mich - i - gan, my Mich - i - gan; But
I sing a State of all the best, Mich - i - gan, my Mich - i - gan; I

great - er song than this is thine, Mich - i - gan, my
sing a State with rich - es blessed, Mich - i - gan, my

Mich - i - gan;   The   whis - per of   the for - est tree,   The
Mich - i - gan;   Thy   mines un - mask   a   hid - den store,   But

thun - der of   the   in - land sea, U - nite in   one grand sym - pho-
rich - er thy   his - to - ric lore, More great the   love thy build - ers

ny Of Mich - i - gan, my Mich - i - gan.
bore, Oh, Mich - i - gan, my Mich - i - gan.

1

USING YOUR TEXTBOOK

Your textbook contains many features that will help you understand and remember the geography, history, and people of Michigan.

TABLE OF CONTENTS

Lists all parts of your book and tells you where to find them

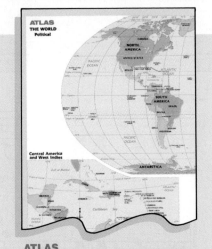

ATLAS
THE WORLD
Political

REVIEWING MAPS & GLOBES

REVIEWING MAPS AND GLOBES

Reviews skills that will help you use the maps in your book

ATLAS

Maps of the world, the United States, and Michigan

LESSON OPENER

Important vocabulary, people, and places introduced in the lesson

Lesson introduction

Asks you to think about what you already know from your book or from your own experience

Question you should keep in mind as you read the lesson

LESSON

3   Timber, Copper, and Iron Ore

READ TO LEARN

Key Vocabulary	Key People	Key Places
industry	Douglass	Muskegon
	Houghton	Saginaw
		Keweenaw Peninsula

Read Aloud

Come listen, young fellows who follow the lakes
In iron ore vessels your living to make,
I shipped in Chicago, bid adieu [good-bye] to the shore,
Bound away to Escanaba for red iron ore.

These words are part of a song that Michigan sailors sang during the 1850s. The vessels, or ships, that they sang about carried iron ore from the Upper Peninsula to factory towns along the Great Lakes. In this lesson you will read how timber, copper, and iron ore helped to bring more settlers and new wealth to our young state.

Read for Purpose

1. **WHAT YOU KNOW:** Who were the first people to mine copper in our state?
2. **WHAT YOU WILL LEARN:** How did timber and mining become important to our state?

THE "GREEN GOLD RUSH"

During the 1830s Michigan was

the forests in the states farther east had been cut down. However

DICTIONARY OF GEOGRAPHIC TERMS

DICTIONARY OF GEOGRAPHIC TERMS

Definition, pronunciation, and picture of major geographic terms

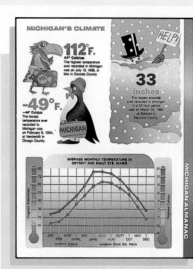

MICHIGAN ALMANAC

Important and interesting facts about Michigan

GAZETTEER

GAZETTEER

Location and pronunciation of all key places and the first page where each is found

GLOSSARY

GLOSSARY

Definition and pronunciation of all key vocabulary and first page where each is found

BIOGRAPHICAL DICTIONARY

BIOGRAPHICAL DICTIONARY

Identifies and pronounces names of key people and lists first page where each is found

INDEX

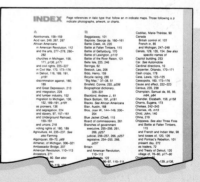

INDEX

Alphabetical list of important subjects and pages where information is found

NATIONAL GEOGRAPHIC

A Look at Michigan

Robots weld car bodies at an auto plant in Wixom.

Detroit residents enjoy a summertime jazz concert held on the banks of the Detroit River.

A great-antlered moose enjoys a meal in Isle Royale National Park.

The sun sets behind the Grand Haven lighthouse along the shores of Lake Michigan.

Ice hockey fans throughout our state watch the Red Wings take the ice.

5

NATIONAL GEOGRAPHIC

Five Themes of Geography

Location
How do people know exactly where things are?

Movement
How do people travel from one place to another?

Region
How is the Great Lakes region different from other regions of the country?

Place
What makes Michigan different from other places?

Human/Environment Interactions
How have people changed the landscape?

Using Globes

Key Vocabulary

continent	hemisphere
ocean	equator

In social studies this year you will learn about our state, Michigan. You will come to understand Michigan's relationship with its neighboring states, with the rest of the United States, and with the world.

The students in this picture are using a globe to learn about Michigan's place on Earth. As you study our state, you, too, will find that maps and globes can be very useful.

Maps and globes can show at a glance what would take a great deal of space to describe in writing. They can be thought of as special "tools." Let's review how to use these tools.

Continents and Oceans

You have probably built or played with model trains or cars. Models look like the originals, only they are much smaller. A globe is also a model. It is a small copy of Earth. Like the earth, it is round. Another name for a round body is *sphere* (sfîr).

A globe shows Earth's seven continents and four oceans. A continent is a very large area of land. An ocean is a very large body of salt water. The students in the picture learned that Michigan is located in North America. The globe helped them understand where Michigan is located in relation to Earth's continents and oceans.

Hemispheres

No matter which way you turn a globe or how you position yourself to look at it, you can see only one half of it at a time. Since a globe is a sphere, what you see is half a sphere. Hemisphere is another word for "half a sphere." *Hemi* means "half."

The map on page 9 shows that Earth can be divided into different hemispheres. Each map shows half of the earth.

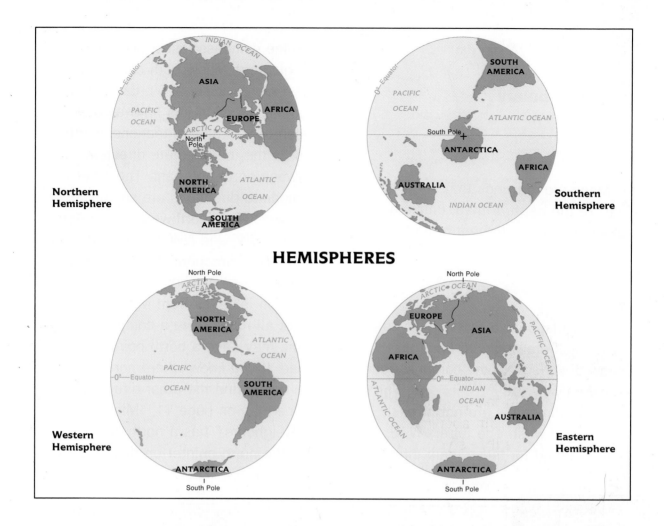

HEMISPHERES

You can also see these different hemispheres by looking at a globe.

The northern half of Earth is divided from the southern half by the **equator**. The equator is an imaginary line that lies halfway between the North Pole and the South Pole. The equator divides Earth into the Northern Hemisphere and the Southern Hemisphere. Look at the map above. How many continents are found in the Northern Hemisphere? How many continents are found in the Southern Hemisphere?

Earth also is divided into the Eastern Hemisphere and the Western Hemisphere. These two hemispheres are separated by another imaginary line, which you will read about on pages 28–31.

1. Name two things that you can learn about the earth from looking at a globe?
2. What is a continent? Name two continents that border the Atlantic Ocean.
3. What does the word *hemisphere* mean?
4. What is the equator?
5. In which two hemispheres is North America located?

9

Using Maps

Key Vocabulary

compass rose

cardinal directions

intermediate directions

symbol

map key

scale

Maps are drawings that show all or part of the earth. A map, unlike a globe, can show the entire earth at one time.

Compass Rose and Directions

Many maps have a compass rose, or a small drawing with lines that show directions. Some compass roses show only cardinal directions. The cardinal directions are north, east, south, and west. The letters *N*, *E*, *S*, and *W* stand for these main directions.

Some compass roses, like the one on this page, show both cardinal and intermediate directions. Each intermediate direction lies halfway between two cardinal directions. Northeast is the intermediate direction between north and east. The other intermediate directions are southeast, southwest, and northwest. The letters *NE*, *SE*, *SW*, and *NW* stand for the intermediate directions. Look at the compass rose on the map. In which direction is Texas from Michigan?

Not all maps have a compass rose. Some may have a north pointer instead. If you know where north is, you can easily find the other directions.

The map on page 11, "Michigan and Its Neighbors," has a north pointer. Use the north pointer on this map to

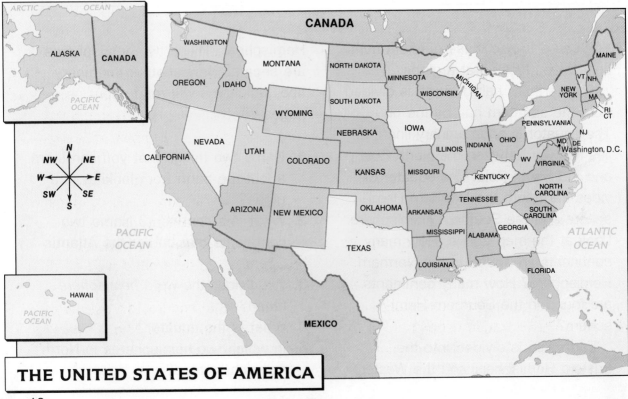

THE UNITED STATES OF AMERICA

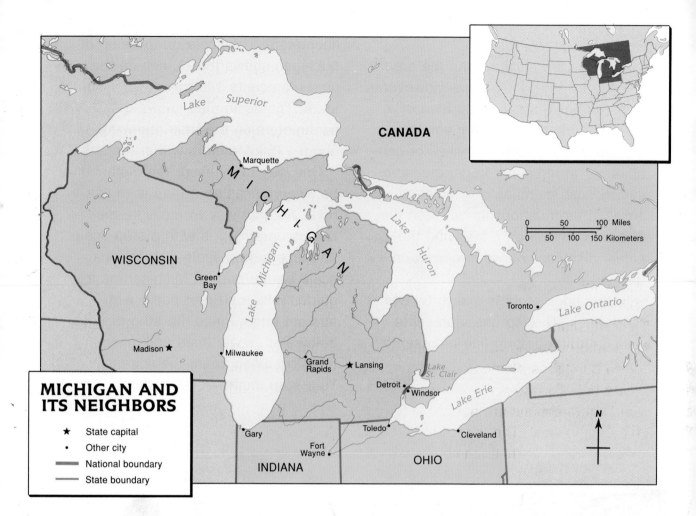

MICHIGAN AND
ITS NEIGHBORS

★   State capital
•   Other city
━━ National boundary
── State boundary

name the states that are found to the south of Michigan. Which lake is found to the west of Michigan?

Symbols and Map Keys

Symbols are used to give information on maps. A symbol is something that stands for, or represents, something else. Symbols are often small drawings of the things that they represent. A drawing of an airplane is often used to represent an airport. Dots are often used to indicate cities and towns. Color is also used as a symbol. You probably know that the color blue often stands for water.

To understand or "read" a map, you must know what the symbols used on the map represent. Most maps have a map key. The map key explains the meaning of each symbol that is used on the map.

Some symbols have the same meaning on different kinds of maps. For example, state boundaries are usually represented by lines. Some symbols mean different things on different kinds of maps.

Look at the map key on the map "Michigan and Its Neighbors." What does a star stand for? What does a dot stand for?

11

Scale

All maps are smaller than the area of the earth that they show. However, maps can give an accurate idea of size. They do this by using smaller measurements, such as inches or centimeters, to represent larger measurements, such as miles or kilometers. Scale is the relationship between the distances shown on a map and the actual distances between places on the earth.

In this book scale is shown by two black lines. The top line represents miles and the bottom line represents kilometers. The scale on the map of Michigan shows that 1 inch on the map represents 140 miles within the state. The scale also shows that 2 centimeters on the map represent about 175 kilometers within the state.

One way to measure the distance between places on a map is to use a ruler. Another way to measure distances on a map is with a strip scale. To make a strip scale, use the map scale on the map of Michigan as a guide. Take a strip of paper with a straight edge. Place the strip of paper below both scale lines and, moving the strip along, mark the distances. Your strip might look like this:

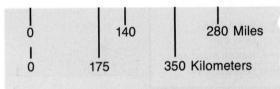

Now use the scale strip to find the distance between Traverse City and Detroit. The map key shows that a black dot stands for a city. Place the 0 (zero) edge of the scale strip on the black dot that stands for Traverse City. Then read the number on the scale strip that is closest to Detroit. You will see that the distance between Traverse City and Detroit is about 350 kilometers (217 mi).

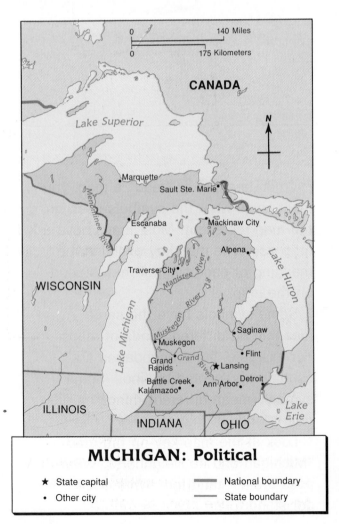

MICHIGAN: Political

★ State capital
• Other city
━━ National boundary
━━ State boundary

1. Why is a compass rose useful to people?
2. What might a map key show?
3. What kind of information do map scales give?

Different Kinds of Maps

Key Vocabulary
grid map
transportation map
product map

There are many different kinds of maps. Some maps show oceans, continents, countries, or states. Other maps help travelers find their way. There are also maps that show where certain products are made. Each kind of map is useful in a different way.

Before using a map, look at the map title. The title tells you what is shown on the map.

Grid Maps

Grid maps make it easier to find places on a map. A grid map is made up of two sets of lines that cross each other to form squares. One set of lines crosses the map from left to right. The spaces between these lines are labeled with letters. The other set of lines crosses the map from top to bottom. The spaces between these lines are labeled with numbers. Each square on the map can be identified by combining its letter with its number. This grid pattern makes it easy to find places on the map or to give their location. Look at the map of Sleeping Bear Dunes National Park. You can find the Visitor Center easily if you know that it is located in square D-2. In which square is South Manitou Island located?

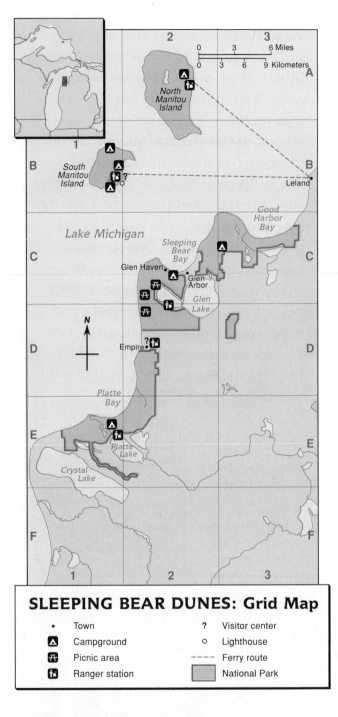

SLEEPING BEAR DUNES: Grid Map

•	Town	?	Visitor center
⛺	Campground	○	Lighthouse
⛱	Picnic area	-----	Ferry route
🚶	Ranger station	�▨	National Park

Transportation Maps

Suppose that you were visiting a city in our state for the first time. A **transportation map** could help you find your way around. A transportation map shows the different ways you can travel from one place to another.

13

Some transportation maps show the routes of railroads, subways, or buses. Others show roads, streets, or highways. Still others show airplane or ship routes.

Look at the transportation map on this page. It shows the downtown section of Detroit. You can visit the many sites of downtown Detroit on foot, by bus, or by trolley. You can also get around another way. Detroit has a train system called the People Mover.

The map below is a transportation map of the People Mover route and the trolley route in downtown Detroit. To find your way around downtown Detroit, you would use a map like the one below.

You can see that this map has colored lines on it. The map key tells you what the colored lines stand for. The red line stands for the trolley route and the green line stands for the People Mover route.

Use the map to answer the following questions: Would you take the trolley or the People Mover if you wanted to go from Millender Center to Bricktown? Which would you take to travel from Hart Plaza to the Old Federal Building?

Many visitors to Detroit like to visit Joe Louis Arena, the home of Detroit's professional hockey team, the Red Wings. Which type of transportation would take you there?

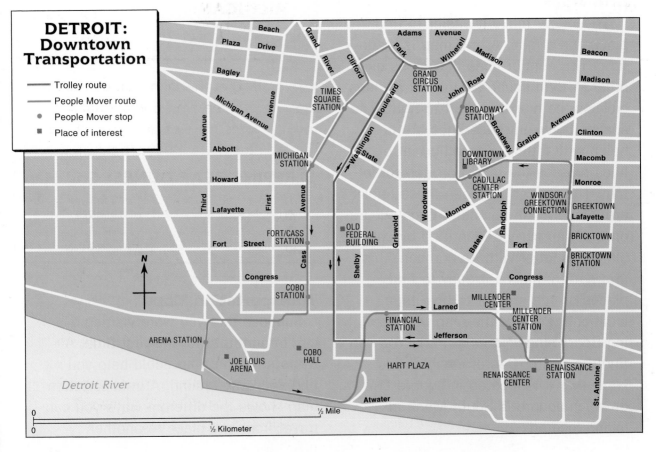

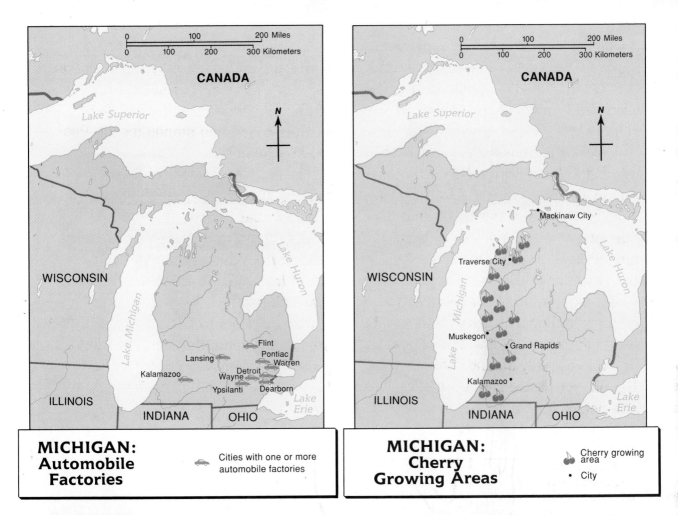

MICHIGAN: Automobile Factories — Cities with one or more automobile factories

MICHIGAN: Cherry Growing Areas — Cherry growing area • City

Product Maps

Suppose that you wanted to find out where a certain product is made or grown. Some maps give you this information at a glance. They are called product maps. Product maps show the kinds of things that are made or grown in a specific area.

The product maps above show where automobiles are made and where cherries are grown in our state. Look at the map keys. They show the symbol that represents each of these products. What is the symbol for automobiles? What is the symbol for cherries? Which product is made or grown near Traverse City?

By looking at the map, you can tell that automobiles are an important product in the southeastern part of our state. Cherries are an important product in southwest Michigan.

1. What are some of the different kinds of maps people use?
2. Look at the grid map on page 13. In which square is Glen Haven?
3. Name two kinds of transportation maps.
4. What can you learn by reading the title of a map?
5. If you were taking a trip through Michigan, which kinds of maps might you use and why?

15

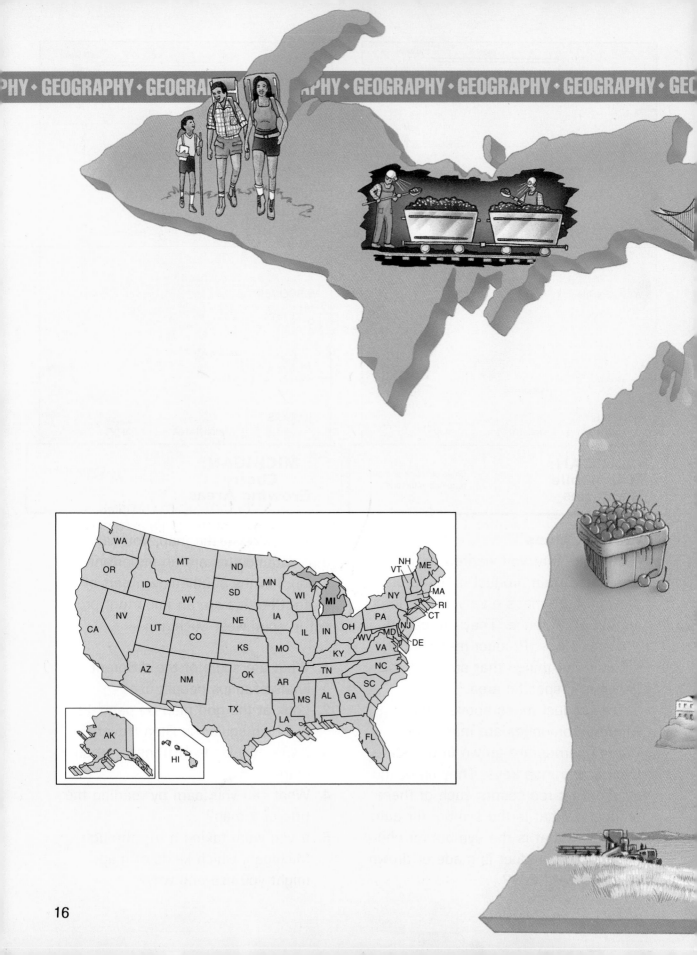

UNIT

1

STUDYING MICHIGAN

WHERE WE ARE

The state that we call home is in the part of the United States known as the Middle West. In our state you can fish in the clear waters of the Great Lakes, ski through white pine forests, or hike through the hills of the Upper Peninsula. You can also catch a glimpse of our state's history at our Capitol Building in Lansing. Let's find out about Michigan—its land and its people.

CHAPTER 1

THE GEOGRAPHY OF MICHIGAN

FOCUS

I like to walk along the beaches looking for shells and stones. I run by the water trying to get as close as I can without letting the waves hit my feet.

Joey Hatton lives in Romeo, which is near several lakes. For Joey, and for most people in our state, being close to the water is one of the best things about living in Michigan. Which of our state's lakes or rivers is near to where you live?

1 Land and Water

READ TO LEARN

Key Vocabulary

peninsula
geography
landform
glacier
basin

Key Places

Great Lakes   Lake Michigan
Lake Huron   Lake Erie
Lake Ontario   Lake Superior

Read Aloud

It was a beautiful country. . . . The soil was as rich as a barnyard, as level as a house floor, and [there were] no stones in the way.

This is how a farmer named John Nowlin described one part of the land of Michigan a long time ago. Do you think it has changed much since then? In this lesson you will read more about the "beautiful country" of Michigan. You will also learn why it looks the way it does today.

Read for Purpose

1. **WHAT YOU KNOW:** What do you enjoy about living in Michigan?
2. **WHAT YOU WILL LEARN:** What is geography? What is the geography of Michigan?

THE SHAPE OF MICHIGAN

Our state has a special shape. Did you know that you can show a "map" of that shape with your hands? Hold out your right hand with its palm facing you and thumb out. Now place your left hand above your right hand, with the thumb slightly lifted. You have just made a "map" of our state's shape.

Now look at the map of Michigan on page 20. As your hands showed, the land of our state is made up of two parts. Each part is a peninsula, or a body of land surrounded almost entirely by water. We call

19

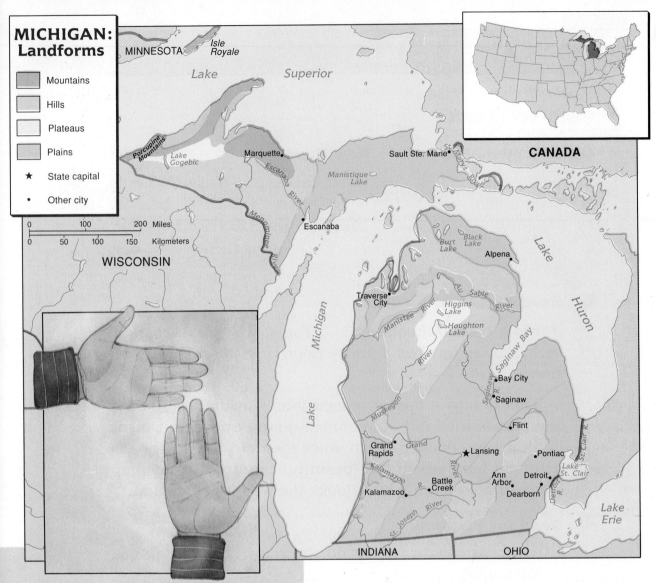

MICHIGAN: Landforms

- Mountains
- Hills
- Plateaus
- Plains
- ★ State capital
- • Other city

MINNESOTA
Isle Royale
Lake Superior
Porcupine Mountains
Lake Gogebic
Marquette
Sault Ste. Marie
Manistique Lake
CANADA
Escanaba River
Menominee River
WISCONSIN
Escanaba
Burt Lake
Black Lake
Alpena
Lake Michigan
Traverse City
Au Sable River
Higgins Lake
Houghton Lake
Manistee River
Lake Huron
Saginaw Bay
Saginaw R.
Bay City
Saginaw
Muskegon River
Flint
Grand Rapids
Grand R.
★ Lansing
Pontiac
St. Clair R.
Lake St. Clair
Kalamazoo R.
Grand R.
Ann Arbor
Detroit
Battle Creek
Kalamazoo
R.
Dearborn
Detroit R.
St. Joseph River
Lake Erie
INDIANA
OHIO

0 — 100 — 200 Miles
0 — 50 — 100 — 150 Kilometers

MAP SKILL: Which of the Great Lakes border both of our state's peninsulas?

these two parts the Upper Peninsula and the Lower Peninsula.

A GREAT LAKES STATE

When you make a map of Michigan's shape with your hands, you are leaving out one important thing—water! Most of our state is surrounded by a group of large lakes known as the Great Lakes.

Look at the map on pages 298–299 of the Atlas. You will see that there are five Great Lakes: Lake Huron, Lake Michigan, Lake Erie, Lake Ontario, and Lake Superior.

The Upper Peninsula is surrounded by Lake Superior, Lake Michigan, and Lake Huron. The Lower Peninsula, which looks like a mitten, is bordered by Lake Michigan, Lake Huron, and Lake Erie. Which one of the five Great Lakes does not touch our state?

OUR NEIGHBORS

Michigan is part of a group of states known as the Great Lakes States. This group also includes Ohio, Indiana, Wisconsin, Minnesota, and Illinois. With the exception of Minnesota and Illinois, all of these states are our neighbors. Michigan is bordered by Ohio and Indiana to the south and by Wisconsin to the southwest. To the north and east, our state shares a water boundary with the country of Canada.

WHAT IS GEOGRAPHY?

Studying maps like the one on page 20 can help you understand our state's geography. Geography is the study of the earth and the way people live on it and use it.

Michigan is one of the 50 states that make up our country. Its shape and its landforms make it different from every other state. A landform is a feature of the earth's surface, such as a valley or a mountain.

MICHIGAN LONG AGO

How did our state's landforms come to look the way they do today? Long ago most of this area was covered with water. Over time, volcanoes erupted and formed high mountains in the Upper Peninsula. Other parts of our state gradually became dry land. Still, much of the land of Michigan remained under water. Fish probably swam through

Many years ago water covered the entire area of Michigan. Animals like the one shown above lived during that time.

the place where your classroom is located today.

After many more years, the whole earth turned extremely cold. This cooling caused glaciers to form. Glaciers are huge sheets of ice that move slowly over the land. Some of these giant sheets of ice crept south over the land of Michigan.

Some of these giant glaciers were 2 miles (3 km) high—more than 10 times as tall as modern Detroit's tallest building. They wore down the mountains and pushed deep holes and ridges into the earth. Like giant bulldozers, the glaciers carried rocks, pebbles, soil, and sand along in front of them.

The fields of southern Michigan are still dotted with boulders that the glaciers carried from the northern part of the state. The glaciers also left huge mounds of sand along the shore of Lake Michigan. You can explore these sand dunes today at Sleeping Bear Dunes National Lakeshore near Traverse City.

LAKES AND RIVERS

The Great Lakes are another gift left by the glaciers. The enormous weight of these glaciers sometimes caused them to carve deep **basins** (bā sinz) in the earth. A basin is a low, bowl-shaped area surrounded by higher land.

When the glaciers melted, these huge basins filled up with water. Over time they increased in size and became the Great Lakes. Meanwhile, many smaller basins became Michigan's 11,000 inland lakes. Our state has so many lakes that there is probably at least one not far from where you live.

Mountains and rivers are both important parts of our state's **geography**

The glaciers helped to form our state's many rivers. They are also responsible for the direction in which these rivers flow. Why? The glaciers left a long, high ridge of ground running north and south through the Lower Peninsula. The land slopes down from this ridge on both sides. As a result, rivers and streams on the west side of this ridge flow into Lake Michigan. Those on the east side flow into Lake Huron or Lake Erie.

A SPECIAL PLACE TO LIVE

You have read about the shape of our state, and learned which lakes, states, and country form its boundaries. You have also read about what our state's land was like long ago and what it is like today. In the next lesson you will read about some other features that make Michigan a special place.

Check Your Reading

1. Name each of the five Great Lakes. Which lake is located farthest north?
2. How did the glaciers cause our lakes to form?
3. GEOGRAPHY SKILL: Which of our neighbors is not part of the United States?
4. THINKING SKILL: What are three questions that you could ask to learn more about the geography of Michigan?

Saving
A RIVER

When Al Martin looked at the Clinton River in the eastern part of the Lower Peninsula in 1987, all he saw was a dying waterway. More than 90 kinds of fish were swimming among household garbage, shopping carts, automobile parts, and fallen trees. Soon deer, raccoons, and other animals would not be able to find any food or fresh water along the riverbanks. Boats were having trouble moving through the garbage.

Martin decided that something had to be done to clean up the Clinton River. At first many people told him that it would be impossible. But Martin believed that volunteers could make a difference. Martin said:

When it comes to saving a river, we must all put forth real physical effort. Keeping the river clean . . . is not any one person's responsibility.

In 1988 Martin began the Clinton River Clean-Up Project. More than 4,000 volunteers from school groups, the Boy Scouts and Girl Scouts, boating groups, and local businesses pitched in to clean up the 70-mile (113-km) waterway. Tons of garbage were removed and boats could finally move easily along the river.

Because of his hard work, Al Martin was presented with the Greater Michigan Foundation's Volunteer Leadership and Community Achievement Award in 1988 and 1989. Martin was also invited to the White House to receive the Take Pride in America Award.

Today the Clinton River Clean-Up Project gathers twice a year to clean up the waterway. But Martin says that cleaning up the river is not enough. He is trying to encourage people to prevent the acts that cause the river to become so jammed. Martin also believes in educating students about the importance of keeping their environment clean. Martin said:

The future of the environment will soon be up to our children. . . . Keeping the river clean is as much their choice as it is ours.

2 Climate and Weather

READL TO LEARN

Key Vocabulary

weather   temperature
climate   precipitation

Read Aloud

If you don't like the weather now, just wait an hour.

You have probably heard this saying before. People in our state often joke about the weather because it seems to change from one hour to the next. Have you ever been surprised by Michigan's weather?

Read for Purpose

1. **WHAT YOU KNOW:** How often does it rain in the part of Michigan in which you live? How often does it snow?
2. **WHAT YOU WILL LEARN:** What effect does climate have on life in our state?

WEATHER AND CLIMATE

The Morris family had moved to Traverse City from Florida a week before school started. Scott and Erica Morris wondered what life would be like in their new home.

"I hope it will be cold enough in January to build an ice rink in the backyard," Scott said.

"Not me," Erica replied. "I hope it will still be warm enough to go canoeing on the Manistee River."

What plans should Scott and Erica make for January? They soon decided to look for more information in the school library.

First Scott and Erica read about weather. Weather is how hot or cold and how wet or dry a place is. Weather can change very quickly.

Next they read about climate. Climate is the type of weather an area has over a period of years. When climate changes, it does so very slowly. While weather affects how we live day to day, climate makes a greater difference in how we plan our year-round activities.

24

TEMPERATURE IN MICHIGAN

Now Scott and Erica read about the different parts that make up climate. One of these parts is called **temperature** (tem′ pər ə chər). Temperature is a measure of how hot or cold the air is.

Why are some places very hot and some places very cold? Temperature is affected by how far above sea level a place is located. It is also affected by how far from the equator a place is located. Look at the world map on pages 294–295 of the Atlas. Places along the equator get the full force of the sun's rays. Places farther north or south get weaker, slanted rays. Since Michigan is a long way from the equator, we have a colder climate than states such as Arkansas and Arizona.

In Michigan the temperature varies widely at different times of the year. The temperature also varies as you travel north or south. In January the average temperature may drop as low as 2°F. (−17°C) in the Upper Peninsula. In the Lower Peninsula, though, the average may be closer to 16°F. (−9°C).

Look at the maps on this page. They show the average temperatures in our state during January and July. As you can see, our summers are much warmer than our winters. Judging from the maps, who do you think got the answer he or she wanted about Michigan's climate—Scott or Erica?

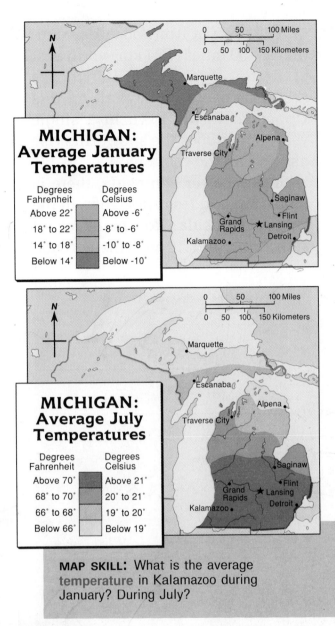

MAP SKILL: What is the average **temperature** in Kalamazoo during January? During July?

PRECIPITATION IN MICHIGAN

Another key part of climate is **precipitation** (pri sip i tā′ shən). We use the word *precipitation* to describe the moisture that falls to earth as rain, snow, sleet, or hail. In Michigan much of the precipitation comes during winter in the form of snow. The amount of snowfall varies from north to south.

The town of Ironwood, for example, is 450 miles (724 km) northwest of Detroit. More than 100 inches (254 cm) of snow may fall on this Upper Peninsula town in a single year! Sometimes the snowdrifts rise as high as the rooftops.

In the Lower Peninsula, there is more rain and less snow than in the Upper Peninsula. How many feet of snow usually fall on Lansing each year? To answer this question, look at the graph on this page.

THE "LAKE EFFECT"

There is one more important influence on Michigan's climate: the waters of the Great Lakes. Because of its size and location, Lake Michigan plays the biggest part in creating the "lake effect."

Look at the diagram on this page. Winds known as the "westerlies" blow across the middle part of the United States for most of the year. These powerful winds, which blow from west to east, usually pass over Lake Michigan. As they blow over the lake, the westerlies change in temperature.

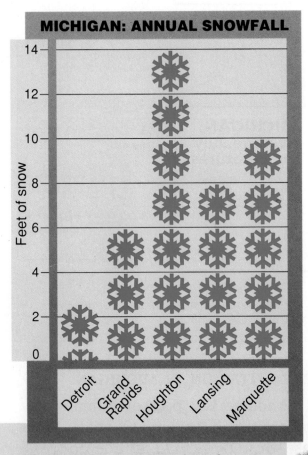

MICHIGAN: ANNUAL SNOWFALL

Feet of snow (y-axis: 0, 2, 4, 6, 8, 10, 12, 14)

Cities: Detroit, Grand Rapids, Houghton, Lansing, Marquette

GRAPH SKILL: How many feet of snow fall in Houghton every year?

DIAGRAM SKILL: In which season does the lake effect cool the westerlies?

Summer

Lake water cools air. Cool breezes blow toward shore.

THE LAKE EFFECT

Winter

Lake water warms air. Warm breezes blow toward shore.

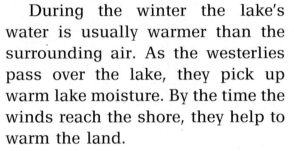

During the winter the lake's water is usually warmer than the surrounding air. As the westerlies pass over the lake, they pick up warm lake moisture. By the time the winds reach the shore, they help to warm the land.

During the summer the effect works in reverse. The lake's water is usually cooler than the surrounding air. This causes the westerlies to cool off as they blow over the lake, and to bring cool breezes inland.

The lake effect influences our climate in two different ways. On one hand, it helps to make our climate more moderate, especially in the Lower Peninsula. The word *moderate* means less extreme—not too hot or too cold.

On the other hand, the lake effect sometimes causes heavy snowfall in the Upper Peninsula. This happens when cold air sweeps across Lake Superior and grows warmer. The warming of the air makes thick snow clouds develop.

CLIMATE AFFECTS PEOPLE

The climate of Michigan brings many visitors to our state. People come here to feel the cool summer breezes, or to see the leaves change color in the fall. In the winter, they come here to go skiing or sledding. Our climate makes Michigan a good place to visit—or to live!

Check Your Reading

1. How does Michigan's distance from the equator affect how hot or cold it is?
2. What is the lake effect?
3. **GEOGRAPHY SKILL:** Why is the average temperature in Marquette lower than the average temperature in Muskegon?
4. **THINKING SKILL:** Predict how life in Michigan might be different if our state had a very hot climate.

Understanding Latitude and Longitude

Key Vocabulary

latitude
parallel
degree
longitude
prime meridian
meridian
global grid

Have you ever tried to describe the location of Michigan to people who have no idea of where it is? How would you begin to explain where our state is located? You could identify the states that border Michigan, but how could you be more exact?

Mapmakers thought about this kind of problem hundreds of years ago. They invented a system of imaginary lines on maps and globes to describe a location. Used together, these lines provide an "address" for any place on earth. Let's look at how they work.

Lines of Latitude

You already know about one of these imaginary lines—the equator. Look at the map on this page, and put your finger on the equator. The equator is the starting line for measuring latitude. Latitude is the distance north

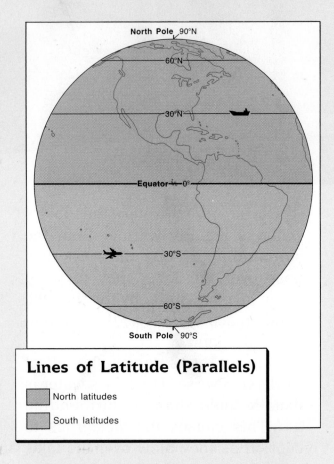

Lines of Latitude (Parallels)

North latitudes

South latitudes

or south of the equator. Lines of latitude are also called **parallels**. Parallel lines never meet and are always the same distance apart.

Each line of latitude has a number. Notice that the equator is labeled 0°, meaning zero **degrees**. Degrees are used to measure the distance between the lines of latitude. The symbol ° stands for degrees. The latitude of the equator is 0°.

Now look at the lines of latitude north of the equator. These parallels are labeled *N* for "north." The latitude of the North Pole is 90°N. The parallels south of the equator are labeled *S* for "south." The latitude of the South Pole is 90°S. Latitude is measured up to 90° north of the equator and up to 90° south of the equator.

Lines of latitude measure degrees north and south of the equator. But as the map shows, the parallels run east and west. Find the small ship on the map. The ship is moving west. Along which parallel is it traveling? Now find the small airplane on the map. On which parallel is it traveling? Is the airplane going east or west?

Lines of Longitude

Now look at the map on this page. It shows lines of longitude. These lines are imaginary lines on a map or globe that measure degrees east or west of the prime meridian. *Prime* means "first." The prime meridian is the first line, or starting place, for measuring lines of longitude. The prime meridian is the line on the map marked 0°. Find the prime meridian on the map.

Lines of longitude are also called meridians. Look at the meridians to the west of the prime meridian. These lines are labeled *W* for "west." The lines to the east of the prime meridian are labeled *E* for "east."

Longitude is measured up to 180° east of the prime meridian and up to 180° west of the prime meridian. Since 180° east and 180° west fall on the same line, this line is marked with neither an *E* nor a *W*.

Unlike lines of latitude, lines of longitude are not parallel to each other. They are not always the same distance apart. Look at the map on this page again. As you can see, meridians are far apart near the equator, but they come together to meet at the North Pole and at the South Pole.

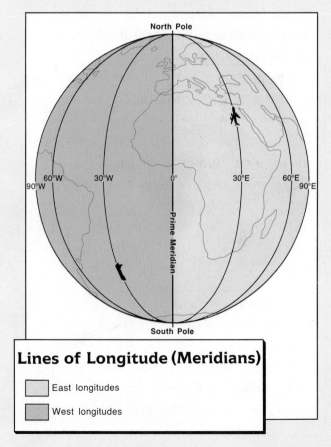

Lines of Longitude (Meridians)

☐ East longitudes

▨ West longitudes

Meridian lines measure degrees east and west. But, as the map shows, the meridians themselves run north and south. Look at the ship on the map on page 29. The ship is moving south. Along which meridian is it traveling? Now look at the airplane on the same map. It is flying over the continent of Africa. In which direction is the airplane on the map traveling?

The Global Grid

In order to use latitude lines and longitude lines to find places, you must combine latitude and longitude on the same map. Look at the world map below. On this map, lines of latitude and longitude form a grid, or a set of crisscrossing lines.

The grid on this map is called a **global grid** because it covers the whole earth. By using the global grid, it is possible to locate places anywhere in the world.

Find the airplane on the map below. Between which lines of latitude is it located? Between which lines of longitude is it located?

Finding Places on a Map

A global grid makes it easy to show where places are located on a map. Look at the map on page 31. Find the city of Tecumseh, Michigan. As you

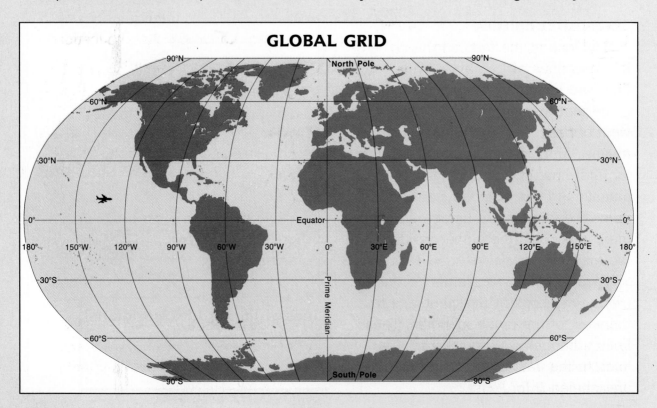

GLOBAL GRID

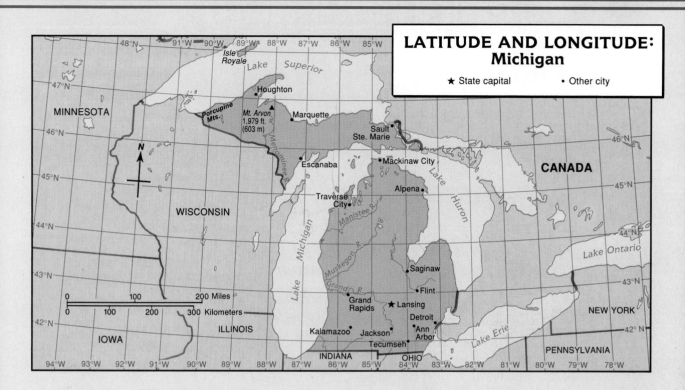

can see, it is located at 42°N latitude. It is also located at 84°W longitude. So we say that its location is 42°N, 84°W. Remember that in locating places on a map, always give latitude first and longitude second.

When a place is not exactly at a point where two lines cross, you have to use the closest lines. Find the city of Flint. It is closest to 43°N, 84°W, so that is the "address" we give it.

If you know the latitude and longitude of a place, you can find its location. There is a city located at about 46°N, 87°W. Put your finger on the latitude line labeled 46°N. Follow the line until your finger passes the 88°W longitude line. Continue until you are almost at the 87°W meridian. What is the city at 46°N, 87°W?

Reviewing the Skill

Use the maps and the information in this lesson to answer these questions.

1. What are lines of latitude and longitude? What do these lines help you to do?
2. What kind of lines are shown on the map on page 28? On the map on page 29? On the map on page 30?
3. What are the latitude and longitude of the city or town closest to where you live?
4. To the nearest degree, what is the latitude and longitude of Lansing, our state capital?
5. Why is it important to understand how to use latitude and longitude on maps and globes?

3 Michigan's Natural Resources

READ TO LEARN

 Key Vocabulary

natural resource   mineral
fertile   timber

Read Aloud

We entered . . . a broad river, with a gentle current, [a] winding course, and heavy wooded banks, with the dark green foliage [leaves] *overshadowing the water.*

A traveler named Henry Schoolcraft wrote this description of the Ontonagon River in 1820. The water and the forests that he described are two parts of nature that remain valuable to the people of Michigan.

Read for Purpose

1. WHAT YOU KNOW: What are some things from nature that you use every day?
2. WHAT YOU WILL LEARN: What are some of Michigan's most important natural resources?

NATURAL RESOURCES

Look around your classroom. What objects can you see that are made from something in nature? The pencils, desks, chairs, books, chalk, and even the windows in your classroom are all made from natural resources. A natural resource is something found in nature that is useful to people. Michigan is lucky to be very rich in natural resources.

MICHIGAN'S SOIL

Every time you step outside in our state, you are walking on one of our most valuable natural resources—dirt! Do you remember the glaciers that you read about in Lesson 1? The glaciers are responsible for this valuable resource. When these huge sheets of ice moved south over the land of Michigan, they brought fertile soil. *Fertile* means "good for growing crops."

Farmers in the middle and southern parts of our state grow corn, wheat, sugar beets, and many other products. Near Lake Michigan, the fertile soil helps farmers to raise fruits and vegetables.

MINERAL TREASURES

Soil is not the only important natural resource beneath your feet. **Minerals** are natural substances located below the earth's surface. Michigan's mineral resources are used by factories throughout our state and nation.

One such mineral resource is iron. Many millions of years ago, volcanoes in what is now northern Michigan formed deep beds of this valuable metal. These beds of iron ore remained undiscovered until about 150 years ago. Then, many people rushed to our state to mine the ore. Today we use iron to make steel for cars, railroads, bridges, and hundreds of other products.

Copper is another mineral found in our state. For many years, mines in the Upper Peninsula supplied most of the copper used in the United States. There is even a town called Copper Harbor at the northern tip of the peninsula.

Look at the natural resources maps on this page to see where these mineral resources can be found in our state. Other mineral resources found in Michigan include limestone and salt.

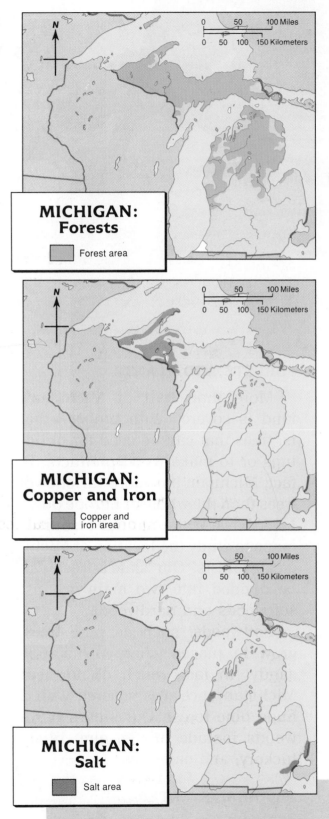

MICHIGAN: Forests

Forest area

MICHIGAN: Copper and Iron

Copper and iron area

MICHIGAN: Salt

Salt area

MAP SKILL: In which area of Michigan is the most salt found? In which area is the most iron found?

Products like these have been made from Michigan's **natural resources**.

FORESTS AND PLANTS

More than half of Michigan's land is covered with **timber**—that is, trees that can be used for buildings or to make wood products. In fact, Michigan has more varieties of trees than the whole of Europe does! Look back at the natural resources maps to study the location of Michigan's forests. Our state's trees can be divided into two main groups: softwoods and hardwoods.

Softwoods, such as pine trees, grow in places where the soil is sandy. In fact, much of northern Michigan once was covered with a huge pine forest. Our state's hardwoods include maple, elm, birch, hickory, and oak trees.

MICHIGAN'S WATER

You have read that the Great Lakes are very important to our state's climate. But did you know that these lakes, along with many smaller ones, are also among our most important natural resources? We use water from these lakes for drinking, washing, and cooking. Michiganians also use this water for boating, swimming, and fishing.

TAKING CARE OF OUR RESOURCES

As you have learned, our state has a great wealth of natural resources. For many years, however, people did not always take care of these resources. Many of our forests, for example, were almost completely cut down.

Today Michiganians are trying to protect our natural resources. We can continue to use them, but we must use them with care. By doing so, we can help to protect Michigan's many natural resources for years to come.

✔ Check Your Reading

1. What is a natural resource?
2. What are some valuable natural resources that Michiganians can find beneath their feet?
3. **GEOGRAPHY SKILL:** Which part of our state is famous for its large amounts of copper?
4. **THINKING SKILL:** Which of our state's natural resources are found above ground? Which resources are found underground?

34

REVIEWING VOCABULARY

climate   natural resource
geography   precipitation
landform

Number a sheet of paper from 1 to 5. Beside each number write the word or term from the list above that best completes the sentence.

1. Timber is an example of a ____.
2. The boy studied ____ to learn about the earth and the ways in which people live on it and use it.
3. The ____ in the desert is hot and dry most of the year.
4. Those rolling hills are an example of a ____.
5. During the winter in Michigan, a great deal of ____ falls in the form of snow; during the summer, it falls as rain.

REVIEWING FACTS

1. Describe the general shape of Michigan.
2. Name the lands and bodies of water that border Michigan.
3. What are two results of the glaciers that once covered Michigan?
4. What are two differences in climate between the Upper Peninsula and the Lower Peninsula?
5. If you wanted to plan what to wear next Sunday, would you need to know the weather or the climate in your community? Explain.

WRITING ABOUT MAIN IDEAS

1. **Writing a Paragraph:** Choose one of Michigan's natural resources. Write a paragraph describing where it can be found, how it came to be there, and how it can be used.
2. **Writing a Letter:** What is your favorite outdoor activity? At which time of year and in which part of Michigan could you best pursue that activity? Write a letter to an out-of-state friend inviting him or her to come and join you in doing that outdoor activity. Tell your friend when to come and where in Michigan you will be going. Explain why you chose that time and place.

BUILDING SKILLS: UNDERSTANDING LATITUDE AND LONGITUDE

Use the map of Michigan on page 31 to answer these questions.

1. After you have located a place on a map, what steps would you follow to find its latitude and longitude?
2. What is the latitude and longitude of Detroit?
3. Which city is located at about 43°N, 86°W?
4. Name a city that is located at approximately the same longitude as Ann Arbor.
5. Why is it helpful to understand latitude and longitude?

CHAPTER 2

THE REGIONS OF MICHIGAN

FOCUS

Michigan is special because it has two peninsulas that are joined by a bridge. I feel special because I get to live right by the spot where they meet.

Renee Fornes lives in Mackinaw City, just minutes away from the Mackinac Bridge. During the summer she sails with her family out under the bridge. In this chapter you will read about the two parts of Michigan that are brought together by "Big Mac."

1 What Is a Region?

READ TO LEARN

Key Vocabulary

region

Read Aloud

We drove a long way the day before to get to St. Ignace (sānt ig' nəs). It wasn't scary at all to walk over the bridge. Helicopters were flying overhead counting people and taking pictures. When we finally got to Mackinaw City at the other end, there were long lines for the buses that took us back to our cars. It was lots of fun.

These are the words of Ben Elling, a fourth grader from Ferndale. Every September on Labor Day, thousands of people like Ben join in a walk across the Mackinac (mak' ə nô) Bridge. They cross from St. Ignace in the Upper Peninsula to Mackinaw City in the Lower Peninsula. In this lesson you will read about these two parts of our state.

Read for Purpose

1. **WHAT YOU KNOW:** How would you describe the part of Michigan in which you live?
2. **WHAT YOU WILL LEARN:** What is a region? What are the names of the two regions of Michigan?

A BIG JUMP

Look at the map on page 38. Can you find St. Ignace, where Ben Elling began his walk across the bridge? At this point Michigan's two peninsulas nearly touch each other. They are so close together on the map that it looks as though you could take a big jump from one peninsula to the other.

The distance, however, is greater than it looks. The Mackinac Bridge

37

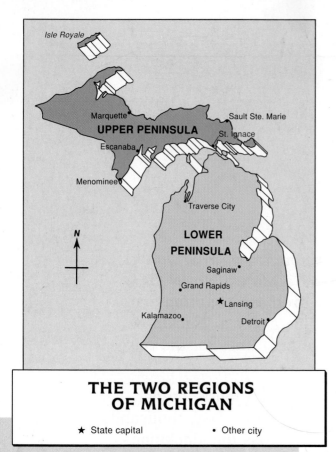

THE TWO REGIONS OF MICHIGAN

★ State capital · Other city

MAP SKILL: You can travel to Detroit (*below, left*) from Menominee (*below, right*) by crossing the Mackinac Bridge (*below, center*). In which of our state's **regions** are these cities located?

is one of the longest bridges in the world. This bridge stretches about 5 miles (8 km)—a distance equal to the length of 88 football fields! No wonder many Michiganians call the Mackinac Bridge "Big Mac."

BRIDGING TWO REGIONS

The distance between the two peninsulas is a "big jump" in another way, too. These two parts of Michigan are very different. It often seems as if you have traveled from one state to another when you cross Big Mac.

In fact, you have traveled from one **region** to another. A region is an area with common features that set it apart from other areas.

Dividing a state into regions can help us to understand its geography. Each region has its own kind of land and its own history. We can learn a great deal about our state by studying its two regions.

Look at the map on page 38 to locate both the Upper Peninsula and Lower Peninsula. Sometimes, Michiganians shorten these names to "the U.P." and "the L.P." In which of these two regions is our state capital located?

TWO DIFFERENT MICHIGANS

How different are Michigan's two regions? Imagine that your family has just taken a long car trip through either the Upper Peninsula or the Lower Peninsula.

If you had visited only the Lower Peninsula, you might say that Michigan is a state with gently rolling hills and farmland. You might write about the big cities with their factories, tall office buildings, and crowds of people. Maybe you would describe the busy highways.

But what if you had visited only the Upper Peninsula? Then you would probably say that Michigan is a state of mountains, tall trees, and waterfalls. You might write about the small towns, the open spaces, and the quiet roads.

Which description of our state would be correct? Both would! Michigan is all of these things. The different ways of life and resources in the two peninsulas together make up the special features of our state.

A STATE OF MANY FACES

In the next two lessons you will read more about both the Upper

Big cities and small farms make Michigan a state of many faces.

Peninsula and the Lower Peninsula. You will study what is special about each region. You will read about the towns and countryside, the work people do, and the fun they have on both sides of Big Mac.

Check Your Reading

1. Why do many Michiganians call the Mackinac Bridge "Big Mac"?
2. What is a region?
3. **GEOGRAPHY SKILL:** Look at the map on page 38. Which of Michigan's two regions makes up the northern part of the state?
4. **THINKING SKILL:** How might your life be different if you lived in the other region of Michigan?

Reading Elevation and Profile Maps

Key Vocabulary

elevation   profile

If you planned to bicycle across Michigan, which kind of map would you find most useful? In Reviewing Maps & Globes you looked at different kinds of maps, such as product maps, a grid map, and a transportation map. Another kind of map is an **elevation** map. Elevation is the height of land above sea level. It is measured in feet or in meters. Elevation at sea level is 0 feet (0 m).

Landforms and Elevation

In Chapter 1 you read about landforms, the shapes that make up the surface of the earth. A landform map like the one on page 20 helps you to understand how the land varies or changes from one region to the next. It will show you the location of the Porcupine Mountains as well as the city of Detroit. However, it will not tell you how high the Porcupine Mountains are or how low the plains are around Detroit. A landform map does not tell you about elevation.

Using an Elevation Map

Look at the elevation map of Michigan on this page. How is it different from a landform map? How is it the same?

The colors on an elevation map show how high the land is. The map key shows the heights the colors stand for.

Look at the key on the elevation map. Which color is used to show elevations above 1,600 feet (486 m)? Find the Porcupine Mountains on the map. What is their elevation?

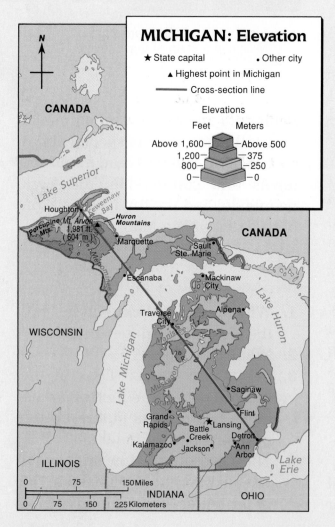

MICHIGAN: Elevation

★ State capital   • Other city

▲ Highest point in Michigan

——— Cross-section line

Elevations

Feet	Meters
Above 1,600	Above 500
1,200	375
800	250
0	0

MICHIGAN: A Profile

Using a Profile

The information on an elevation map can be used to draw a **profile** (prō′ fīl). A profile is a side view of a part of the earth. It shows how the surface would look if an up-and-down cut were made through the earth along a line. Look at the diagram above. It shows a profile of Michigan along a line from Houghton in the Upper Peninsula, through Traverse City, to Detroit in the Lower Peninsula. Find the red line on the elevation map to the left. This is called the cross-section line. It shows the area covered by the profile.

The lines on the profile are for reading elevation. Study the profile and compare it with the elevation map on the left. Use the profile to figure out the elevation of Traverse City. Then use the elevation map to find the same information. Which one lets you read elevation more accurately?

By using a profile like this one, you could plan your bicycle trip across Michigan. The profile would show where you would have to bicycle uphill and where you would bicycle downhill.

Reviewing the Skill

1. What is the difference between a landform map and an elevation map? In what ways are the two kinds of maps similar?
2. Which part of Michigan has the highest elevations?
3. What is the highest elevation in Michigan?
4. Use the profile map to figure out the elevation of Detroit.
5. Suppose that you wanted to bicycle from Saginaw to Lansing. Would you be bicycling toward a higher or lower elevation?
6. Why is it helpful to be able to read an elevation map and a profile?

41

2 The Lower Peninsula

READx TO LEARN

Key Vocabulary

tourist   suburb
population   agriculture
manufacturing   recreation

Key Places

Detroit   Muskegon River
Grand River   Grand Rapids
Saginaw River   Lansing

Read Aloud

What a devilish country it is where they have bears for watchdogs.

These are the words of a French traveler who visited Michigan's Lower Peninsula in the summer of 1831. He found that Detroit was "a little town of two or three thousand" people. When he visited Saginaw, he came upon a few settlers clearing land for farms. To his surprise, a bear was chained outside one cabin to serve as a watchdog! As you will learn in this lesson, many things have changed a great deal since then in the Lower Peninsula.

Read for Purpose

1. **WHAT YOU KNOW:** Have you ever traveled throughout the Lower Peninsula? What did you see?
2. **WHAT YOU WILL LEARN:** What is special about the Lower Peninsula?

THE LOWER PENINSULA TODAY

The French traveler you read about was named Alexis de Tocqueville (ə lek′ səs ′də tōk′ vil). He was one of the first tourists in Michigan. A tourist is a person who travels for enjoyment.

Today millions of tourists come to the Lower Peninsula every year. Many visit the same sites that De Tocqueville visited. However, most of these places have changed a great deal since 1831.

Modern-day visitors to Detroit find a large city, famous throughout

42

the world for its automobile factories. In other parts of the Lower Peninsula, they see shopping malls and farms. And today, not a single family has a bear for a watchdog.

THE LAND OF THE LOWER PENINSULA

Find the Lower Peninsula on the map on this page. As you have already read, this region is shaped like a mitten. Which of the Great Lakes surrounds the "thumb" of this mitten?

At the beginning of Chapter 1 you read a statement made by an early farmer in our state. This Michiganian described our land as "level as a house floor." Certainly this description fits the land of the Lower Peninsula! Most of the land in this region is fairly low and flat. As you move inland from the shore, the land becomes slightly more hilly. In general, though, very little of the Lower Peninsula rises far above the level of the sea.

You have already read about how the glaciers left many rivers and lakes in our state. Three major rivers that flow through the Lower Peninsula are the **Grand River**, the **Saginaw River**, and the **Muskegon River**. This region also contains many of our 11,000 inland lakes.

PEOPLE AND FACTORIES

The Lower Peninsula is the home of most of Michigan's **population**.

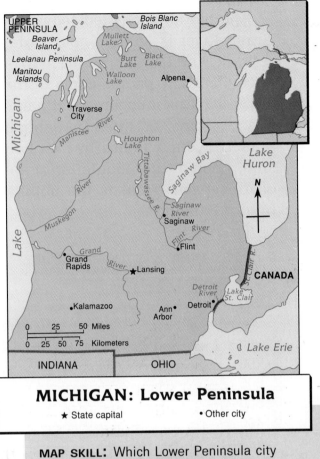

MICHIGAN: Lower Peninsula

★ State capital   • Other city

MAP SKILL: Which Lower Peninsula city is located closest to Canada? Which is located closest to the Manitou Islands?

Population means "the number of people living in a place." In 1990 our state had a total population of 9,179,661 people. About 8,900,000 of the Michiganians live in the Lower Peninsula. Most of these people live in cities and large towns in the southern half of the region.

Many of the cities in the Lower Peninsula grew because of their location near a river. **Grand Rapids**, for example, is located on the Grand River. Early settlers used the river to float logs downstream to the sawmills in Grand Rapids.

43

Another large city located on the Grand River is Lansing, our state's capital. Find Lansing on the map on page 43. Many people come to this city to visit its museums and parks. Others come to attend Michigan State University in nearby East Lansing. Look at the population graph on this page. What is the population of Lansing?

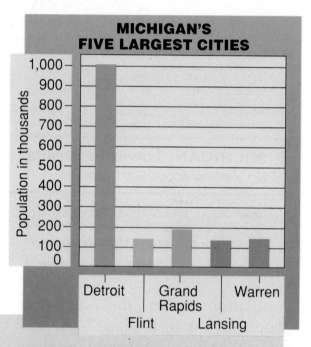

MICHIGAN'S FIVE LARGEST CITIES

Population in thousands

1,000	
900	
800	
700	
600	
500	
400	
300	
200	
100	
0	

Detroit   Grand Rapids   Warren
Flint   Lansing

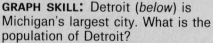

GRAPH SKILL: Detroit (*below*) is Michigan's largest city. What is the population of Detroit?

The Lower Peninsula is also a center for manufacturing, or the making of products with the use of machinery. The factories throughout this region produce everything from automobiles to furniture to guitars. Manufacturing centers in the Lower Peninsula include Battle Creek, Flint, and our largest city—Detroit.

METROPOLITAN DETROIT

Find Detroit on the map on page 43. As you can see, this city is located on the Detroit River, which joins Lake Erie and Lake St. Clair.

Detroit has been Michigan's largest community for almost 300 years. In 1990 Detroit was the seventh-largest city in the United States. But metropolitan Detroit is even larger. What do we mean when we say "metropolitan Detroit"? This phrase includes not only the city itself but also the surrounding communities, or suburbs. About 4 million people out of metropolitan Detroit's 5 million people live in these suburbs. In Chapter 10 you will read more about Detroit and its importance to Michigan.

FARMING IN THE LOWER PENINSULA

The Lower Peninsula is famous for its agriculture (ag' ri kul chər). Agriculture is the business of growing crops and raising animals. You have already read in Chapter 1 about the lake effect. By keeping temperatures moderate in western Michigan, the lake effect helps farmers in the Lower Peninsula.

The "Fruit Belt," which runs along the shore of Lake Michigan, produces peaches, pears, apples, plums, and berries. Another important area for farming is the "thumb" of the "mitten," where apples and dairy products are produced.

Use the map on page 43 to locate the Leelanau (lē′ lə nô) Peninsula. Much of this area is covered with enormous cherry orchards. In fact, so many cherries are grown here that Traverse City is often known as the "Cherry Capital of America."

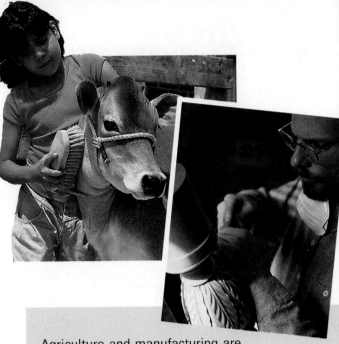

Agriculture and manufacturing are important parts of life in the Lower Peninsula.

MIDDLE MICHIGAN

Most of the communities you have just read about are located in the southern part of the Lower Peninsula. The northern part of the region also has much to offer.

Once this area was a major center for logging. Logging is the business of cutting down trees, cutting them into logs, and transporting the logs to sawmills. In the last few years, oil and natural gas have also become important natural resources produced in this area.

Recreation is also an important part of life in this part of Michigan. We use the word *recreation* to describe the activities people do to enjoy themselves. Many people who live in southeast Michigan travel "up north" for vacations.

MICHIGAN'S "MITTEN"

You have just learned about our state's Lower Peninsula. In the next lesson you will read about the region on the other side of Big Mac— the Upper Peninsula.

Check Your Reading

1. Name three major rivers of the Lower Peninsula.
2. How would you describe the land of the Lower Peninsula?
3. **GEOGRAPHY SKILL:** Look at the map on page 43. Which water route might you take to travel from Lansing to Grand Rapids?
4. **THINKING SKILL:** Name four products of the L.P. Then classify them as agricultural products or manufactured products.

Legacy

READ TO LEARN

■ **Key Vocabulary**

tall tale   lumberjack

■ **Read for Purpose**

1. **WHAT YOU KNOW:** How have geologists explained the formation of the Great Lakes?
2. **WHAT YOU WILL LEARN:** How does this story about Paul Bunyan explain the creation of the Great Lakes?

Paul Bunyan and the Great Lakes

retold by
Tom Pohrt

In Chapter 1 you read about how glaciers formed the Great Lakes long, long ago. The following tall tale gives a very different view of the making of the Great Lakes. A tall tale is a funny, exaggerated story. This tall tale is about the hero of America's lumberjacks, Paul Bunyan. A lumberjack is a person who cuts down trees for a living.

Paul Bunyan was a make-believe giant—a kind of "super-lumberjack"—who was the favorite subject of lumberjacks' stories. In their stories, no job was ever too big or too hard for Paul and his friend Babe, the Big Blue Ox. Together, according to the tall tales, they changed the face of Michigan and the United States.

THE WINTER OF THE BLUE SNOW

One of the worst winters Paul ever worked through was the Winter of the Blue Snow. It was so cold that words froze as everyone began to talk, and Paul had to send for a frozen-word translator from Alaska. It was so cold that the snow itself turned blue, even before it hit the ground.

One night during that terrible winter, Paul heard a crashing roar in the forest behind his camp. He ran outside and found a giant ox calf, obviously lost and cold, knocking down pine trees as it stumbled through the forest. Paul brought the huge calf back to his cabin, warmed and fed him, and the two soon became fast friends.

Paul decided to call his friend Babe, the Blue Ox. Babe's fur was white when he was born, but he had turned blue while lost for six days in the blue

47

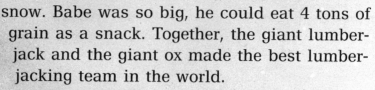

snow. Babe was so big, he could eat 4 tons of grain as a snack. Together, the giant lumberjack and the giant ox made the best lumberjacking team in the world.

Paul and Babe set out into the Winter of the Blue Snow to log, or cut, trees in the great valleys of Michigan. Somewhere early on, however, Paul lost his left mitten. Strong and determined, he kept on cutting timber day in and day out, even though his left hand was becoming colder and colder. With every swing of his ax, poor Paul could only think about how sorry he was that he had lost his left mitten, and how dearly he wanted it back.

On they went, logging a valley that stretched for hundreds of miles. Once they reached the end of that valley, Paul and Babe walked eastward to another great valley. They continued logging northwards in that valley until they had weaved their way back home. By that time, Paul's left hand was frozen stiff, which put him in a rather grumpy mood. But when he turned around to look back at the job he had done, Paul let out a thunderous laugh. Having been able to think of nothing else, Paul had logged the land into the shape of a big mitten!

PAUL AT WORK

It took Paul and Babe two months to haul all of the timber out of those valleys. By the time they got back to Paul's camp, Babe's iron shoes were worn right down to the hooves. Paul, too, was mighty tired and cold.

But his work was not yet finished. For these were the days when glaciers were still pushing their way south from the North Pole. And one of these big ice fields was now closing in and threatening Paul's own camp. As usual, though, Paul was way ahead of the game and had already come up with a plan.

With a clever glint in his eyes, Paul mined some iron out of the rich Michigan rock to make new shoes for his friend Babe. A great fire was built up, and Paul began to hammer away at the iron that had been heated. Great white sparks flew off and hit the surface of the crusty old glacier surrounding Paul's camp. Small streams of water began to flow from the melted spots.

As Paul finished each of Babe's four enormous shoes, he would toss it into the glacier behind him so that it could cool. Each time, a giant hiss rose up in the air as white-hot metal met ice. Soon the small streams became rivers. The rivers flowed into the valleys that Paul and Babe had just cleared, and five new Great Lakes were created.

AN ICE–COLD LAKE

In time, the Winter of the Blue Snow came to an end and a blisteringly hot summer followed. As bucket-sized drops of sweat poured down his forehead, Paul vowed to be better prepared for the heat of summer the next time around.

The next winter, Paul and his crew of lumberjacks anchored large blocks of ice to the bottom of Michigan's new lake, Lake Superior. There they were kept in storage. Whenever the crew wanted to cool down the following summer, Paul would dive down into the water and cut loose one of the ice-cold blocks from the bottom of the lake.

Paul anchored ice blocks to the bottom of Lake Superior each year until his last winter in Michigan. When Paul decided to move on, the bottom of the lake remained paved with ice blocks. This is the secret of why Lake Superior is always so very, very cold.

Check Your Reading

1. According to this tall tale, how did the Great Lakes become filled with water?
2. GEOGRAPHY SKILL: Why did Paul log the land of Michigan into the shape of a mitten?
3. THINKING SKILL: Put all the events of this story in the order in which they happened.

3 The Upper Peninsula

READ TO LEARN

Key Vocabulary

strait
lock

Key Places

Straits of Mackinac
Mount Arvon
Porcupine Mountains

Marquette
Sault Ste. Marie

Read Aloud

[There] was sweet fern, growing ankle high, to walk through, and clumps of jack pines; a long undulating [hilly] *country with frequent rises and descents. . . .*

This is how Ernest Hemingway, a famous American writer, described Michigan's Upper Peninsula. In this lesson you will learn about the land of this region and the people who live there.

Read for Purpose

1. **WHAT YOU KNOW:** Which Great Lakes surround the land of the Upper Peninsula?
2. **WHAT YOU WILL LEARN:** What is special about the Upper Peninsula?

HEADING FOR THE UPPER PENINSULA

Ernest Hemingway first traveled to the Upper Peninsula about 80 years ago. At that time, this region was difficult to visit. No bridge connected the two peninsulas. Some travelers reached the U.P. by driving up the long, dusty roads of northern Wisconsin. Others crossed by ferry from the Lower Peninsula.

Today the trip is much easier. You have already read about the Mackinac Bridge. Big Mac allows people to cross easily from the L.P. to the U.P.

Big Mac stretches across the **Straits of Mackinac**. A **strait** is a narrow waterway that connects two larger bodies of water. Look at the map on page 53. Which lakes are joined by the Straits of Mackinac?

51

The Pictured Rocks along the shore of Lake Superior attract many visitors to the Upper Peninsula.

A TRIP THROUGH THE UPPER PENINSULA

What is the geography of the Upper Peninsula? One way to study the landforms of this part of Michigan is to take an imaginary trip.

Imagine that you have just crossed the Mackinac Bridge to St. Ignace and have begun to drive northwest. At first, you will see rolling hills much like those of the northern part of the Lower Peninsula. As you drive farther, however, you will reach high, rugged country.

As you can see from the map on page 53, traveling in this direction will quickly take you to the rocky shore of Lake Superior. The famous poet Henry Wadsworth Longfellow described this part of Michigan in his popular poem, *The Song of Hiawatha*.

> *On the shores of Gitchee-Gumee*
> *Westward by the Big-Sea Water*
> *Come unto the rocky headlands,*
> *To the Pictured Rocks of*
> *sandstone.*

What did Longfellow mean when he wrote about the "Pictured Rocks"? He was talking about the towering, reddish slabs of sandstone on the shore of Lake Superior. Over many years, winds and water from the lake have carved these rocks into interesting shapes. Some people think that these shapes look like "pictures" of human faces, animals, or buildings.

For ships sailing on Lake Superior, these rocks are as dangerous as they are beautiful. So many ships have crashed along this rough and rocky shoreline that it is often called the "Graveyard Coast."

MOUNTAINS AND WATERFALLS

If you continue west toward the Wisconsin border, you will soon see Mount Arvon, Michigan's highest peak. This peak towers 1,981 feet (604 m) above the surrounding land. Still farther west are the steep slopes of the Porcupine Mountains. Find these mountains on the map on page 53. Many skiers flock to this mountainous area each winter.

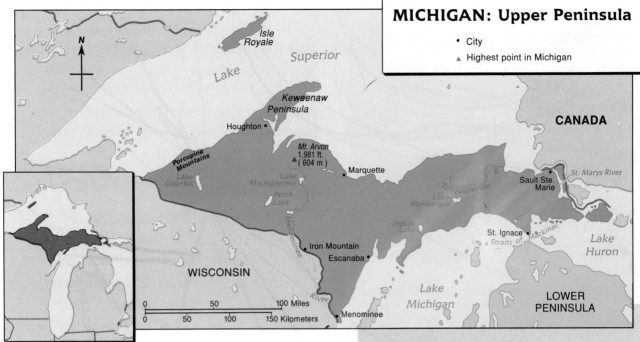

MAP SKILL: The Upper Peninsula has many lakes and rivers. Into which Great Lake does the Tahquamenon River flow?

You will also find many lakes, rivers, and waterfalls throughout the Upper Peninsula. In the eastern part of the region, the Tahquamenon (tä kwä′ mə nun) River drops 52 feet (16 m) to form Michigan's largest waterfall.

MINERAL TREASURES

Do you remember making a map of Michigan's shape with your hands? When you made the shape of the Upper Peninsula with your left hand, your thumb formed the Keweenaw (kē′ wi nô) Peninsula. Find this other "thumb area" on the map on this page.

The Keweenaw Peninsula is rich in iron, limestone, and other minerals. It is most famous, however, for the copper buried beneath its soil. In fact, this area is often called Michigan's "Copper Country."

Marquette, the region's largest city today, grew after a mineral treasure was discovered here. Few people lived in Marquette until the discovery of iron in the early 1850s. Then, the city became a shipping center for the mining companies. Today iron mining remains Marquette's biggest business.

THE SOO LOCKS

Another important feature of the region is located at Sault Ste. Marie (sü sānt mə rē′). Find this city on the map on this page. As you can see, it is located on the St. Marys River, which connects Lake Superior to Lake Huron.

For many years it was impossible for ships to sail between these

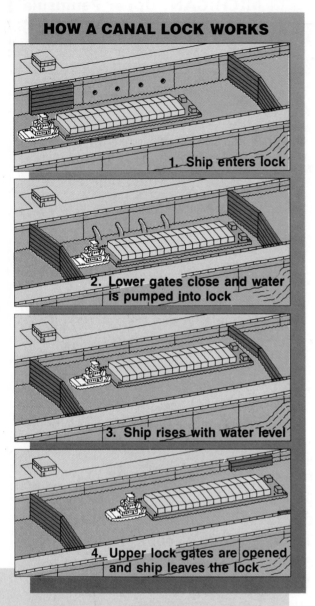

HOW A CANAL LOCK WORKS

1. Ship enters lock

2. Lower gates close and water is pumped into lock

3. Ship rises with water level

4. Upper lock gates are opened and ship leaves the lock

DIAGRAM SKILL: What happens after the ship enters the lock?

two Great Lakes. Why? Lake Superior is 22 feet (7 m) higher than Lake Huron. As the water of the St. Marys River flows south from Lake Superior into Lake Huron, it drops 19 feet (6 m) over a series of waterfalls near Sault Ste. Marie. No ship could sail across this drop.

To solve this problem, a canal and a system of **locks** were built at Sault Ste. Marie during the 1850s. The "Soo Locks" work like a water elevator. Look at the diagram on this page to see how a lock system raises or lowers a ship.

THE "YOOPERS"

The Upper Peninsula makes up one third of the land of Michigan. However, only about 319,000 people, or 1 of every 30 Michiganians, make their home here. These people often call themselves the "Yoopers"— their way of saying "U.P.'ers." They are proud of their region and their way of life.

OUR STATE'S REGIONS

In this chapter you have read about the land and geography of the Lower Peninsula and the Upper Peninsula. In the next chapter you will read about the first people to live in the land of Michigan.

Check Your Reading

1. What is the highest point in Michigan?
2. Why were the Soo Locks built?
3. **GEOGRAPHY SKILL:** What are three routes that you could take to travel from the Lower Peninsula to the Upper Peninsula?
4. **THINKING SKILL:** In what ways are the Upper Peninsula and the Lower Peninsula different? In what ways are they similar?

REVIEWING VOCABULARY

agriculture   region
lock   strait
manufacturing   suburb
population   tourist
recreation

Number a sheet of paper from 1 to 9. Beside each number write the word from the list above that best matches the definition.

1. A device that is used to raise or lower a boat from one part of a river or canal to another
2. One of the communities surrounding a city
3. An area with common features that set it apart from other areas
4. Activities that people do to enjoy themselves
5. The business of growing crops and raising animals
6. A person who travels for enjoyment
7. A narrow waterway connecting two larger bodies of water
8. The making of products with the use of machinery
9. The number of people who live in an area

REVIEWING FACTS

Number a sheet of paper from 1 to 10. Beside each number write the name of the Michigan region that is associated with each item.

1. factories
2. Grand River
3. copper mining
4. Soo Locks
5. Fruit Belt
6. Porcupine Mountains
7. Cherry Capital of the World
8. Lansing
9. Marquette
10. Tahquamenon Falls

WRITING ABOUT MAIN IDEAS

1. **Writing an Explanation:** In which region of Michigan would you rather live if you were: (a) a fruit farmer? (b) a skier? (c) an automobile manufacturer? or (d) a mine operator? Answer each part of the question with a sentence that gives the reason for your answer.
2. **Writing a Poem:** Choose the region of Michigan that you would like to live in or visit. Write a poem that captures the mood of that region so that others will understand why you would choose to live or visit there.

BUILDING SKILLS: READING PROFILES AND ELEVATION MAPS

1. What is a profile?
2. What is an elevation map?
3. Is the elevation of Traverse City higher or lower than Lansing?
4. What is the highest point of elevation in Michigan? How is it shown on the profile?

REVIEWING VOCABULARY

Number a sheet of paper from 1 to 5. Beside each number write **C** if the underlined word is used correctly. If it is not, rewrite the sentence, using the word correctly.

1. <u>Geography</u> includes the study of landforms.
2. The <u>climate</u> in Upper Michigan is colder and snowier than the climate in Lower Michigan.
3. Lake Michigan, Lake Huron, Lake Superior, and Lake Erie are among Michigan's <u>natural resources</u>.
4. Lake Michigan is a <u>region</u> of Michigan.
5. The <u>population</u> of Michigan is made up of all the lakes and rivers of the state.

WRITING ABOUT THE UNIT

1. **Writing a Paragraph:** Most residents of Michigan live in the L.P. Write a paragraph explaining why the landforms, resources, and climate of the L.P. have made it attractive to so many people.
2. **Writing a List:** People have changed Michigan's environment in many ways. They have built bridges, farmed the land, and dug for minerals. Make a list of at least five specific examples of ways in which people have changed the natural environment of Michigan.
3. **Writing a Magazine Ad:** Choose one of the regions of Michigan. Write a magazine advertisement that would make tourists want to visit that region. Think of a catchy slogan to use in the ad. Describe pictures that you might want to include.

ACTIVITIES

1. **Designing a Flag:** Each state in the United States has its own flag. (You can see a picture of the Michigan state flag on pages 232–233.) The design of each flag often has a special meaning that is related to the history or geography of the state. Perhaps each of Michigan's regions should have a flag, too. Design a flag for one of Michigan's regions. Then write a few sentences explaining your design.
2. **Working Together to Make a Scrapbook:** Collect newspaper or magazine articles and pictures that relate to the geography of Michigan. Then, with a group of classmates, arrange your articles and pictures according to their subjects. Paste them on pieces of construction paper to make the pages of a book. Add a cover and a table of contents. Make a class library so that everyone can see them.

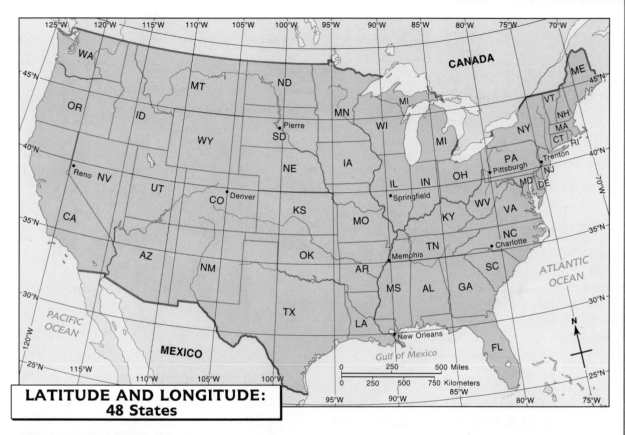

LATITUDE AND LONGITUDE:
48 States

BUILDING SKILLS: UNDERSTANDING LATITUDE AND LONGITUDE

Use the map of the United States above to answer the following questions.

1. What are lines of latitude? What are lines of longitude?

2. Identify one line of longitude that passes through Michigan.

3. Which line of latitude forms the northern boundary of Kansas?

4. Which city is located at 30°N, 90°W?

5. Why is it important to understand lines of latitude and longitude?

LINKING PAST, PRESENT, AND FUTURE

Suppose that you were asked to put together a collage of pictures in order to show the people of the future what Michigan is like today. Which pictures would you include? List the pictures that you would include in your collage. Then write a paragraph explaining why you chose those pictures.

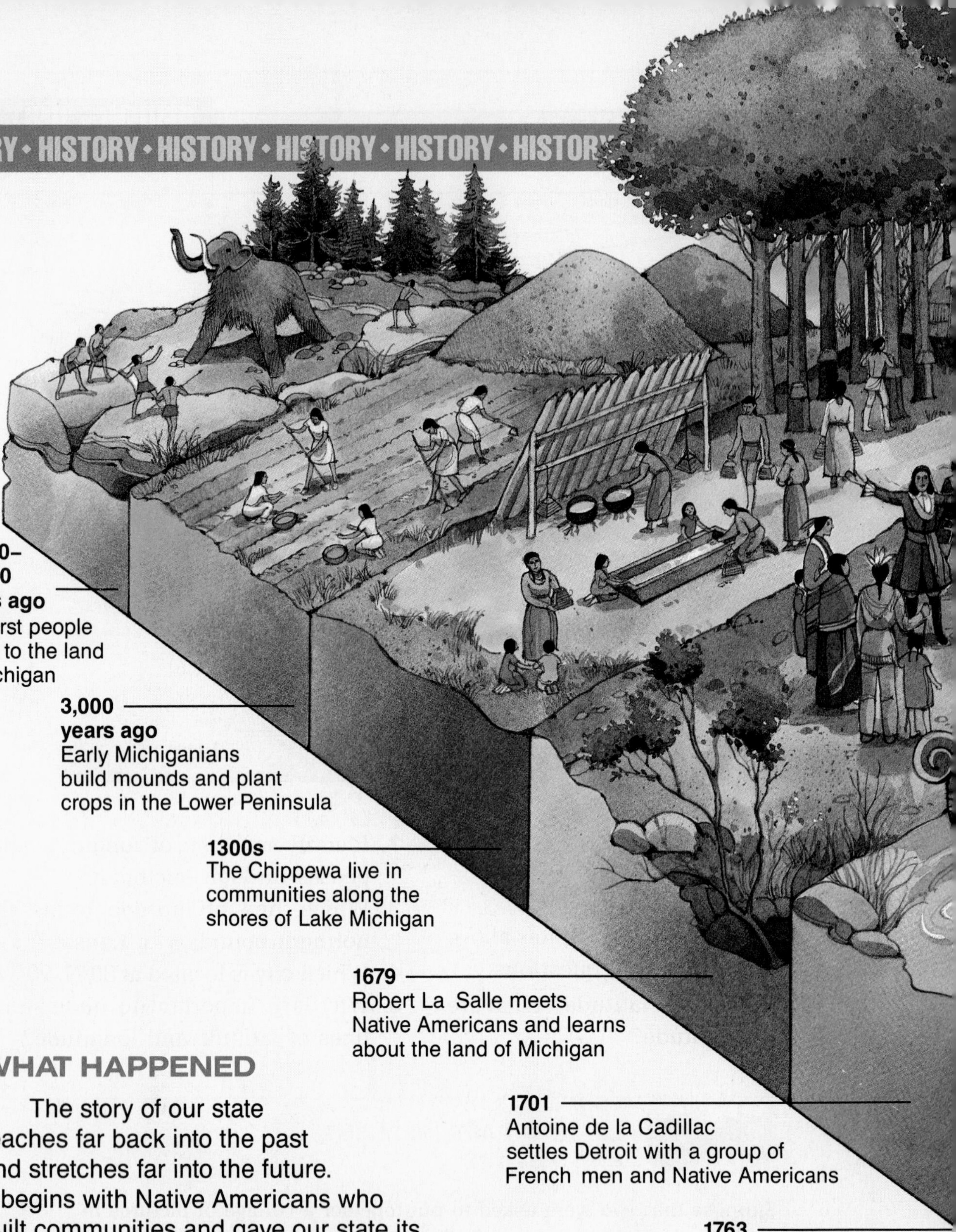

**10,000–
20,000
years ago**
The first people
come to the land
of Michigan

**3,000
years ago**
Early Michiganians
build mounds and plant
crops in the Lower Peninsula

1300s
The Chippewa live in
communities along the
shores of Lake Michigan

1679
Robert La Salle meets
Native Americans and learns
about the land of Michigan

WHAT HAPPENED

The story of our state
reaches far back into the past
and stretches far into the future.
It begins with Native Americans who
built communities and gave our state its
name. The story continues with French traders
and British soldiers who came to Michigan and
started settlements. In this unit you will read about
these early Michiganians.

1701
Antoine de la Cadillac
settles Detroit with a group of
French men and Native Americans

1763
Chippewa prepare
to take over Fort
Michilimackinac
during Pontiac's
Rebellion

58

UNIT 2

EARLY MICHIGAN

CHAPTER 3

THE FIRST PEOPLE OF MICHIGAN

FOCUS

My favorite dance is the Sneak Up. It is a traditional dance where you move your knees up and down. The drum beats fast. Then everything stops. That's why they call it the Sneak Up.

Steve Alberts lives in Mount Pleasant. He dances during powwows and other celebrations. This is one way in which he keeps his Chippewa heritage alive.

1 The Early Native Americans

READ TO LEARN

Key Vocabulary

history   artifact
prehistory   ceremony
archaeologist

Key Places

Bering Strait
Beringia

Read Aloud

I never knew my people to want for anything to eat or to wear, as we always had plenty of wild meat and plenty of fish, corn, vegetables, and wild fruits. I thought . . . that my people were very happy in those days.

These are the words of Andrew J. Blackbird, an Ottawa Indian who lived in northern Michigan. In 1887 Blackbird wrote a history of his people. In this lesson you will learn that long before American Indians began to write, they passed down their history in other ways.

Read for Purpose

1. **WHAT YOU KNOW:** What do you think are some of the ways in which we can learn about people who lived long ago?
2. **WHAT YOU WILL LEARN:** Who were the first people to live in the land of Michigan?

HISTORY AND PREHISTORY

We use the word **history** to describe past events that have been preserved in written records. In addition to writing, these records may include photographs, drawings, maps, and many other things that teach us about the past.

The first Michiganians did not leave any written records behind. Why? The reason is that they lived thousands of years before the invention of writing.

To describe the period before writing was invented, we use a different word—**prehistory**. You can

Archaeologists learn about the past by digging up artifacts. These artifacts tell them how people lived long ago.

understand the difference between *prehistory* and *history* by remembering that *pre* usually means "before" or "earlier."

How, then, do we learn about prehistoric people, who lived before there were cameras, books, paper, and pens to record their stories? This is the job of a special kind of scientist called an archaeologist (är kē ol' ə jist).

Archaeologists study the way people lived a long time ago. They do this by digging up the remains of ancient villages and tombs, or burial sites. They study the tools, weapons, pottery, and other objects that earlier people left behind. These objects are called artifacts.

For an archaeologist, each artifact is like a clue. Each artifact can help to solve part of the mystery of how people lived long ago.

THE FIRST AMERICANS

Archaeologists have studied artifacts left behind by the first Americans. These objects tell us that those first people probably came to North America from Asia. But how did they reach the North American continent from Asia?

Look at the map on pages 300–301. As you can see, a body of water called the Bering Strait lies to the west of Alaska. This strait separates North America from Asia. Thousands of years ago, when glaciers still covered the land, much of the water in the oceans was also frozen. As a result, the water level of the oceans dropped. The floor of the Bering Strait became dry land that formed a land bridge between Asia and North America. This "bridge" is called Beringia (ber' ən gē ə).

Asian hunters and gatherers probably walked across the land bridge to come to North America. They followed herds from place to place in search of food. Some of them may have learned how to make boats and then sailed along the shore of the land bridge. Look at the map on page 63 to trace the route of these first Americans. What a hard trip it must have been, on foot or by boat!

Over the next several thousand years, hunters and gatherers moved farther south and east. Eventually they came to live all over North and South America.

These first Americans later became known as Indians. Today we often call them Native Americans. When we use the word *native* in this way, it means "one of the first people to live in a land."

THE FIRST MICHIGANIANS

The first Native Americans arrived in the land of Michigan about 11,000 years ago. They wandered into Michigan searching for food after the glaciers began to melt.

We call these first Michiganians Paleo-Indians, which means "old" or "early" Indians. Because they were prehistoric people, we know about them only by studying the artifacts that they left behind.

Archaeologists have uncovered evidence of these early people near Detroit and in other parts of our state. They have found such artifacts as broken stone tools, spear points, and the remains of a hearth, or fireplace. The Paleo-Indians used their stone weapons to hunt the large animals, such as mammoths, that lived in Michigan thousands of years ago.

THE OLD COPPER PEOPLE

About 8,000 years ago, another group of Native Americans began settling in the Upper Peninsula. Unlike the earlier groups of people, who often moved around were hunters and gatherers, these Native Americans stayed for longer periods in one place. They built villages along the shores of Lake Michigan and Lake Superior.

MAP SKILL: The first Americans made these spear points (*above*). In which direction did they travel after crossing the land bridge?

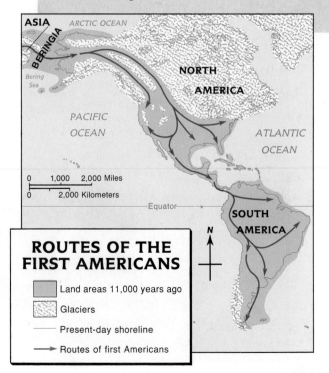

ROUTES OF THE FIRST AMERICANS

- Land areas 11,000 years ago
- Glaciers
- Present-day shoreline
- Routes of first Americans

These people made an important discovery. Scratching at the rock and soil of Isle Royale and the Keweenaw Peninsula, they found a strange reddish substance—copper! You read about this important natural resource in Chapter 1. Soon these Native Americans learned to scrape the copper out of the earth by using wooden and stone tools. They became North America's first copper miners.

These Native Americans also discovered that they could soften the copper by heating it. This process allowed them to shape it into tools, weapons, and jewelry. Archaeologists who found these people's copper artifacts have named them the Old Copper People.

The Old Copper People dug mines like this one in the Upper Peninsula and used the copper to make tools and jewelry.

THE MOUND BUILDERS

About 3,000 years ago the Native Americans of Michigan began to settle in permanent communities. These people are often known as the Mound Builders. This is because they built huge piles of earth, or mounds, in many parts of what is now called Michigan.

One of the largest mounds that they built was located near modern-day Grand Rapids. This mound no longer exists. Other mounds were destroyed when the land they were on was cleared for farms or for buildings. However, more than 600 mounds still exist in our state today. You can visit one of these mounds in Bronson Park, which is in Kalamazoo.

Why did the Native Americans build these mounds? Archaeologists believe that the Mound Builders held ceremonies (ser'ə mō nēz) at the mounds. A ceremony is an act or a set of acts that people perform on a special occasion. These early Michiganians may have gathered at the mounds for ceremonies such as funerals, or to hear speeches.

Many of the mounds built by Native Americans have been destroyed, but you can see this one today in Grand Rapids.

We have learned much about these prehistoric Indians by studying the artifacts they left behind in the mounds. We know that they made pottery, jewelry, carved pipes, musical instruments, and figures of animals and humans.

Archaeologists also believe that the Mound Builders must have traveled long distances to trade with other Native Americans. Why do they think this? Some of the materials used by these people came from the Rocky Mountains and from the area near the Gulf of Mexico.

MICHIGAN'S INDIANS

As you have read, Native Americans probably first reached the North American continent by crossing Beringia. Over a period of many years, these Indians spread across the whole continent, including the land of Michigan. In the next lesson you will read about other Native American groups that made their homes on Michigan soil.

Check Your Reading

1. How do we learn about people who lived before the invention of writing?
2. How did the first Americans reach North America?
3. How did the Old Copper People get their name?
4. **GEOGRAPHY SKILL:** Why can we no longer take the same route from Asia to North America that the first Americans took?
5. **THINKING SKILL:** Compare and contrast the way of life of the Paleo-Indians with that of the Mound Builders.

Decision Making

Key Vocabulary

decision

Every day you make dozens of **decisions**, or choices. You decide what to wear, what to eat, what friends to play with, and when to study. Some decisions are easy to make; others are hard. Once you make a decision, you have to accept the results. So you try to make the decision that is best for you. In this lesson you will learn some steps to follow when making decisions.

Trying the Skill

In Lesson 1 you read about the Mound Builders. You also read that archaeologists have found artifacts that tell us about the Mound Builders' way of life.

Let's imagine that there is a farmer named Rose Rummel who discovers a piece of prehistoric pottery while plowing her field. What should Rose Rummel do about her discovery? Read the paragraphs below, and note the way in which Rose makes a decision.

There may be more artifacts near this one. I must decide whether to call in an archaeologist or to dig by myself.

If I call in an archaeologist, he or she will know how to dig properly. But it might take several days to dig, and I won't be able to plant my crops right away.

If I don't call in an archaeologist, I might destroy some important artifacts by mistake.

I think that it is best to call in an archaeologist.

1. What does the farmer have to make a decision about?
2. Which choices does she identify?
3. Why was the farmer's decision difficult to make?

HELPING YOURSELF

The steps on the left will help you to make good decisions. The example on the right shows how Rose Rummel made her decision.

One Way to Make a Decision	Example
1. State your goal, or what it is you want to do.	The farmer's goal is to find as many important artifacts as possible.
2. Identify some actions that you could take in order to reach your goal.	The farmer can dig up the artifacts herself, or she can call in an archaeologist.
3. Identify what might happen as a result of each choice.	If the farmer calls in an archaeologist, he or she will be able to dig up the field properly. But the farmer won't be able to plant her crops while waiting. If the farmer digs up the field herself, she might destroy some important artifacts.
4. Choose the action that is most likely to help you reach your goal.	The best choice is to call in an archaeologist.

Applying the Skill

Now apply what you have learned. Imagine that you want to buy a house near Grand Rapids. You cannot afford to spend a lot of money. For this reason you must try to get the "most house" for the least amount of money. One choice is to build a house with the help of friends. Building a house by yourself would take too much time.

Another choice is to buy an old house that does not cost very much because it needs repairs. A third choice is to build a house in Grand Rapids, where the prices are lower.

1. What is your goal?
   a. to buy your own home
   b. to move out of Grand Rapids
   c. to live in an old house

2. Which choice do you *not* consider?
   a. renting a house
   b. buying an old house
   c. building a new house

3. What is an advantage of buying an old house?
   a. It would need a lot of repairs.
   b. It would be close to work.
   c. It would not cost very much.

Reviewing the Skill

1. What is the first thing you must do when you are making a decision?
2. What are some steps that you can follow in order to make a good decision?
3. Why is it important to make good decisions?

2 The Three Fires

READON TO LEARN

 Key Vocabulary

culture
clan
religion

 Read Aloud

O Great Spirit
Whose voice I hear in the winds,
And whose breath gives life to
  all the world . . .

Let me learn the lessons
You have hidden in every
  leaf and rock.

This is a prayer from one of Michigan's Native American groups. It shows the way in which these groups valued the natural resources surrounding them. In this lesson you will learn more about the way of life of these Native Americans.

 Read for Purpose

1. **WHAT YOU KNOW:** How did the Mound Builders get their name?
2. **WHAT YOU WILL LEARN:** Who were the "Three Fires"?

MICHIGAN'S INDIAN GROUPS

For some reason that we do not know, the Mound Builders' way of life slowly disappeared. In the meantime, however, other Native American groups had begun to arrive and take their place.

Around 1,000 years ago, several Native American groups left their homes along the eastern coast of North America and migrated westward. They may have been looking for new hunting grounds. Perhaps they were forced off their lands by other Indian groups. Whatever the reason, they began a long, slow journey toward the Great Lakes.

Several of these groups settled in the Upper Peninsula and the Lower Peninsula of present-day Michigan.

The largest groups were the Chippewa (chip′ ə wä), the Potawatomi (pot ə wä′ tə mē), and the Ottawa (ot′ ə wə). The Chippewa, who were also called the Ojibwa (ō jib′ wä) by the French, settled in the Upper Peninsula and in the northeastern part of the Lower Peninsula. The Ottawa built settlements along the shore of Lake Michigan and in southeastern Michigan. The Potawatomi made their home in the southern part of the Lower Peninsula. Look at the map on this page to see where these three groups of Native Americans lived in 1760. In which direction would a Chippewa have traveled to visit a Potawatomi village?

THE THREE FIRES

The Chippewa, the Ottawa, and the Potawatomi had a special name for themselves—the "Three Fires." The three groups that made up the Three Fires thought of themselves as a family. The Ottawa called the Chippewa their "older brother" and the Potawatomi their "younger brother." The three groups shared a common **culture**. Culture is the way of life of a group of people. They had many customs and beliefs in common. All three groups spoke the same language, called Algonkian (al gong′ kē ən). Look at the chart on this page to see some of the many names of places in present-day Michigan that come from the

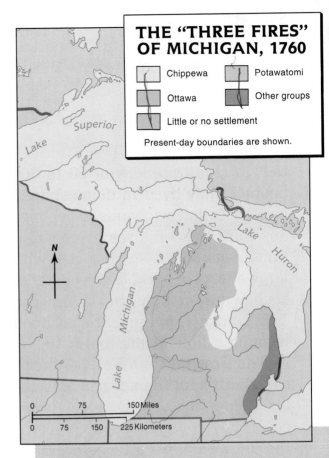

THE "THREE FIRES" OF MICHIGAN, 1760

Chippewa	Potawatomi
Ottawa	Other groups
Little or no settlement	

Present-day boundaries are shown.

MAP SKILL: Which Native American group settled in both the Upper Peninsula and the Lower Peninsula?

CHART SKILL: What does the Algonkian word *Kalamazoo* mean?

MICHIGAN: INDIAN PLACE NAMES

Indian Word	English Meaning
Cheboygan	Chippewa water
Escanaba	flat rock
Kalamazoo	reflecting river
Leelanau	delight of life
Manitou	Great Spirit
Michigan	great lake
Munising	island in a lake
Petoskey	rising sun
Sidnaw	small hill by a creek
Tahquamenon	dark water

Algonkian language. Does the name of your community sound as if it may have come from a Native American word?

VILLAGE LIFE

The people of the Three Fires settled in small villages of 50 to 300 people. They lived in dome-shaped houses called wigwams. The Indians built these houses by covering frames made of small trees with large sheets of bark. In the center of each wigwam they dug a fire pit. The smoke from the fire escaped through a hole in the roof.

The fires that the Native Americans built kept them warm all winter. When the weather grew very cold, they covered the entrance to the wigwam with a large deerskin to keep the heat inside.

In Chippewa and Potawatomi villages, each person was part of a clan. A clan is a group made up of different family members: mothers, fathers, aunts, uncles, grandparents, and, of course, children. These clans were often named after animals, such as turtles, crabs, or bears. Each clan had its own stories, heroes and symbols.

WORKING AND PLAYING TOGETHER

The Three Fires worked hard to provide enough food to last them through the winter. They planted large gardens of corn, beans, squash, potatoes, and pumpkins. They gathered nuts and berries, and harvested wild rice from nearby lakes and rivers. In the spring they made maple syrup from the sap of maple trees.

The people of the Three Fires used Michigan's natural resources to make canoes, clothing, and wigwams.

The people of the Three Fires were also experts at hunting and fishing. Indian hunters often traveled hundreds of miles in search of buffaloes, moose, elk, and deer.

How do you think all of these important jobs got done? As in any community, different people were good at different jobs. Some Indians spent most of their time hunting. Others prepared food. Still others served as teachers or builders. Each person used his or her talents to help do the work of the village. Some tasks, such as teaching the children, were shared by everyone.

The whole village also joined together to celebrate the harvest and other important events. These festivals were a time for singing, dancing, and games.

Storytelling also played a special part in this culture. Children learned to be good listeners. The stories they heard around the fire were part of their education.

NATIVE AMERICAN BELIEFS

Among the people of the Three Fires, religion was an important part of daily life. Religion is the way people worship the God or gods they believe in.

An important part of the religion of the people of the Three Fires was the belief in *manitous* (man i′ tüz), or spirits. These people believed manitous lived everywhere in the world, in many different things such as a bird or a stone. Children learned that manitous could even give them extra strength in times of danger. For this reason children often carried objects with them such as a feather or a stone.

The people of the Three Fires believed that all things—earth, plants, and animals—should be used carefully. They hunted and fished for only as much as they needed to eat. If a hunter was lucky enough to kill a deer, he would share it with the other people of the village. By sharing such "gifts" from the earth, the Three Fires helped one another and their community.

HUNTERS AND TRADERS

Although they had similar ways of life, the groups of the Three Fires were different in some ways, too. Because the Chippewa lived in the far north, where the growing season is short, they lived mostly by hunting and fishing. By contrast, the

Drums, belts, and cloth were among the goods traded throughout the Great Lakes region by the Three Fires.

Potawatomi, who lived farther south, became skilled farmers. Like many of the farmers who live in Michigan today, the Potawatomi took advantage of the lake effect to grow huge vegetable gardens.

The Ottawa were well known as skilled traders. In fact, the word *Ottawa* means "to trade." Each Ottawa family owned a trade route, and only the members of that family were allowed to use it. Loading their birchbark canoes with goods such as furs, copper, corn, and sunflower oil, the Ottawa traveled throughout the Great Lakes region. They traded goods with their "older brother" the Chippewa, and with their "younger brother" the Potawatomi. They also traded with nearby Native American groups such as the Menominee, the Miami, and the Huron.

SHARING THE LAND

The Chippewa, the Ottawa, and the Potawatomi were held together by their family relationships and by their need to help each other. Together these Native Americans cared for the land and shared its gifts. In the next chapter you will read about how their lives changed when the first Europeans arrived.

Check Your Reading

1. Which groups made up the Three Fires?
2. Why was storytelling important among all three groups?
3. What did the Native Americans in Michigan eat?
4. **GEOGRAPHY SKILL:** Why did the Chippewa rely on hunting more than on farming?
5. **THINKING SKILL:** List three questions that you might have asked an Ottawa in order to learn more about his or her culture.

72

READ TO LEARN

Key Vocabulary

myth

Read for Purpose

1. **WHAT YOU KNOW:** How have scientists explained the formation of Michigan's Sleeping Bear Dunes?
2. **WHAT YOU WILL LEARN:** What story did the people of the Three Fires tell about the formation of Sleeping Bear Dunes?

SLEEPING BEAR DUNES

retold and illustrated by Tom Pohrt

In the last lesson you read about the Three Fires of Michigan. During long winter nights, members of the Three Fires gathered inside their warm, fire-lit wigwams and told myths about the world around them. A myth is a story that explains the beliefs of a group. The following story was told by the people of the Three Fires to explain how the Great Manitou, or Great Spirit, created three of Michigan's most famous landforms.

A TIME OF TROUBLE

Long ago when animals could talk, Bear lived by the western shore of Lake Michigan with her two cubs. In the great forest that bordered the lake, they ate their fill of berries and nuts. When they were thirsty, they drank from the cool blue waters of the lake. Bear taught her cubs, "We must always be thankful to the Great Manitou for giving us life and all good things."

One summer, though, rain did not fall on Bear's forest home for many weeks. The earth cried out for water, but it received none. Then one night a big storm came. Thunder shook the earth. A bolt of lightning set the forest ablaze. As flames swept through the forest, Bear shouted to her cubs, "Quickly! Follow me to the lake!"

Bear and her cubs waded into the dark waters of the lake and began swimming as hard as they could away from the burning land. All through that night they continued to swim toward the distant shore on the other side of the lake. But in time the brave little cubs became so tired that they could go no further. Just as the early-morning light revealed the dim shape of land in the distance, the younger cub sank beneath the waves. The older cub struggled on for a few more miles, but then it, too, disappeared beneath the waves.

Bear did all that she could to help her two cubs, but she could not save them. Heartbroken, Bear managed to swim the remaining miles to the distant land. There, she dragged herself up onto the beach, where she soon fell into a deep sleep.

THE GREAT MANITOU'S GIFT

As Bear lay there sadly, the Great Manitou itself spoke into her ear. "Take Heart," the voice said. "Because you and your cubs always thanked me for giving you life and all good things, so I shall take you with me into the Land of the Spirits. Your cubs are already waiting for you to join us there."

To honor the courage of Bear's two cubs, the Great Manitou created two small islands to mark the places in the lake where the cubs' struggles had ended. He called one of them North Manitou Island and the other South Manitou Island.

As for Bear, the Great Manitou covered her body very gently with a blanket of soft, white sand. And to this day, Bear continues to rest under the sandy beach known as Sleeping Bear Dunes.

Check Your Reading

1. How do you think this myth might have made people of the Three Fires feel when they looked at Sleeping Bear Dunes and North Manitou Island and South Manitou Island?
2. Why do you think people tell myths? Can you think of any other myths that people have told?
3. **THINKING SKILL:** List three questions you could ask the members of the Three Fires to learn more about their belief in the Great Manitou.

3 Life in a Chippewa Village

READ TO LEARN

▪ Key Vocabulary

migrate

▪ Read Aloud

First the Creator Kitche Manitou made rock, water, fire, and wind. From these things he created the sun, earth, moon, and stars. And finally, he added plants, animals, and last of all, human beings.

Stories like this one helped Chippewa children to understand the world around them. In this lesson you will read about what life might have been like for two Chippewa children who lived in Michigan long ago.

▪ Read for Purpose

1. **WHAT YOU KNOW:** How would you describe a typical day in your own life?
2. **WHAT YOU WILL LEARN:** What was life like for a ten-year-old Chippewa?

DAILY LIFE OF THE CHIPPEWA

In the last lesson you read that the Chippewa settled in the Upper Peninsula and in the northeastern part of the Lower Peninsula. You read about their villages, their clans, and their beliefs. But how did a ten-year-old Chippewa spend his or her day during the 1500s? In a village near the coast of Lake Huron, daily life might have been something like this. . . .

LESSONS FOR WAAGOSHENHS

"Come and see the fog over the bear cub islands!" Waagoshenhs (wä′ gō shenz) calls to his sister Pitcheh (pich′ ə). His voice echoes across the water. "They look like they're floating in the clouds!"

"At least you remember *that* story," Pitcheh teases as she runs to catch up with him.

Waagoshenhs does not laugh. Last night at the fire he had been

Chippewa girls and boys learned much about their own culture by listening to stories and legends.

talking to his friends while the men of the village were telling stories. His mother had scolded him for his lack of respect. "You chattered like a noisy goose," she said.

He is sorry that he has disappointed his mother. His parents and the other adults of the village are always very kind. They do not spank or slap the children, even when they behave badly. But the adults want the children to listen carefully when they speak or show them how to do things. This is the village "school" for Waagoshenhs, Pitcheh, and their friends.

"What did I miss last night?" asks Waagoshenhs.

"The legend about how our tribe got its name," his sister tells him.

"One of my favorites," he says. He looks down at his moccasins and laughs. "Even though I did not listen last night, I will always remember that our neighbors gave us the name Chippewa because it means "pucker up." They call us that because the top seam on our moccasins puckers up!"

Waagoshenhs enjoys learning about the language of his people. He knows that many of its words have special meanings. For instance, his own name means "Little Fox." When he grows up, he will be known as Waagosh, which means just "Fox." That animal will always be his special protector.

In a Chippewa village there were many different chores to do.

Most girls are named after a bird or some gentle animal. His sister's name, Pitcheh, means "Robin." But Waagoshenhs's baby sister does not yet have a name. Soon, however, she will be one year old, and her parents will ask an older member of the village to choose a name for her. It is a great honor to be asked to name another's child. A special feast will be held for the occasion. Everyone will join the celebration.

Of course, each of the children in the village also has a nickname. Waagoshenhs sometimes thinks his baby sister should be nicknamed "Squawking Bird."

CHORES FOR WAAGOSHENHS

"We must stop walking along the lake and get back to the village," Waagoshenhs says.

It is already autumn. The cold, wet wind blowing in from the lake makes Waagoshenhs's cheeks sting. Soon, before the snow comes, the families of the village will pack their belongings and migrate inland to their winter hunting camps. To migrate means to move from one area to another.

"They will have more lessons for us and more work, too," Pitcheh agrees as they hurry home.

Today the boys in the village are going to follow the men on a hunt. Waagoshenhs has his bow and arrows ready. Maybe they will be able to shoot ducks or geese. The men have taught him how to imitate

78

these birdcalls and how to make decoys. Today they will also show the boys how to set snares, or traps, for deer and rabbits.

"Never kill an animal for sport," Waagoshenhs's father warns him, as the hunting party moves through the forest. "We must hunt only what we need to feed our families."

On other days, the boys watch the men in the village who are experts at catching fish. These men teach the boys to make nets and to spear fish.

CHORES FOR PITCHEH

Pitcheh, meanwhile, has hurried off to find her mother. Today's lesson will be on drying meat and fish. Pitcheh has already learned how to butcher and skin animals, and how to tan their hides.

"But I would much rather hunt," Pitcheh says to her mother. Her grandmother overhears her. She gently reminds Pitcheh that every job is equally important.

"We women must work in the village so that we can tend the small children," says the old woman. "I will show you how to make pottery containers, Pitcheh."

Pitcheh hurries to work beside her grandmother. She loves her mother and her grandmother, and wants to be like them when she is older. She wants them to be proud of her.

THE GRAND MEDICINE SOCIETY

Just as Pitcheh wants to be like her mother, Waagoshenhs wants to be like his father. Waagoshenhs

The Chippewa got their name from moccasins like these.

to ask the spirits to watch over the village. They also lead the ceremonies when the harvest is good or the hunt is successful.

"I am very proud of my father," Waagoshenhs thinks, as the hunting party crosses a shallow stream. He looks down at his moccasins again and smiles happily. "I am lucky to be Little Fox among these people whose shoes pucker up," he says to himself.

THE "FIRST PEOPLE"

You have just read about the daily lives of a Chippewa brother and sister. Along with the Ottawa and the Potawatomi, the Chippewa called themselves the Anishnabeg (ə nish′ nə beg). This word means the "first people." In the next chapter you will read about the new arrivals who joined these first people in the land of Michigan.

admires the way that many people in the village come to his father for help and advice.

One reason for his father's importance is that he is a member of the Grand Medicine Society. He knows how to treat illness with herbs. He tells villagers which seeds and plants will make them stronger and healthier.

The Midewiwin (mi′ də wi win) Society is another name for the Grand Medicine Society. The word *midewiwin* means "magical doings." Members of the society, such as Waagoshenhs's father, know how

Check Your Reading

1. What kinds of names were given to Chippewa children?
2. How did Chippewa boys and girls get an education?
3. Why were medicine men like Waagoshenhs's father important to Chippewa communities?
4. THINKING SKILL: In what ways were Pitcheh's chores different from Waagoshenhs's chores? Which chores would you have preferred to do?

REVIEWING VOCABULARY

archaeologist   migrate
artifact   religion
culture

Number a sheet of paper from 1 to 5. Beside each number write the word from the list above that best completes the sentence.

1. In the winter, the people of the clan ____ from their summer home to a warmer place.
2. The ____ studies the lives of prehistoric people.
3. The group's ____ includes its customs and beliefs.
4. The arrowhead that was left behind by the people who lived here long ago is an example of an ____.
5. The way people worship is called ____.

REVIEWING FACTS

Number a sheet of paper from 1 to 5. Beside each number write **T** if the statement is true. If the statement is false, rewrite it to make it true.

1. The earliest Americans probably came to North America across the Gulf of Mexico.
2. The earliest Indians in Michigan were the Old Copper People.
3. The Mound Builders used the mounds as winter homes.
4. The reason that Native American adults told their children stories was to help them to fall asleep.
5. Members of the Grand Magic Society knew how to heal people and how to ask the spirits to look after a village.

WRITING ABOUT MAIN IDEAS

1. **Writing a Comparing Paragraph:** Review what you have learned about the clans of the Chippewa and the Potawatomi. How are their families the same as or different from your family? Write a paragraph comparing and contrasting your family with theirs.
2. **Writing a Summary Paragraph:** Review the information about the beliefs of the people of the Three Fires, which appears on page 71. Write a paragraph summarizing the information.

BUILDING SKILLS: MAKING DECISIONS

1. What steps should you take to help you make good decisions?
2. Think of a decision that you must make soon. Perhaps you have to decide how you want to celebrate your birthday. Use the decision-making steps to reach a decision.

CHAPTER 4

EUROPEANS ARRIVE

FOCUS

Living in the old days must have been hard. Fur traders had a lot of work to do. They did things like weaving and sharpening tools.

Demar Cranford lives in Port Huron, where he learned about the lives that fur trappers lead in Michigan 300 years ago. In this chapter you will read about why these Europeans came to Michigan.

1 The French Explorers

READ TO LEARN

Key Vocabulary

expedition
colony
Northwest Passage
missionary

Key People

Christopher Columbus
Samuel de Champlain
Etienne Brulé
Jean Nicolet
Jacques Marquette

Key Places

New France
St. Ignace

Read Aloud

The weather is agreeable as we begin to canoe on the great expanse of water. . . . We see banks so high that when an [Indian] stands on one, he appears no larger than a crow. It is a most incredible thing that the waves of the lake should have such strength, to make banks so high and water so deep.

These are the words of Pierre Radisson (rä dē sōn′), a French trader who explored the southern coast of Lake Superior in 1658. In this lesson you will read about the first Europeans to arrive in the land of Michigan.

Read for Purpose

1. **WHAT YOU KNOW:** What can you learn by exploring a new place?
2. **WHAT YOU WILL LEARN:** Which parts of Michigan did the French explorers visit?

NEW ARRIVALS

For thousands of years, Native Americans were the only people living in North America. The Vikings, a people from Scandinavia, may have sailed to the present-day island of Newfoundland almost 1,000 years ago. However, they left no settlements behind.

In 1492 Christopher Columbus a European explorer, landed on San Salvador, an island in the Bahamas. At first, Columbus believed that he

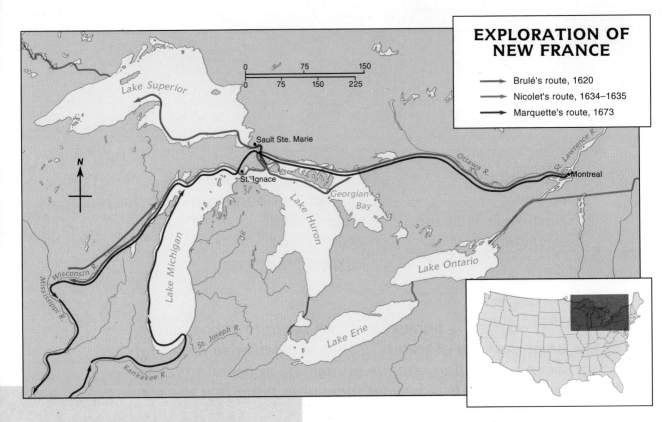

EXPLORATION OF NEW FRANCE

→ Brulé's route, 1620
→ Nicolet's route, 1634–1635
→ Marquette's route, 1673

Lake Superior

Sault Ste. Marie

St. Ignace

Georgian Bay

Lake Huron

Lake Michigan

Ottawa R.

St. Lawrence R.

Montreal

Lake Ontario

Wisconsin R.

Mississippi R.

St. Joseph R.

Lake Erie

Kankakee R.

0 75 150
0 75 150 225

MAP SKILL: Samuel de Champlain (*below*) was one of the first European explorers to visit North America. Which European explorer first traveled on Lake Michigan?

The Granger Collection

had sailed to the eastern coast of Asia. Others soon realized that Columbus had reached a continent unknown to Europeans.

In the years following Columbus's voyage, many rulers in Europe began sending explorers across the Atlantic Ocean. The explorers were eager to claim new lands for their own countries. They also hoped to find precious metals such as gold and silver.

These explorers led **expeditions** (ek spi dish′ ənz) into both South America and North America. An expedition is a journey made for a special purpose.

NEW COLONIES

During the early 1600s, Spain, France, and Britain had established **colonies** in North America. A colony is a place or settlement that is ruled by another country.

These European colonies had many different purposes. Some of

84

Native Americans provided transportation, food, and information to the French explorers in the Great Lakes.

them served as bases for explorers to use while they searched for riches. Others were founded by people looking for land, adventure, or more freedom than they had experienced in Europe.

Few Europeans saw anything wrong in claiming the lands on which Native Americans already lived. The newcomers thought that they could teach the Indians their own religion, Christianity, and their way of life. However, most of these European colonists depended on the Indians to learn how to survive in their new homes. In a strange and often dangerous country, these Europeans were the students rather than the teachers.

THE FRENCH REACH MICHIGAN

French explorers soon claimed most of the land that is now Canada. In 1608 the French started a colony called New France. The center of this colony was located on the site of present-day Quebec City in eastern Canada.

Samuel de Champlain (də sham plān′), the founder of the colony, had come to America as an explorer and mapmaker. Part of his goal in founding New France was to search for a direct water route through the North American continent to the Pacific Ocean. People like Champlain hoped that this route, called the Northwest Passage, would make trading with Asia easier.

The Northwest Passage never existed. The French, however, sent many expeditions in search of it. One of these expeditions was led by Etienne Brulé (ā′ tyen brü lā′). Use the map on page 84 to trace the route of his journey.

Around 1620 Brulé set off from Georgian Bay with a small group of Indian guides. They paddled their canoes across Lake Huron and up into the St. Marys River. Struggling against the current, they canoed upstream until they reached the rapids, or the *sault*. As you read in Chapter 1, the waterfall they saw is the present site of the Soo Locks.

Brulé may have continued farther upstream and sailed along the shore of Lake Superior. In any case, he certainly went ashore somewhere during this long journey. This made him the first European to reach the land of Michigan.

A ROUTE TO THE WEST

Champlain did not give up his dream of finding the Northwest Passage. The French had begun to hear rumors of an Indian group called the "People of the Sea." If these people lived near the Pacific Ocean, perhaps they traded with people in Asia. In that case, the French reasoned, these Indians could probably show them the quickest route through North America.

Hoping to locate this group, Champlain sent out another expedition. **Jean Nicolet** (nik ə lā′) and his guides set out from New France in 1634. No one is sure of exactly which route they traveled. However, Nicolet's group crossed the Straits of Mackinac and followed the shore of the Upper Peninsula to what is now Wisconsin. Nicolet probably caught a glimpse of the Lower Peninsula as he traveled west. The map on page 84 will help you to follow Nicolet's probable route.

Nicolet's small group passed through several Indian villages. Almost all the Native Americans they met had never seen a European before. Can you imagine how strange each group must have appeared to the other one? A member of the expedition recorded the effect that Nicolet had on one Native American village.

> *He wore a great robe . . . with flowers and birds of many colors. No sooner did they see him than the women and children fled, at the sight of a man who carried thunder in both hands—for thus they called the two pistols that he held.*

For the most part, the Native Americans treated Nicolet like an important visitor. Nicolet, however, never found the "People of the Sea" or the Northwest Passage.

A FRENCH SETTLEMENT

The next Europeans to visit this land were **missionaries**. A missionary is a person who teaches his or her religion to other people who

Native Americans welcomed Jean Nicolet as he traveled through their land in search of the **Northwest Passage**.

Jacques Marquette, a French **missionary** founded Michigan's first European settlement at Sault Ste. Marie.

have different beliefs. The king of France sent missionaries to North America to teach Native Americans about the Christian religion.

In the 1660s a missionary named Jacques Marquette (zhäk mär ket´) arrived in Michigan. After traveling widely around the Great Lakes region, he founded Michigan's first European settlement at Sault Ste. Marie in 1668. Within a few years, Marquette decided to start a second settlement called St. Ignace. Find St. Ignace on the map on page 84.

Many Huron and Ottawa came to live near St. Ignace. As time passed, Marquette became very friendly with them. However, he was not able to convince many Huron and Ottawa to become Christians. They wanted to follow their own way of life and religious beliefs.

A NEW MAP OF MICHIGAN

During the early 1600s, French explorers began to travel to the land of Michigan. None of these explorers ever found the Northwest Passage that they were seeking. But they did bring back valuable knowledge about the geography of the Great Lakes region.

Check Your Reading

1. Why did the French, British, and Spanish rulers send explorers to North America?
2. Why did French explorers try to find the Northwest Passage?
3. Who was Jacques Marquette?
4. **GEOGRAPHY SKILL:** Which areas did the French explore during their search for the Northwest Passage?
5. **THINKING SKILL:** How were the lives of Michigan's Indians different from those of the European explorers? How were they the same?

87

Reading Time Lines

Key Vocabulary

time line

You have read that Native Americans reached the land of Michigan thousands of years ago. You also have read that Europeans explored the Mississippi River hundreds of years ago.

When you see phrases such as *500 years ago* or *in 1492*, you are reading about events that took place in the past. Because time is hard to imagine, we can use a **time line** to help us see how dates and events fit together. A time line is a diagram that shows when events took place. It also shows the order in which events happened and the amount of time that passed between events.

Reading a Time Line

The time line below shows some of the important events in the history of the exploration of our state. The name of each event is written beneath the date on which it happened. The earliest event is located on the left end of the time line. The latest event is on the right end. Therefore, you read a time line from left to right. What is the earliest date on the time line? What is the latest date?

A time line is divided into equal parts. Each part of the time line represents a time period. This time period can be short, such as 1 month, or it can also be long, such as 100 years. Into what time periods is the time line below divided?

To read a time line, begin by reading the title. Then look for the earliest and latest events. What is the first

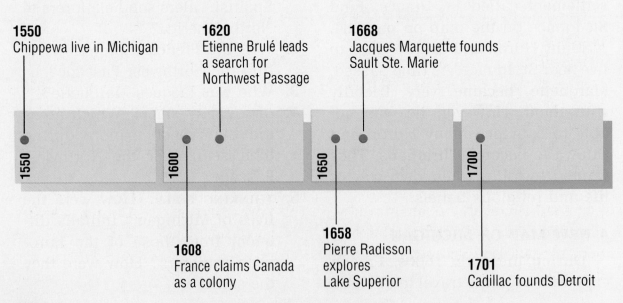

1550
Chippewa live in Michigan

1620
Etienne Brulé leads a search for Northwest Passage

1668
Jacques Marquette founds Sault Ste. Marie

1550

1600

1650

1700

1608
France claims Canada as a colony

1658
Pierre Radisson explores Lake Superior

1701
Cadillac founds Detroit

CALENDAR TIME LINE

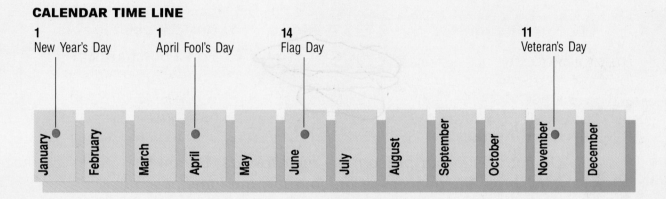

1
New Year's Day

1
April Fool's Day

14
Flag Day

11
Veteran's Day

January | February | March | April | May | June | July | August | September | October | November | December

event on the Michigan time line? What is the last event recorded on that time line?

Look again at the time line on page 88 to see the order in which the events took place. Did Etienne Brulé lead an expedition in search of the Northwest Passage before or after France claimed Canada as a colony?

Making a Time Line

Time lines can be made for different purposes. They can be divided into time periods such as an hour, a day, or a week. Look at the "Calendar Time Line" above. How many months are shown on the time line?

Now make a time line of your own, using the calendar year. Place January, the first month of the year, on the left, and December, the last month of the year, on the right. Mark off sections of equal size for each month of the year.

Next, include dates and events that are special within each month. For example, within January you might write *January 1, New Year's Day*. You may want to include other dates and events, such as the beginning of a school vacation, your birthday, or a national holiday. Try to include one event within each month.

Reviewing the Skill

1. What is a time line?
2. In which year did Jacques Marquette found Sault Ste. Marie?
3. How many years are shown on the time line on page 88?
4. How many years passed between the time that France claimed Canada as a colony and Étienne Brulé's search for the Northwest Passage?
5. Why is it important to know how to use a time line?

2 Traders and Settlers

READ TO LEARN

Key Vocabulary

barter
voyageur
stockade

Key People

Robert La Salle
Antoine de la Cadillac

Key Places

Fort Pontchartrain

Read Aloud

Do not waste your pity on me, dear friends. I know the hardships, the dangers of the journey, the loneliness of the life to which I am going. Yet I am eager to go.

A French woman named Marie-Thérèse Cadillac (mä rē tā rez´ kä´ dē yäk) spoke these words to her friends in 1701. She was about to leave Quebec to live in the new French settlement of Detroit. In this lesson you will learn what life was like for her and the other settlers in the tiny outpost of Detroit.

Read for Purpose

1. **WHAT YOU KNOW:** What was the location of the first European settlement in the land of Michigan?

2. **WHAT YOU WILL LEARN:** Why was the fur trade important in the settlement of the land of Michigan?

FRANCE AND THE GREAT LAKES

As the French explored more of the Great Lakes area, they decided to build a series of forts. These forts would help them to protect the territory they had claimed.

The king of France granted permission to certain explorers to build forts and trade with the Indians. One such explorer was Robert La Salle (lə sal´), a young teacher who was eager for adventure.

In 1674 La Salle built a fort and began trading with the Native Americans near present-day Montreal. Five years later, he set off with fourteen men to explore the western part of New France.

La Salle sailed down the western coast of Lake Michigan. On November 1, 1679, the expedition arrived at what is now St. Joseph. High on a bluff overlooking the lake, La Salle and his men built Fort Miami, the first fort in the Lower Peninsula. Use the map on this page to trace the route of La Salle's expedition.

THE FUR TRADE

Europeans enjoyed wearing hats, capes, and coats trimmed with fur. However, because animals with fur were rare in Europe, only the wealthy could afford to buy such clothing. When the explorers first arrived in North America, they were surprised to find Native Americans using fur for clothing and blankets. French officials discovered that New France had many beavers, foxes, otters, minks, wolves, and other animals with fur. They saw an opportunity for great wealth.

Because they knew how to find and trap the animals, Native Americans soon became an important part of the fur business. French fur companies sent trappers to work with the Chippewa, Ottawa, Huron, and other Indian groups. The French forts quickly became centers for trading. In these rough outposts, traders and Native Americans met to **barter**, or trade one good for another. The French bartered ribbons, cloth, beads, and guns in exchange for furs.

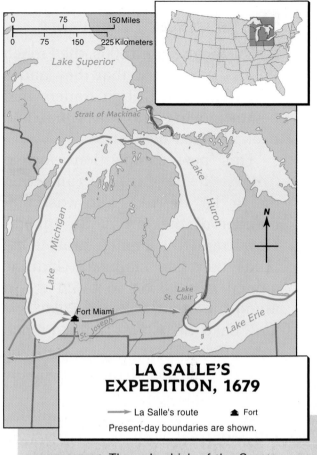

LA SALLE'S EXPEDITION, 1679

→ La Salle's route   ▲ Fort
Present-day boundaries are shown.

MAP SKILL: Through which of the Great Lakes did La Salle travel during his journey in 1679?

Frenchmen known as **voyageurs** (voi ə zhərz′) transported the furs from the trading posts to Quebec. They loaded the furs onto canoes and paddled as much as 100 miles (161 km) a day. Often they would reach an area at which it was necessary to travel overland from one river to another. Here the voyageurs carried the furs and canoes on their backs. This load could weigh as much as 400 pounds (180 kg)! After the furs were delivered to Quebec, they were shipped across the ocean to France.

THE BEGINNING OF DETROIT

During the late 1600s, the French traders discovered that they had a new rival. The British traders had begun moving into areas that had been claimed by France.

This new competition worried **Antoine de la Cadillac** (än′ twän də lə kä′ dē yäk), who was commander of the fort at St. Ignace. How could the French protect the lands they had claimed? Cadillac gained permission to build a fort along the strait between Lake Erie and Lake St. Clair. If the French controlled this strait, they would be able to keep the British out of the upper Great Lakes.

In the summer of 1701 Cadillac left Montreal with 50 soldiers, 50 workmen, 100 Native Americans, and 2 priests. Cadillac's nine-year-old son also made the trip. On July 24 the expedition landed at the narrowest point on the strait. Cadillac and his men immediately set to work building **Fort Pontchartrain** (pän′ chər trān). Sometimes the words *du Détroit* (dù dē troit′), which mean "on the strait" in French, were added to the fort's name. After some years Detroit became the name for the town that grew around the fort.

BUILDING A FORT

Cadillac and his men began by cutting down trees along the bank. They used logs to build a tall fence, or **stockade**. Although the French were friendly with many Native American groups, some Indians disliked their new neighbors. The

DIAGRAM SKILL: French forts served as meeting places for French and Native American traders. In which building did these people barter?

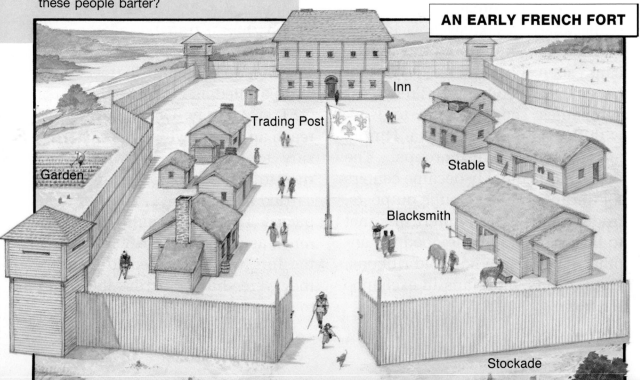

AN EARLY FRENCH FORT

Inn

Trading Post

Stable

Garden

Blacksmith

Stockade

stockade would help protect the settlement from attack.

Inside the stockade the men built log houses with sod roofs. You can see what this fort looked like in the diagram on page 92.

Cadillac wanted his settlement to be more than just an outpost with a handful of soldiers, like the fort at St. Ignace. He wanted to establish a colony with craftspeople, shopkeepers, and farmers. Just one year after founding the new settlement, Cadillac wrote a report to the governor of New France.

> *First we built Fort Pontchartrain and our houses; then I had some land cleared and wheat sown by October 7th. This wheat . . . came up very fine, and was harvested on July 21st. I have a fine garden with vines and fruit trees. . . . Next year I will have a mill built.*

Eventually, long, narrow farms stretched out from the river like ribbons. When the men were not defending the fort, they farmed or worked in the little town of Detroit. Women worked in the fields, prepared meals, and sewed clothing. Children helped by tending the crops and bundling furs.

As the settlement grew, thousands of Native Americans who were friendly with the French began to live around the fort. Cadillac welcomed them. The Indians brought furs that they bartered for French pots, pans, needles, and other tools.

The Granger Collection

Antoine de la Cadillac landed along the Detroit River in 1701. Within ten years Fort Pontchartrain grew into a busy settlement.

HERE TO STAY

The land that La Salle had explored in 1679 soon became a very important area for the French fur trade. By the time the Cadillacs left Detroit in 1710, the little fort had grown into a busy colony. In the next lesson you will read about the new challenges that the French settlers and the Indians faced.

Check Your Reading

1. Where was the first French fort built in the Lower Peninsula?
2. Why was fur important to the French explorers?
3. What role did the Native Americans play in the fur trade?
4. **THINKING SKILL:** Predict how the Native American way of life might have been different if the Indians had not wanted to trade with the French.

Should the Chippewa Have Special Fishing Rights?

As you have read in Chapter 3, fishing was a way of life for Waagoshenhs, his family, and all the people of the Three Fires. But in the 1700s and 1800s settlers wanted the Native American lands for themselves. In a series of agreements, the people of the Three Fires sold the land that is now Michigan to the United States government. The Chippewa, however, kept their right to fish in Michigan.

Today, some Chippewa still fish in Lake Michigan in order to earn a living. They obey Chippewa fishing laws. The Chippewa do not have to obey Michigan fishing laws. For example, they fish with large nets, which is against state law. The Chippewa also fish for lake trout, which other Michiganians are not allowed to do. Some Michiganians think it is unfair for the Chippewa to have special fishing rights.

Many Michiganians argue that the Chippewa should follow state fishing laws. But the Chippewa say that fishing has been their way of life for many hundreds of years. They had to give up their land to the United States government and do not want to give up their fishing rights, too. Should the Chippewa have special fishing rights?

Two DIFFERENT Viewpoints

The Chippewa Should Have Special Fishing Rights

James Bransky is a lawyer for the Michigan Indian Legal Services. He says that the Chippewa are only asking for what is rightfully theirs. Bransky explains:

> The Chippewa gave the United States government almost everything they had. [Now] all they are asking is to keep their fishing rights.

Fishing rights are very important to Albert LeBlanc, a Chippewa from Bay Mills. He earns his living from fishing.

> We will do nothing to hurt the lakes or the fish—this is our livelihood from year to year.

- According to James Bransky, why are the Chippewa asking to keep their fishing rights?

The Chippewa Should Not Have Special Fishing Rights

Robert W. Davis, who was a congressman from Michigan, thought that it was unfair for the Chippewa to have special fishing rights. He tried to pass a law to require that all Michiganians have the same fishing rights. Part of this law would have said:

> . . . All groups [should] equitably [fairly] and peacefully participate in the sharing of the resources. . . .

A charter boat owner from Traverse City believes it is unfair that he has to obey different fishing laws from the Chippewa. He says:

> I'm treated like a second-class citizen because Indians can fish for whatever they want and I can't.

- Why does the charter boat owner think that he is being treated like a second-class citizen?

BUILDING CITIZENSHIP

1. Why do some Michiganians believe that the Chippewa should keep their fishing rights?
2. Why do other Michiganians want the Chippewa to obey Michigan's fishing laws?
3. Which side do you think makes the stronger case? Why?

3 The French and Indian War

 Key Vocabulary

slavery
French and Indian War
treaty

 Read Aloud

I take possession of this country in the name of . . . our king. This land is his.

On June 14, 1671, a French official made this announcement to a gathering of Native Americans near Sault Ste. Marie. As you will read, however, the French were not the only Europeans to claim this land.

Read for Purpose

1. WHAT YOU KNOW: How would you describe the relationship between the French fur traders and Michigan's Native American groups?
2. WHAT YOU WILL LEARN: How did Michigan become a British colony?

THE BRITISH START COLONIES

Like the French, many British explorers searched for the Northwest Passage. They had no more luck than the French had in finding it. However, the British did start 13 colonies along the Atlantic coast.

Over time, these colonies began to flourish. The British colonists grew tobacco, rice, and other crops. They also bartered with the Indians for furs. Most of these goods were shipped back to Britain.

THE BRITISH COLONIES GROW

Encouraged by this new source of wealth, British leaders urged more people to migrate to America. Thousands of British families made the trip across the Atlantic Ocean. Thousands more came from countries such as Germany, Scotland, and Ireland.

Still other people were brought to these colonies against their will. During the 1600s, many thousands of African captives were shipped across the Atlantic in chains. Some had been captured by Europeans. Other captives were sold to Europeans by other Africans. After arriving in America, they were forced into slavery. Slavery is the practice of making one person the property of another person. Enslaved Africans were forced to work without pay on plantations in the colonies.

The 13 colonies grew much more quickly than the settlements in New France did. By 1750 about 2 million people lived in the British colonies. Only 60,000 people had settled in New France.

As the British colonies grew more crowded, farmers and traders slowly began to move northwest. As you have read, the French and the British both claimed the same lands. These areas were between the Ohio River and the Mississippi River and between the St. Lawrence River and the Great Lakes.

NATIVE AMERICAN ALLIES

Ever since the British and the French arrived in North America, they had been friendly with different Native American groups. Most of the groups in New France preferred the French over the British. Still, when the British began to offer a wider variety of goods in exchange

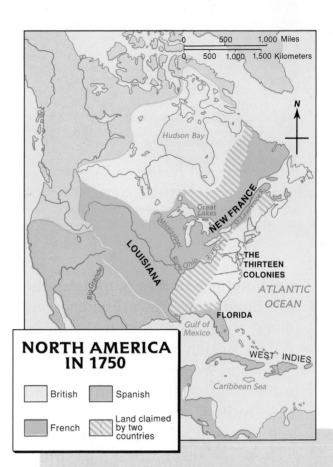

NORTH AMERICA IN 1750

British   Spanish

French   Land claimed by two countries

MAP SKILL: The population of the British colonies was growing rapidly in 1750. In which direction could these colonists move to find more land?

for their furs, some Native Americans began to trade with them. This led to increased fighting over the fur trade among different Indian groups.

WAR BEGINS

In 1754 the French built Fort Duquesne (dü kān'), near present-day Pittsburgh. Since the British had also claimed this area, they decided to attack the French. A 22-year-old British colonist named George Washington led an army of 150 men against the fort. At first,

By the end of the 1700s Detroit had grown into an important town. In 1760 it first became a British settlement.

Washington's forces captured the fort. Soon, however, a French army forced them to retreat to Virginia.

The British attack against Fort Duquesne began the French and Indian War. French settlers and their Indian allies battled British colonists and soldiers for six years.

None of the battles took place on Michigan soil. However, Ottawa and Chippewa from northern Michigan joined the French army in the fighting at Fort Duquesne.

DETROIT FALLS

As the war dragged on, the French began to lose. The British had a larger army, a bigger fleet of ships, and better weapons.

In 1760 the British captured Quebec. Then, British troops marched onward to take over the remaining forts in New France. On November 29, 1760, they reached Detroit. Down came the French flag, which had flown over the settlement for almost 60 years. The British flag quickly took its place.

Three years later France and Britain signed a treaty ending the war. A treaty is an agreement between two countries. In the Treaty of Paris, France gave up all its land claims in North America.

A NEW FLAG

Throughout the 1700s, relations between the French and British settlers in North America grew more tense. In 1754 war broke out. The French and Indian War ended with the defeat of France.

Check Your Reading

1. Why did the British settlers begin moving into lands claimed by the French?
2. Why did many Native American groups choose to side with the French instead of the British?
3. Explain how the French and Indian War got its name.
4. THINKING SKILL: What are three questions you might ask in order to learn more about the French and Indian War?

4 Chief Pontiac's Rebellion

READ TO LEARN

Key Vocabulary
Pontiac's Rebellion
Proclamation of 1763

Key People
Chief Pontiac

Key Places
Fort Michilimackinac

Read Aloud

Drive [the British] away; wage war against them. I love them not. They know me not. They are my enemies, they are your brothers' enemies.

Several hundred Indians gathered near Detroit on April 27, 1763, and listened to the Ottawa chief Pontiac speak these words. He was angry at the way his people had been treated. In this lesson you will read about why the Indians wanted to drive the British off their land, and what happened when they tried.

Read for Purpose

1. **WHAT YOU KNOW:** How would you feel if somebody were to take away the land on which you live?
2. **WHAT YOU WILL LEARN:** Who was Chief Pontiac, and why did he lead an army against the British?

THE BRITISH ANGER NATIVE AMERICANS

After the British took control of the French forts and land, they no longer felt a need to win the Indians' trust. They stopped giving the Indians gifts. They made new rules for the Native Americans.

The Indians had lost many men during the French and Indian War. Many Indian villages had been destroyed. These Native Americans needed British goods to rebuild their communities.

The Indians also needed to hunt, fish, and farm the land in order to live. When the French lost the war, however, British colonists began pushing westward onto Indian land. The Indians knew that there were many more British colonists than there were French. Indian leaders grew worried and angry.

AN INDIAN LEADER

Chief Pontiac argued that the Native Americans must join together to force the British off their land. Half Chippewa and half Ottawa, Pontiac was born in an Ottawa village near Detroit around 1720. Because of his intelligence, bravery, and gift for speaking, the Ottawa chose him as a leader.

There were three large Indian villages near Detroit. A Potawatomi village was located about 2 miles (3.2 km) down the Detroit River from the fort. A group of Huron lived across the river on the spot where Windsor, Canada, is today. An Ottawa village also stood on the Canadian side of the river. Pontiac traveled among these groups, speaking about the need to join together and fight the British.

Chief Pontiac was an important leader of the Ottawa. He believed that Native Americans should fight against the British colonists.

The Granger Collection

THE BATTLE FOR DETROIT

In the Read Aloud you read that Pontiac held a meeting with many of these Indians in April 1763. There he announced his plan to capture Fort Pontchartrain.

A few days later, Pontiac and 60 of his best warriors traveled to the fort for a "peace council" with the British commander. They carried tomahawks, knives, and sawed-off muskets under their blankets.

When they entered the fort, Pontiac and his men saw that something was wrong. The shops had been closed and locked. Soldiers stood ready with their muskets. The commander stood waiting with his pistol and sword. Clearly, someone had told the British about the Indians' plan. No longer able to surprise their enemies, the Indians turned and left without fighting. They returned to their nearby villages.

However, Pontiac's forces hadn't given up. Within a few days, the Indians began to attack the fort from the outside. They fired burning arrows over the stockade and attacked anyone who entered or left the fort. They also tried to keep ships from bringing supplies to the British soldiers.

This battle continued for 153 days! Still, Pontiac and his warriors were unable to force the British army to surrender the fort. By the time autumn began, the Indians needed to return to their villages and prepare for the winter. The battle for Fort Pontchartrain was over.

OTHER BATTLES

Pontiac's actions in Detroit led Indians to attack other British forts. By July 1763 Native Americans had managed to capture all but three British forts in the area west of the Ohio River. Look at the map on this page to find the sites where these battles were fought. These battles were known as Pontiac's Rebellion.

The Indians used a clever plan to capture Fort Michilimackinac. They knew that the British king's birthday was on June 4. A Chippewa chief suggested to the fort commander that the Indians and the British join together in a celebration. As part of this celebration, some visiting Sauk Indians would play a ballgame against the Chippewa outside the fort.

On June 4 the soldiers came out of the fort to watch the game. Chippewa women stood around the fort wrapped in blankets. The Indians began their game of *baggataway*, which was similar to lacrosse.

At one point, the wooden ball was thrown into the fort. The players rushed in after it. As they passed through the gates of the fort, the players grabbed the weapons that the women were holding under their blankets! Once inside, the Indians killed 20 soldiers and took control of the fort.

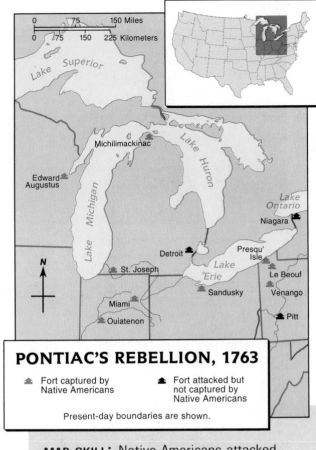

PONTIAC'S REBELLION, 1763

🔺 Fort captured by Native Americans

🔺 Fort attacked but not captured by Native Americans

Present-day boundaries are shown.

MAP SKILL: Native Americans attacked many British forts during 1763. Which forts did not fall to Native American forces during that year?

THE REBELLION ENDS

The Native Americans fought fiercely to defend the land that the British were taking from them. There were acts of cruelty on both sides. But because the British had more weapons and supplies than the Native Americans, they managed to hold onto key forts. The French, who had fought with the Indians in the past, had surrendered to the British in 1763. They could no longer help their old friends.

Eventually, Pontiac became convinced that Indians could not win a

Native American soldiers surrounded Fort Detroit for 153 days. As winter came, however, they returned to their villages to care for their families.

war against the British. He promised to spend the rest of his life working for peace with the British. As he traveled among the different Native American groups and told them to "bury their hatchets," he kept this promise.

The Native Americans had not defeated the British. However, they had succeeded in forcing the British to pay attention to them. The British began giving them gunpowder and other goods again. The British government made the traders treat the Native Americans more fairly.

The British also made a promise to the Indians in the **Proclamation of 1763**. A proclamation (prok lə mā′ shən) is something that is officially announced to the public. The British promised that all land west of the Appalachian Mountains would be set aside for the use of the Indians only. This land included what is now the state of Michigan.

NATIVE AMERICAN LOSSES

Although the Native Americans were unable to defeat the British, they did win a promise to preserve their homeland. For a few years, the Proclamation of 1763 prevented new settlers from coming to the land of Michigan. In the next chapter, you will read about the birth of a new nation and how that nation changed the lives of Pontiac's people.

Check Your Reading

1. Why were the Indians fearful when the British took over the French forts and land?
2. How did Pontiac's Rebellion come to an end?
3. **GEOGRAPHY SKILL:** How was the Proclamation of 1763 to have helped the Indians who lived in the land of Michigan?
4. **THINKING SKILL:** Why did Pontiac's choice to attack Detroit seem to be the best choice for Native Americans at the time?

REVIEWING VOCABULARY

colony   slavery
expedition   treaty
missionary

Number a sheet of paper from 1 to 5. Beside each number write the word from the list above that best matches the definition.

1. A place or settlement that is ruled by another country
2. The practice of making one person the property of another person
3. A person who teaches his or her religion to others who have different beliefs
4. A formal agreement between two countries
5. A journey made for a special purpose

REVIEWING FACTS

1. Why did Samuel de Champlain found New France?
2. Who was the first European to reach the land of Michigan?
3. Who was Jacques Marquette? Which communities did he start?
4. Why was fur trapping and trading a useful business in New France?
5. How did Antoine de la Cadillac try to prevent British traders from competing against French fur traders?

6. Why did the French and Indian War take place?
7. What was the Treaty of Paris?
8. Who was Chief Pontiac?
9. What did Pontiac do when he realized that the Indians could not defeat the British?
10. What was the main requirement of the Proclamation of 1763?

WRITING ABOUT MAIN IDEAS

1. **Writing a Description:** Study the map of La Salle's route on page 91. Describe his route by using the correct direction words, so that someone who had not seen the map could picture his journey.
2. **Writing a Character Sketch:** Review the information about Chief Pontiac on pages 100–101. Then write a short character sketch, explaining the kind of person he was.

BUILDING SKILLS: READING TIME LINES

Copy the time line on page 88, and then answer these questions.

1. What is a time line?
2. Which centuries are shown on the time line?
3. Add the following event to the time line: 1658—Pierre Radisson explores Lake Superior.

REVIEWING VOCABULARY

archaeologist   migrate
artifact   missionary
colony   ceremony
culture   slavery
expedition   treaty

Number a sheet of paper from 1 to 10. Beside each number write the word from the list above that best completes the sentence.

1. At the end of the War of 1812, France and Britain signed a ____ in which they agreed that France would give up its land claims in North America.
2. This piece of prehistoric pottery is an example of an ____.
3. The people ____ to better hunting grounds each summer.
4. La Salle led an ____ through the Great Lakes region.
5. Marquette was a ____ who tried to teach his religion to Indians.
6. The ____ tried to learn more about the lives of prehistoric peoples.
7. Early people held a ____ to celebrate a special occasion.
8. In the British colonies, people practiced ____, which allowed them to own other people.
9. Religion is part of a group's way of life, or ____.
10. New France was a ____ of France, which controlled it.

WRITING ABOUT THE UNIT

1. **Writing a Comparison:** Compare the arrival of the first Native Americans in Michigan with the arrival of the first Europeans. Consider questions such as: Why did they come? How did they get here? What did they find?
2. **Writing a Speech:** Imagine that you are Chief Pontiac and the year is 1763. The Rebellion is over and you are traveling among Indian groups, trying to convince them to make peace with the British. Write a speech that Pontiac might have given to persuade the Native Americans to make peace.

ACTIVITIES

1. **Making a Diorama:** Review the information about Fort Pontchartrain in Chapter 4, Lesson 2. Then make a diorama of the fort.
2. **Working Together to Conduct Research:** Divide into three groups to learn more about the Three Fires. Each group should concentrate on one of the following topics: their clothing, their homes, their ways of hunting or farming, their legends, their beliefs. Prepare a written report or series of illustrations with captions based on your research.

BUILDING SKILLS: MAKING DECISIONS

Imagine that you are Chief Pontiac and the year is 1763. The Indians have been fighting the British for months. The British have issued the Proclamation of 1763. You must decide whether the Indians should keep fighting the British or make peace. You want to do what is best for the Indians.

1. Your decision should help you to
   a. make up your mind.
   b. reach your goal.
   c. be popular with the Indians.
2. You should first
   a. think about your choices and the possible results of each one.
   b. ask some other Native American leaders what they think.
   c. decide what is best for all the Native Americans.
3. Why is it important that Pontiac make a good decision in this case?

 **LINKING PAST, PRESENT, AND FUTURE**

As you have read, archaeologists study people who lived a long time ago. In order to learn more about people's lives, archaeologists look at artifacts, such as tools, weapons, and pottery. Suppose that archaeologists of the future wanted to learn more about life in Michigan today. Which artifacts do you think would help them learn about our state? Name four or five artifacts that would represent life in Michigan today.

1805
Detroit burns to the ground

1813
The Americans defeat the British at the Battle of Put-in-Bay

1837
Michigan becomes a state

1830s
Pioneers rush to buy land that had been owned by Native Americans

1853
The Soo Canal is built connecting Lake Superior and Lake Huron

WHAT HAPPENED

You have already read about the first people to live in our state. But the whole story has not yet been told. In this unit you will read about how Michigan became part of a new country. You will also read about the challenges faced by Michigan's Native Americans and a terrible war that tore our young country apart.

1850s
Black and white Michiganians help people escape from slavery to freedom along the Underground Railroad

1864
Soldiers of the First Michigan Colored Regiment march through Michigan towns before fighting in the Civil War

106

UNIT 3

MICHIGAN JOINS THE UNITED STATES

UNITED STATES LAND OFFICE

CHAPTER 5

MICHIGAN BECOMES A STATE

▼ FOCUS ▼

I like to see the displays of different things that have been uncovered at the fort. They show how people lived long ago. But my favorite part of Fort Michilimackinac is the cannons.

Alexandra Felski lives in Cheboygan, at the northern tip of Michigan's Lower Peninsula. She likes to go to nearby Fort Michilimackinac to learn about what life was like in Michigan many years ago.

1 Michigan and the American Revolution

READ TO LEARN

Key Vocabulary
frontier
tax
American Revolution

Key People
Henry Hamilton
Jean de Sable

Key Places
Fort St. Joseph

Read Aloud

In the fort there are four English officers, 17 men, and a considerable quantity of all sorts of goods which they use to purchase corn . . . from the neighboring Indians.

These words are from a letter written by a Spanish soldier, Don Francisco Cruzat (crü sät), in 1781. He and his men had just taken over Fort St. Joseph, near present-day Niles. In this lesson you will read about the different countries that battled for control of the land of Michigan. You will also read how a new country, the United States, was born.

Read for Purpose

1. **WHAT YOU KNOW:** Why were European nations interested in controlling the land of Michigan?
2. **WHAT YOU WILL LEARN:** How did the land of Michigan become part of the United States?

BRITAIN ANGERS THE COLONISTS

You read about the Proclamation of 1763 in Chapter 4. In this proclamation, the British promised that all lands west of the Appalachian Mountains would be saved for the Native Americans. Look at the Atlas map on pages 298–299 to see the land included in this area.

The proclamation pleased the Native Americans. But it made the colonists very angry. More colonists hoped to move to the frontier, the term they used for the land at the edge of their settled area. Now the

109

A battle in Lexington, Massachusetts began the **American Revolution** in 1775. American leaders signed the Declaration of Independence a year later.

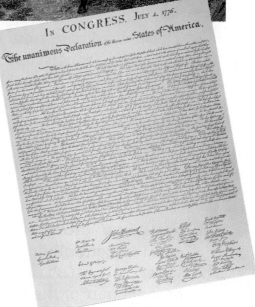

British had closed the frontier to new settlement. Many colonists who wanted to move west felt that they had been cheated.

The British king, George III, also angered the colonists in other ways. He announced that more troops would be sent to North America to protect the lands along the frontier. These extra troops would cost money, of course. To raise the money, the British government insisted that the colonists pay new taxes. A tax is money that people pay to support their government.

The American colonists were forced to pay a tax each time they bought a newspaper or a calendar. They paid a tax to obtain official papers such as marriage licenses.

They even paid a tax when they bought playing cards!

THE COLONIES BREAK AWAY

Tensions between the colonists and the British continued to grow. The colonists began secretly training their own troops. On April 19, 1775, battles broke out between American and British soldiers near

110

Boston, in the small towns of Lexington and Concord. The American Revolution had begun. A revolution is a sudden, total change in government, usually by force.

The new nation's independence became official 15 months later. On July 4, 1776, representatives from each of the 13 colonies signed the Declaration of Independence. This document, which was written by Thomas Jefferson, announced that the colonies

> *are, and of Right ought to be, Free and Independent States . . . and that all political Connection between them and the State of Great-Britain is and ought to be totally dissolved.*

The rebellious colonists called their new nation the United States of America. Nobody suspected that the war would last until 1783.

THE WAR IN THE WEST

The land of Michigan played an important part in the American Revolution, although no battles were fought here. Henry Hamilton, the commander of the British army along the frontier, had his main outpost at Detroit. As long as British soldiers remained in their forts throughout Michigan, they could control much of the Great Lakes area. They also used the forts in Michigan as bases to launch raids into the area that is now Indiana, Ohio, and Kentucky.

Henry Hamilton, commander of Fort Detroit, traded gunpowder with Native Americans. Powderhorns, such as this one, were used to keep gunpowder dry.

Hamilton worked hard to gain the help of the Native Americans. The British gave the Indians wagonloads of gifts. In one year of the war, these gifts included 12,000 pounds (5,450 kg) of gunpowder, 4,000 blankets, 10,000 needles, and 100 dozen black silk handkerchiefs!

INDIAN AND BRITISH RAIDS

The Native Americans were glad to accept these gifts. However, they had their own reasons for helping the British. Despite the Proclamation of 1763, American settlers had already begun moving west of the Appalachian Mountains. If the colonies won their independence, there would be nothing to prevent a flood of settlers from taking over Native American lands.

To discourage the settlers, the Indians sent raiding parties into present-day Kentucky and into other areas. These raids were meant to chase the settlers back east and to warn others against coming west.

In one raid Michigan Indians captured Kentucky's famous leader, Daniel Boone. The Indians brought Boone back to Detroit.

In another raid, this time under the command of a British officer, Indians captured Jean de Sable (zhän də säb′ lə). Born in Haiti, De Sable was one of the first people of African descent to live in the Great Lakes area. The British worried that De Sable might be spying for the American colonists. They kept him prisoner on Mackinac Island and in Detroit for several years. De Sable later remained in Michigan to trade with the Native Americans near the site of present-day Port Huron.

THE FORT OF FOUR FLAGS

In the Read Aloud you read about Fort St. Joseph, located near what is now Niles. This British fort played only a small role during the American Revolution. However, the fort is famous for being the only place in Michigan over which four flags have flown—the French, British, Spanish, and American flags.

In 1781 a group of Spanish and Native American soldiers traveled north from St. Louis. When they reached Fort St. Joseph, they found it almost empty. Most of the British soldiers were off fighting the Americans. Historians are still not sure why the Spanish and Native American soldiers took over Fort St. Joseph. In any case, they left after only one day!

CHART SKILL: Flags of four different countries flew over Fort St. Joseph. When did the American flag first fly there?

FLAGS OVER FORT ST. JOSEPH

1671–1760
France

1760–1781
Great Britain

1781
Spain

After 1781
United States

THE WAR ENDS

At first, the American Revolution went badly for the colonists. The British army was bigger and better equipped, and British troops soon won several victories.

Over the years, however, the colonists began to wear the British down. The Americans were fighting on their home territory. It was easier for them to get food and supplies. Halfway through the war, they also gained help from the government of France. The French sent troops, ships, arms, and clothing. On October 19, 1781, the British army finally surrendered to the Americans at Yorktown, Virginia.

Look at the map on this page to see the area that now became the United States of America. According to the treaty that the British made with the Americans, the land of Michigan was part of this new country. But when it came time for the British to leave their forts in Detroit and on Mackinac Island, they refused! They stayed in Michigan for years while the two countries continued to argue.

AMERICAN INDEPENDENCE

You have read about how the 13 colonies gained their independence. The land of Michigan became part of this new, independent country. In the next lesson you will read about Michigan's early days as part of the United States of America.

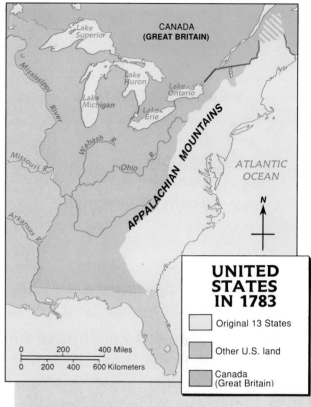

MAP SKILL: Which river formed the western border of the United States in 1783?

Check Your Reading

1. Why were the American colonists angry with the British government?
2. Who was Jean de Sable, and why was he captured by the British?
3. **GEOGRAPHY SKILL:** Which landform did the Proclamation of 1763 forbid American colonists to move beyond?
4. **THINKING SKILL:** List three possible courses of action that the Native Americans of Michigan could have taken when the American Revolution began.

2 The Michigan Territory

READ TO LEARN

Key Vocabulary

territory
pioneer
Treaty of Greenville

Key People

Anthony Wayne
William Hull
Augustus Woodward

Key Places

Northwest
Territory

Read Aloud

Sir—

The United States have succeeded to [gained] *a great deal of property at Detroit.*

In 1796 the British finally left Detroit. On that occasion the letter above was sent to George Washington, who was the President of the United States. In this lesson you will read about how the new nation organized the land it had won.

Read for Purpose

1. **WHAT YOU KNOW:** In what ways is your community divided into different areas or neighborhoods?
2. **WHAT YOU WILL LEARN:** How did the United States organize the land that it won from the British?

THE NORTHWEST TERRITORY

When the land of Michigan became part of the United States, it formed part of a huge frontier area. This area was called the Northwest Territory. A territory is land that belongs to a country but is not a state of that country. Look at the map on page 115 to see the Northwest Territory.

The leaders of the 13 original states soon agreed on two important laws that shaped the Northwest Territory. One of these was called the Land Ordinance of 1785. This law stated that the land of the Northwest Territory would be measured and mapped once the Native Americans had sold it to the United States government. Few of the leaders who

114

wrote the Land Ordinance thought that the Native Americans might prefer to stay where they had lived for many generations.

The second law was called the Northwest Ordinance of 1787. It stated that at some time in the future the Northwest Territory would be divided into three, four, or five new states. One of these states would be Michigan. Until then, the President would appoint a governor and other officials for the Territory. The Northwest Ordinance made slavery illegal in the Northwest Territory. But people who already owned slaves could keep them.

BATTLE AT FALLEN TIMBERS

Pioneers had begun moving into the Northwest Territory as soon as the British were defeated. A pioneer is one of the first people to move into a frontier area.

The arrival of American pioneers worried Native Americans. Desperate to save their lands, some Indian groups began to attack the pioneers.

President George Washington wanted this fighting stopped. He chose General Anthony Wayne to command a new western army. On August 20, 1794, Wayne's army met a Native American army led by Chief Blue Jacket in Ohio. The two forces fought for only one hour before the Indians surrendered.

A tornado had recently hit the area where the battle was fought,

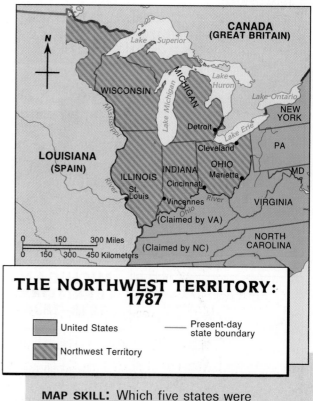

THE NORTHWEST TERRITORY: 1787

☐ United States   —— Present-day state boundary

▨ Northwest Territory

MAP SKILL: Which five states were created from the Northwest Territory?

knocking down many trees. For this reason the battle came to be known as the Battle at Fallen Timbers.

In the summer of 1795, Native American chiefs met with Wayne at Greenville, Ohio. A Chippewa chief known as Bad Bird spoke for the Ottawa, Chippewa, and Potawatomi of Michigan. Bad Bird promised that these groups would no longer fight against Americans. The chiefs also agreed to give up large areas of land in southeastern Michigan.

This agreement was called the Treaty of Greenville. It was the first of many land treaties the Nativ~ Americans would make w~ United States government.

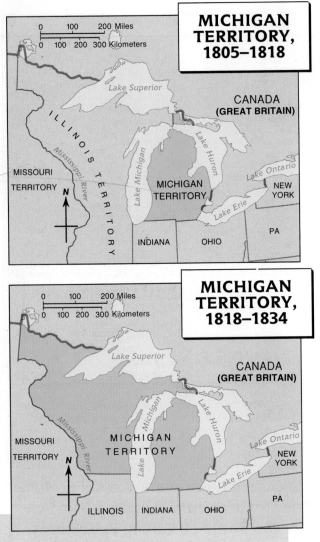

MICHIGAN TERRITORY, 1805–1818

MICHIGAN TERRITORY, 1818–1834

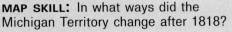

MAP SKILL: In what ways did the Michigan Territory change after 1818?

DETROIT GROWS

When the British left Detroit in 1796, it was a village of about 500 people. One visitor wrote in 1793:

> *The inhabitants of the town are as great a mixture as I ever knew in any one place. English, Scotch, Irish, Dutch, French, Americans from different states, with black and yellow [people] . . . and . . . Indians of different tribes.*

The population also included several enslaved African Americans. There had been African American and Indian slaves at Mackinac Island and Detroit since the time of Cadillac. When the British took over in 1763, some army officers from other states had brought their slaves to this new outpost.

MICHIGAN TERRITORY

The population of the Northwest Territory grew rapidly as Indian lands went up for sale. By 1803, Ohio's population was over 60,000. According to the Northwest Ordinance, as soon as a territory's population reached this number, it could ask to become a new state. Ohio became the seventeenth state in 1803.

The population of Michigan grew more slowly. Still, by 1803 more than 3,000 people lived in and around Detroit alone. Michiganians asked the national government to make Michigan a territory.

In 1805 the United States government agreed to form the Michigan Territory. Look at the map on this page. You will see that in 1805 only part of the Upper Peninsula was included in the Michigan Territory. The boundaries would change several more times in the following years. President Thomas Jefferson appointed William Hull to be Michigan's territorial governor. The people of Detroit began making plans to welcome the new governor.

DETROIT IN FLAMES

Hull received a very different welcome from the one he had expected. Just a few days before he arrived, Detroit burned to the ground! It was a windy day on June 11, 1805. A bakery worker stepped outside to clean his pipe at about 9:00 A.M. The hot ashes from his pipe blew into a pile of hay in a nearby stable. The stable caught on fire, and from there the flames raced from building to building.

People ran into the burning buildings to grab clothing, furniture, and groceries. They piled them into boats and canoes, which they then hauled out onto the Detroit River. Tables, chairs, beds, and chests lined the riverbank.

By 1:00 in the afternoon, only 1 of the town's nearly 200 buildings remained standing. According to one citizen, "nothing was to be seen of the city except a mass of burning coals, and chimney-tops stretching like pyramids into the air. . . ."

One of the new territorial judges had many ideas about how to rebuild Detroit. Augustus Woodward had studied the plans for the country's new capital of Washington, D.C. He drew up a similar street plan for the new city of Detroit. Look on this page to study Woodward's plan. The circular parks and wide avenues extending in all directions would help to make Detroit a bustling frontier city.

Augustus Woodward designed a plan for Detroit that is still part of that city's street pattern today.

A NEW TERRITORY

The Detroit fire was a sad beginning for the Michigan Territory. But the citizens quickly started to rebuild their capital, and the future looked bright for the new territory.

✔ Check Your Reading

1. Where was the Northwest Territory located?
2. Why did fighting break out between Native Americans and pioneers along the frontier?
3. What did the Northwest Ordinance say about slavery in the Northwest Territory?
4. **THINKING SKILL:** What are three questions you could ask Augustus Woodward to learn more about his plan for Detroit?

Comparing Local Maps

Throughout this book you have been using maps to help you to understand the history and geography of Michigan. Each of the different maps helped you to learn something about our state. What have you learned about our state from the maps in this book?

As you have seen, maps show information in a special way. Each map, however, usually shows only one kind of information. By comparing maps that show different kinds of information, you can learn even more about the state of Michigan.

Making Comparisons

The first step in comparing maps is to figure out what you are comparing. Ask yourself the following questions.

- Am I comparing maps that show different information *about the same place*?
- Am I comparing maps that show similar information *about two different places*?

You can answer these questions by looking at the map title and the labels on each map. Study the two maps on these pages. Do they show the same place? How can you tell? What does the map below show? What does the map on page 119 show?

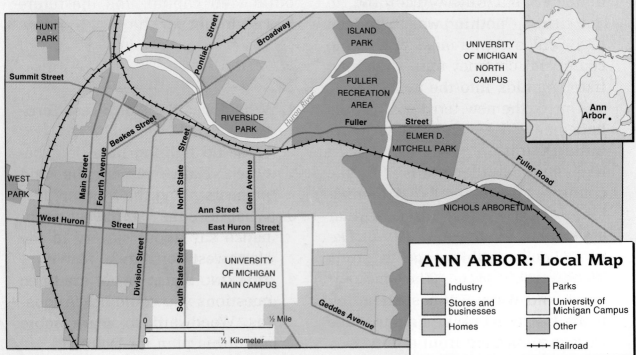

ANN ARBOR: Local Map

Industry	Parks
Stores and businesses	University of Michigan Campus
Homes	Other
	+++ Railroad

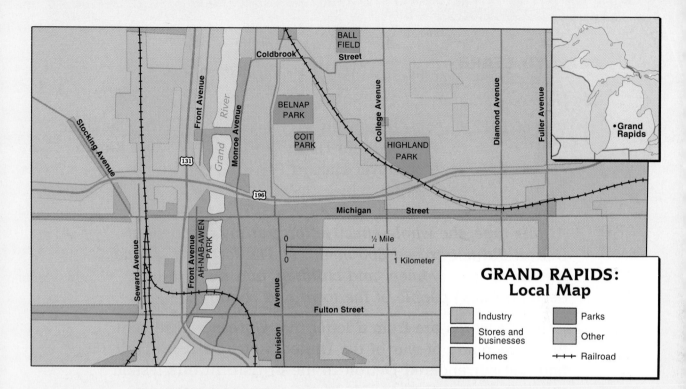

GRAND RAPIDS: Local Map

Key	
Industry	Parks
Stores and businesses	Other
Homes	┼┼┼┼ Railroad

Next read the information each map gives. Use the map keys to find out what the different colors stand for. Which color shows industry in Grand Rapids? What does the color pink stand for in the maps of both Ann Arbor and Grand Rapids?

Then look for similarities in and differences between the information on the two maps. Which city has the larger area with homes?

Finally, make statements based on the information provided on the two maps. Based on the information presented on the map on page 118, which of the following statements about Ann Arbor is true?

- Most of the people who live in Ann Arbor are farmers.

- Ann Arbor's business area is smaller than the area where people live.

Reviewing the Skill

Compare the maps of Ann Arbor and Grand Rapids to answer the following questions.

1. What are the three main uses of land in both Ann Arbor and Grand Rapids?

2. For what purpose is most of the land in Ann Arbor used? For what purpose is most of the land in Grand Rapids used?

3. What can you learn from comparing maps that give similar information about two different places?

4. How is it helpful to compare two or more maps?

119

3 The War of 1812

READ TO LEARN

Key Vocabulary

War of 1812

Key People

Tecumseh
William Henry Harrison
Oliver Hazard Perry

Key Places

Fort Mackinac
River Raisin

Read Aloud

At this time, the whole effective force at my disposal at Detroit did not exceed 800 men. . . . The fort at this time was filled with women, and children, and the old and decrepit [sick] people of the town and country.

These words are from a letter that Governor Hull sent to the secretary of war of the United States in 1812. Hull had just surrendered Detroit to the British. In this lesson you will read about how Michigan came under the control of a European nation for the last time.

Read for Purpose

1. **WHAT YOU KNOW:** Which European nations had previously claimed the land of Michigan?
2. **WHAT YOU WILL LEARN:** How did the War of 1812 change the Michigan Territory?

TENSION ON THE FRONTIER

Governor Hull was anxious to attract more American settlers to the Michigan Territory. But most of the land in the territory still belonged to Native American groups. Hull set up meetings with Indian leaders to pressure them to sell their lands to the United States.

In 1807 a group of Chippewa chiefs signed the Treaty of Detroit. Some Indian leaders did not want to sell their land. Tecumseh, a Shawnee chief, was one of these leaders. He began to organize Indian groups from Michigan to the Gulf of Mexico in an effort to slow down American settlement along the frontier.

British officials and traders were happy to see the tension grow between the Native Americans and the Americans. The British gave the Native Americans guns and tomahawks with which to attack American settlers. The British navy also stopped American ships sailing in the Atlantic Ocean.

Many Americans were angered by the actions of the British and the Indians. Some thought that the only way to stop the attacks on American settlers and ships was to fight back. Congress declared war on Britain in 1812, beginning the War of 1812.

THE WAR IN MICHIGAN

As soon as the war began, the British rushed into Michigan. In August 1812 a group of British and Native American soldiers landed on Mackinac Island. Rather than attacking Fort Mackinac directly, they dragged a huge cannon up to the top of the hill behind the fort. When the Americans saw the cannon pointed down from above, they surrendered without firing a shot. Look at the map on this page to see the location of Fort Mackinac.

Governor Hull was in charge of the fort at Detroit. The British began firing cannons at the city from across the river. Hull knew that the British would have the help of many Native American soldiers. Worried that his army would soon be outnumbered, he surrendered Detroit.

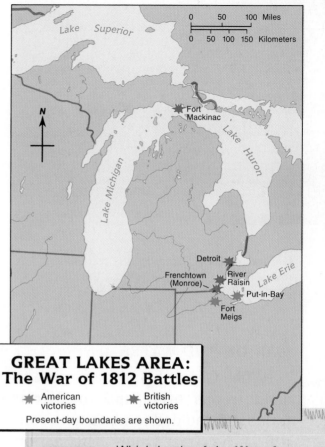

GREAT LAKES AREA:
The War of 1812 Battles
American victories   British victories
Present-day boundaries are shown.

MAP SKILL: Which battle of the War of 1812 was fought near the Upper Peninsula?

The Americans were determined to retake Detroit. Within a few months, General William Henry Harrison sent an army from Ohio to drive the British away.

American troops met the British and Indians in a battle on the River Raisin, near present-day Monroe. Although many soldiers from both sides died, the Americans lost the battle. The next morning, Native Americans returned to the River Raisin. Angry that so many of their people had died in battle, they attacked the wounded American soldiers left on the battlefield.

121

Lieutenant Oliver Hazard Perry rowed from one ship to another during the Battle of Put-in-Bay.

WAR ON THE WATER

When General Harrison's plan to send troops over land to Detroit failed, he decided to try to take control of the Great Lakes. This action would cut off an important British supply route to Detroit.

Lieutenant Oliver Hazard Perry set out to meet the British fleet at Put-in-Bay on Lake Erie. Look at the map on page 121 to see where this naval battle took place. Perry raised a blue flag high above his ship that read, *Don't Give Up the Ship*. When his men saw the flag go up, they let out a loud cheer. This was the signal to attack!

Perry's ship was soon battered into pieces by British cannonballs. Perry took down his flag, rowed in a small boat through gunfire to another ship, and hoisted the flag again. After hours of close fighting, the British fleet surrendered. Perry

sent a famous message to General Harrison: "We have met the enemy, and they are ours."

After their defeat at the Battle of Put-in-Bay, the British abandoned Detroit. General Harrison pushed on after them. In the meantime the Indian leader Tecumseh was killed in a battle in Canada. With their leader gone, the Native Americans stopped fighting alongside their British allies.

In 1814 the British and the Americans signed a treaty ending the war. According to the treaty, Britain kept Canada and the United States kept its territory on the frontier.

THE WAR ENDS

The Americans fought hard during the War of 1812 to keep their new country independent. The British, the Americans, and the Indians all lost many of their leaders and young soldiers.

Check Your Reading

1. Why did Tecumseh organize groups of Native Americans?
2. How did the British capture Fort Mackinac?
3. **GEOGRAPHY SKILL:** Why did General Harrison want to take control of the Great Lakes?
4. **THINKING SKILL:** Predict what might have happened if Governor Hull had not surrendered Detroit to the British.

4 Indians Lose Their Land

READzTO LEARN

Key Vocabulary
Treaty of Saginaw

Key People
Lewis Cass

Read Aloud

We are here to smoke the pipe of peace, but not to sell our lands. . . . Your people trespass upon our hunting grounds. You flock to our shores . . . our land melts like a cake of ice; our possessions grow smaller and smaller. . . . Our children want homes; shall we sell from under them the spot where they spread their blankets? We have not called you here.

O-ge-maw-keke-too (ō gə mô kə gē tō), a Chippewa chief, spoke these words to Lewis Cass, governor of the Michigan Territory, in 1819. Cass had traveled to Saginaw Bay to meet with Native American leaders. He hoped to buy more land for the United States. In this lesson you will learn what happened at this meeting.

Read for Purpose

1. **WHAT YOU KNOW:** How would you feel if you were forced to move from your home?
2. **WHAT YOU WILL LEARN:** How were our state's Native Americans forced to leave their land?

LAND AND SETTLERS

After the War of 1812, **Lewis Cass** became the governor of the Michigan Territory. He hoped that the territory's population would soon reach the number necessary for statehood. However, new settlers required new lands to settle on.

You already have read that Governor Hull purchased a large part of the Lower Peninsula from the Chippewa in 1807. Now Governor Cass hoped to buy even more land from the Native Americans. This would encourage more settlers from the East to make the trip to Michigan.

123

THE TREATY OF SAGINAW

In September 1819, Cass called a meeting of Michigan chiefs to be held near what is now Saginaw. A huge council house was built, and almost 4,000 Native Americans came for the discussions. Cass told the Indians that the government wanted to buy 6 million acres (2.4 million ha) of land. In return, he offered the Indians $3,000 in silver coins. When the Indians hesitated, he reminded them that the President, "the Great White Father at Washington . . . had whipped the English king and the Indians, too."

Some of the Indians began to consider the offer. Michigan's Indians had been weakened by their losses during the War of 1812. Their British allies had left Michigan forever. At the same time, these Native Americans had grown more and more used to non-Indian goods such as guns, needles, pots, and pans. Perhaps it made sense after all to accept the silver that Cass had offered.

After he signed the Treaty of Saginaw, Lewis Cass explored the northern part of the Michigan Territory.

Many Indians continued to resist selling their lands. Cass soon found a way to influence them. He learned that Jacob Smith, a trader who lived among the Native Americans, had been advising the chiefs not to sign the treaty. Cass offered this trusted friend of the Indians a large area of land for free. In return, Smith advised his Native American friends to sign the Treaty of Saginaw. They followed his advice, and 6 million acres of Michigan's land passed into the government's hands.

The government began to divide the land into sections that could be sold. Plans were made to build roads across the Lower Peninsula to make settlement easier. Governor Cass had gotten the land that he wanted. However, for Michigan's Native Americans, the Treaty of Saginaw meant the loss of their homeland forever.

CASS EXPLORES NEW LANDS

Cass was anxious to explore other Native American land in the northern part of the Michigan Territory. He set out with an expedition that included Henry R. Schoolcraft, a geologist and an explorer. You read a statement made by Schoolcraft in Chapter 2.

The members of the expedition paddled canoes out to Mackinac Island. Then they traveled along the shore of Lake Superior. Cass realized that the land of northern Michigan was even more valuable than he had thought. The land he explored included beautiful rivers, vast forests, and useful minerals. These resources would soon attract many settlers to Michigan.

LOST LANDS

Starting in 1807, Michigan's Native Americans gradually gave up their lands in the Lower Peninsula. By 1836 the government had the entire peninsula. Look at the map on this page to see the land that the Native Americans lost.

As American settlers arrived in Michigan, they quickly cleared the land for farming. As farming became more important, the fur trade came to an end. By the mid-1820s, most of Michigan's beavers were gone. And without the fur trade, the traders, merchants, and the United States government had little use for the Native Americans.

INDIAN REMOVAL

During the late 1830s the government began forcing Michigan's Indians to move to unsettled areas in

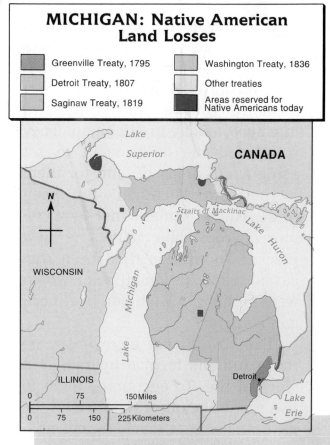

MICHIGAN: Native American Land Losses

- Greenville Treaty, 1795
- Detroit Treaty, 1807
- Saginaw Treaty, 1819
- Washington Treaty, 1836
- Other treaties
- Areas reserved for Native Americans today

MAP SKILL: Michigan's Native Americans signed treaties (*below*), giving up their land. In which year did they give up the land near the Straits of Mackinac?

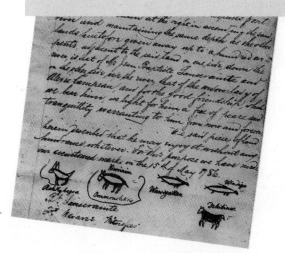

the far west. Government agents first rounded up Potawatomi from southwest Michigan, and marched them on a long trip toward Kansas.

125

Some managed to escape and return to their homes in Michigan. Others fled to Canada, where the British government welcomed them.

Many Ottawa and Chippewa managed to stay in Michigan. They persuaded the government to set aside small areas of land for them in northern Michigan. But even these Native Americans were removed from their homes to new places. Thousands died from diseases, such as smallpox, which were brought to Michigan by American settlers.

The government also pressured these Indians to give up their old ways of life. To encourage them to live more like other Americans, the government sent teachers and missionaries among the Indians. Still, these Native Americans struggled to keep their old customs and culture.

Years later, Simon Pokagon, a Potawatomi from Michigan, reminded a group of Americans that his people had paid a terrible price for the growth of America.

And you who live here . . . do not forget that this success has been at the sacrifice of our homes and a once-happy race.

PIONEER GAINS, INDIAN LOSSES

As you have read, Native Americans gradually sold their lands in the Michigan Territory to the United States government. The Indians were forced to leave their homes. Sometimes they were removed to locations as far away as Kansas. Meanwhile, settlers from the East bought the former Indian lands and began to build farms. In the next lesson, you will read how the Michigan Territory became our nation's twenty-sixth state.

Some Native Americans, such as this group of Potawatomi, stayed in Michigan and worked to keep their culture alive.

Check Your Reading

1. Why did Lewis Cass want to attract more settlers to Michigan?
2. How did Lewis Cass persuade Native Americans to sell their land in the Lower Peninsula?
3. How did the end of Michigan's fur trade affect the Native Americans?
4. **THINKING SKILL:** What were some arguments for and against the Native Americans' signing the Treaty of Saginaw?

5 Statehood

READ TO LEARN

Key Vocabulary

constitution   compromise
canal   legislature
Toledo War

Key People

Stevens T. Mason

Key Places

Toledo Strip
Ann Arbor

Read Aloud

*The admission of Michigan into the Union was cele-
brated in this city on Thursday last, with . . . the firing of
a salute of 26 guns. In the evening the scene was opened
with bonfires and [fireworks].*

In January 1837 Michigan finally became a state. As
this article in the Detroit *Free Press* reported, the event
was a cause for Michigan's settlers to celebrate. But as
you will read in this lesson, becoming a state had not
been easy. First, Michigan had to fight a little "war"
with Ohio.

Read for Purpose

1. **WHAT YOU KNOW:** How did Michigan become part of
   the United States?
2. **WHAT YOU WILL LEARN:** Which steps did Michigan take
   in order to become a state?

A GROWING TERRITORY

In 1831 Lewis Cass left Michigan
for Washington, D.C., to become an
adviser to President Andrew Jackson. Cass had done much to make
Michigan better known in the east.
Partly because of his efforts, the
population of the territory was
growing very quickly. By the mid-
1830s, Michigan was the fastest-
growing area in the country.

How did the news about Michigan spread? Letters from people
who had moved to Michigan encouraged others back east to make
the trip. For example, Martha White

127

was a widow who had come to Michigan from Massachusetts. She settled in Lapeer with her eight children. In one letter, she wrote to a friend about the "good life" in her new home.

We have all good things here, one barrel of molasses, one-and-a-half of sugar, and so you see we live upon the fat of the land. As for . . . snakes, mosquitoes, and rats, I have seen none, and flies are not an inhabitant of this region.

By 1835 Michigan's population had increased to more than 85,000. This number was well above the population of 60,000 that the Northwest Ordinance required for a territory to become a state.

Stevens T. Mason was Michigan's first and youngest governor.

"THE BOY GOVERNOR"

As the population grew, many Michiganians thought that it was finally time for the Michigan Territory to become a state. The governor, Stevens T. Mason, agreed to discuss the issue with Congress.

Mason was often called "the boy governor" because he had begun running the Michigan Territory in 1831, when he was only 20. At that time, Mason actually served as secretary of the territory rather than governor. However, he handled most of the territory's business for the governor, George Porter. When Porter died in 1834, Mason took over as acting governor.

WRITING A CONSTITUTION

Before a territory could become a state, it had to have a constitution approved by Congress. A constitution is a plan of government. The people of Michigan quickly elected a group of 91 men to write a constitution for the state.

On May 11, 1835, this group met in Detroit. Of the 91 men, 45 were farmers. Others were merchants, lumbermen, and lawyers. At the time, neither women, African Americans, nor Native Americans were allowed to vote. For this reason, none of these groups was represented at the meeting in Detroit.

Within 45 days the constitution was ready. Michigan voters approved the constitution in October

1835. They also elected Stevens T. Mason as the state's first governor.

However, the United States Congress refused to approve Michigan's new constitution. President Andrew Jackson, who was supposed to sign the document admitting Michigan as a state, also refused to approve it. The problem was caused by a piece of land along the Michigan-Ohio border known as the Toledo Strip.

THE TOLEDO WAR

What was the Toledo Strip? During the 1830s the state of Ohio was building a canal to connect Lake Erie to the Ohio River. A canal is a waterway that is dug across land for ships to travel on. The builders assumed that Toledo would be Ohio's lake port at the northern end of the canal. Michiganians claimed that the strip of land on which Toledo was located belonged to Michigan.

Michigan and Ohio residents were fighting over the strip of land even as Michigan's constitution was being written. When Governor Robert Lucas of Ohio sent men to mark the strip as Ohio territory, Governor Mason sent a small Michigan army to follow them. Ohio residents raised a small army of their own. The Toledo War had begun.

Michiganians started singing the "Toledo War Song." This verse predicted that Governor Lucas would be frightened away by the "howling" of the Michiganians.

When we got down to Toledo,
Old Lucas was not there.
He had heard that we were
Coming and ran away with fear.
To hear the wolves a-howling
Scared the poor devil so,
He said, before he'd fight
Them, he'd give up Toledo.

The Toledo War never amounted to more than a great deal of shouting and a few black eyes. But some people think that Michiganians earned the nickname, "Wolverines," during this war. Ohioans may have compared the Michigan soldiers to these tough animals.

Congress finally stepped in to propose a compromise. A compromise is an agreement in which each

MICHIGAN AND THE TOLEDO STRIP, 1837

Toledo Strip
Western Upper Peninsula

CANADA
Lake Superior
0   75   150 Miles
0   75   150   225 Kilometers
N
WISCONSIN
Lake Michigan
Lake Huron
MICHIGAN
Lake Erie
INDIANA
OHIO

MAP SKILL: Which Great Lake bordered the eastern edge of the Toledo Strip?

129

Michigan's **legislature** voted in 1847 to move the state capital to Lansing. The first state capitol building (*right*) was built in the same year.

side gives up a little of what it wants. The members of Congress suggested that Ohio should get the Toledo Strip. In exchange, the western part of the Upper Peninsula would be added to Michigan.

This compromise was approved at a meeting in **Ann Arbor**. Michiganians gave up 468 square miles (1,212 sq km) of land and the harbor at Toledo. In return, they gained more than 13,000 square miles (33,670 sq km) of land in the Upper Peninsula. On January 26, 1837, President Jackson signed the bill that made Michigan the twenty-sixth state.

A NEW CAPITAL

The capital of the new state was to remain in Detroit until a permanent place was chosen. Representatives from Ann Arbor, Jackson, Marshall, De Witt, Dexter, Eaton Rapids, Grand Blanc, Byron, and Lyons each argued that his own town should be the new capital.

The **legislature** (lej′ is lā chər) of Michigan finally made a decision in 1847. A legislature is a group of people who have the power to make laws. The members of the legislature agreed to locate the capital in a newly-settled community—the township of Lansing in Ingham County.

THE TWENTY-SIXTH STATE

After the Toledo War had been settled, Michigan finally became a state in 1837. With a new state capital and a new nickname—the "Wolverines"—Michiganians faced an exciting future.

Check Your Reading

1. Who was the first governor of the state of Michigan, and why was he called "the boy governor"?
2. What is a constitution?
3. How was the Toledo War finally settled?
4. **THINKING SKILL:** Predict what might have happened if Michigan had received the Toledo Strip instead of the western part of the Upper Peninsula.

REVIEWING VOCABULARY

Number a sheet of paper from 1 to 5. Beside each number write **C** if the underlined word is used correctly. If it is not, rewrite the sentence using the word correctly.

1. The bustling city was located on the <u>frontier</u>.
2. The storekeeper paid a <u>tax</u> to the man when he bought the new shovel.
3. Before Michigan became a state, its people had to write a <u>treaty</u> for Congress to approve.
4. Each side received part of what it wanted under the <u>compromise</u> plan.
5. The members of the <u>legislature</u> traveled west to become settlers in the new land.

REVIEWING FACTS

1. Why did the British and the colonists begin fighting the American Revolution?
2. What did the Northwest Ordinance of 1787 state?
3. What was one cause of the War of 1812?
4. Name three ways in which the lives of the Native Americans had been disturbed by American settlers by the late 1830s.
5. What was the cause of the Toledo War? What was the compromise that Congress proposed to end the conflict?

WRITING ABOUT MAIN IDEAS

1. **Writing a Paragraph:** You have read about two treaties—the Greenville and the Saginaw—between the Great Lakes Indians and the United States government. Write a paragraph explaining the main goal of each treaty. Explain what each group gained or lost as a result of signing each agreement.
2. **Writing a Letter:** Imagine that you are serving under Lt. Oliver Perry on a ship in Lake Erie. Write a letter home to a friend telling about a naval battle in which you have fought.

BUILDING SKILLS: COMPARING MAPS

1. Why is it useful to compare maps?
2. What is the first step you should take when comparing maps?
3. How can the information in the map key be helpful in comparing maps?
4. Look at the maps of Michigan in the Atlas on pages 304 and 305. How are these maps similar? How are they different?

CHAPTER 6

LIFE IN A NEW STATE

FOCUS

The mine was dark and there was an old man pushing a cart full of rocks. The sounds of axes and hammers were all around me. It would be scary to work underground!

Jaleasha Minor lives in Lansing, our state capital. Sometimes she visits the copper mine and the other exhibits at the State Musuem. In this chapter you will read about copper and other natural resources that brought many new people to Michigan.

1 Changes on the Frontier

READ TO LEARN

Key Vocabulary

surveyor
immigrant

Key Places

Erie Canal

Read Aloud

If you are all coming out, it will be necessary for you to fetch [bring] your beds and bedclothes . . . and also some cooking utensils, and fetch any clothes that are worth wearing . . . [and] any good books you have.

John Lathers wrote this advice to his brothers and sisters in 1839. They were about to leave County Cavan in Ireland to join him in Nankin, Michigan. In this lesson you will read more about the people who came to Michigan. How did they get here? From where did they come?

Read for Purpose

1. **WHAT YOU KNOW:** When did your family first come to Michigan? From where did they come?
2. **WHAT YOU WILL LEARN:** What were some of the changes that affected life on the Michigan frontier?

LAND FOR SALE

In Chapter 5 you read that the United States government bought huge areas of land from the Native Americans. As soon as these lands were purchased, the government sent surveyors to measure them. A surveyor uses special tools to measure the government land and mark it into squares.

The surveyors then made maps that looked like checkerboards, on which the streams, the hills, and the types of soil and trees on each square of land were shown. Government land offices opened across Michigan. People could go to offices in Detroit, Monroe, White Pigeon, and Flint to look at the maps and choose the land they wanted to buy.

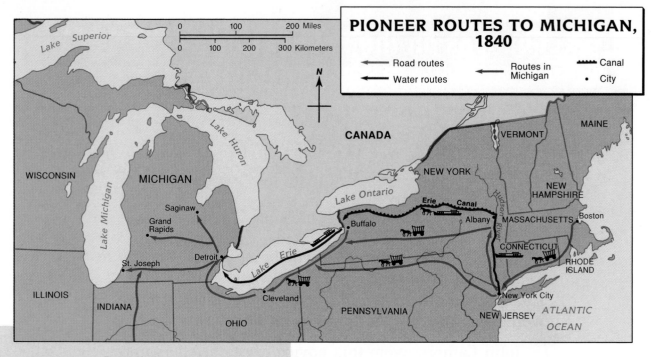

PIONEER ROUTES TO MICHIGAN, 1840

Road routes
Water routes
Routes in Michigan
Canal
City

MAP SKILL: Describe one water route and one land route that pioneers could take from New York City to Detroit.

Of course, everybody hoped to buy the best land. Some people would travel to the land offices at night in order to be the first in line when the office opened in the morning. Fortunately, much of the land in Michigan was very cheap. In 1820 a settler could buy 80 acres (32 ha) of land for just $100. A farm of this size could be worked by a single pioneer.

TRAVELING TO MICHIGAN

Many pioneers traveled to Michigan along dirt roads that followed the routes of Indian trails. These roads were full of holes, stumps, and bumps. One woman who came to Pinckney in Livingston County from New York described her journey to a friend: "I never met so many accidents in so short a journey. Drenched in the mud, overturned in the ditch, [and] jolted to a jelly. . . ."

The state government built corduroy (kôr' də roi) roads to make the journey of settlers easier. These roads were made of logs laid side by side. Although corduroy roads were bumpy, they helped to keep wagons and animals from becoming stuck in the mud in rainy weather.

Corduroy roads made the journey to Michigan more comfortable. However, easier ways of making the trip soon became available.

THE *WALK-IN-THE-WATER*

On the morning of August 27, 1818, people saw an amazing sight on the Detroit River. Trailing clouds of smoke, a long boat cut through the choppy water. Instead of sails, two enormous wooden paddle wheels moved the *Walk-in-the-Water* toward the city. This was the first steamboat to arrive in Detroit!

Ordinary sailboats need windy days in order to be able to travel. Since the *Walk-in-the-Water* was powered by steam engines, it could travel in any weather. Now, trips from Buffalo to Detroit could be made twice a week. Steamboat travel soon became very popular.

THE ERIE CANAL

In 1825 travel to Michigan became easier than ever. After eight years of hard work, the Erie Canal was finally opened. The Erie Canal stretched 363 miles (584 km) across New York State and connected the Hudson River with Lake Erie. Now people could travel all the way from the Atlantic Ocean to Michigan by water. Trace the route of the Erie Canal on the map on page 134.

The Erie Canal looked like a small river. It was only 4 feet (1.3 m) deep and 42 feet (14 m) wide. Passengers traveled on flatboats—large wooden boats built like a box. These flatboats were pulled along by horses, who walked along the edge of the canal on a road called a towpath. A letter written by one passenger in 1826 told of the danger of standing on the flatboat's deck.

This is done at the risk of being scraped off by the bridges, many of which are so low as to leave scarcely enough room for my body. . . . I . . . spread myself on [the deck] as flat as a lizard.

Look again at the map on page 134 and study the routes that settlers took to Michigan.

AMERICAN PIONEERS

During the early years of statehood, two out of every three Michigan pioneers came from western

The Erie Canal made travel to Michigan easier. Passengers rode on flatboats that were pulled by horses.

New York or New England. These people were called "Yankees." They gave Michigan's new towns names like Vermontville, Boston, and New Baltimore to remind themselves of their old hometowns.

Sometimes groups of families came together. For example, the town of Romeo in Macomb County was settled by 60 New Englanders who came on the Erie Canal in 1827.

African Americans also began to settle in Michigan. After gaining their freedom from slavery in other states, many made the trip north to the farming community of Calvin Township in Cass County. Other African American farm families settled around the town of Marshall, in Calhoun County.

However, Detroit continued to draw most of these newcomers because many different kinds of work were available in the growing frontier town. In 1840 there were 700 African Americans in Michigan. By 1850 the number had increased to more than 2,600.

Like the Yankee settlers, black Michiganians started their own churches and schools. As their population grew, African Americans opened schools, stores, stables, and other businesses. They also became an important group among those who worked to end slavery in the Southern states.

EUROPEAN PIONEERS

Michigan also began to attract **immigrants** (im′ i grənts) from many different countries throughout Europe. An immigrant is a person who leaves one country in order to come and live in another.

From which countries did these European settlers come? By 1850

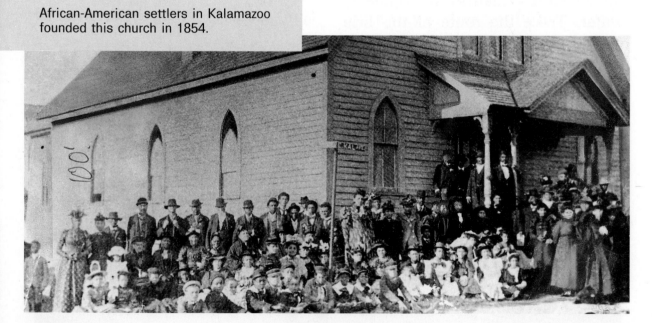

African-American settlers in Kalamazoo founded this church in 1854.

thousands of immigrants from Ireland, Germany, England, Wales, and Scotland lived in Michigan. Still others came from the Netherlands, Finland, Norway, Sweden, and nearby Canada.

Like the Yankees, these settlers gave their towns names that reminded them of home. Some towns were named Berlin, Dublin, Denmark, and Holland.

A FARMING STATE

By canal, steamboat, or over rough frontier roads, settlers poured into Michigan. Between 1830 and 1840 the population grew from 31,640 to 212,267.

Most of these settlers came here to farm. Rather than growing only enough to feed their families, some Michiganians began growing wheat and corn to sell. They sometimes used their earnings to buy items that earlier settlers would have made themselves, such as furniture, tools, and shoes.

To grind the wheat and corn into flour and meal, mills were built across the state. Other businesses began making bags for the mills. Still others built wagons to haul the grain and flour. As you can see, the products of Michigan's farmers went far beyond their own fields.

A GROWING STATE

During the early years of statehood, Michigan's population skyrocketed. Pioneers from Europe and

Steamboats carried newcomers from the East across the Great Lakes to their new homes in Michigan.

other parts of the United States arrived by wagon and by boat. As they built settlements and farms across Michigan, they changed life in our state forever.

Check Your Reading

1. Why were people eager to be first in line at the land offices?
2. From where did the new residents of Michigan come between 1830 and 1850?
3. In which areas of Michigan did African Americans settle during the early 1800s?
4. **THINKING SKILL:** Name two examples of things that government leaders did in the 1800s to reach their goal of having people move onto frontier land.

Reading Line and Circle Graphs

Key Vocabulary

graph   line graph   circle graph

In the last lesson you read about how pioneers and immigrants began settling in Michigan. A **graph** can show you the population growth of Michigan over a period of many years. A graph is a diagram that allows you to compare different facts and figures. Graphs can show a lot of information with the use of very few words.

Reading a Line Graph

One kind of graph is a **line graph**. A line graph shows changes that have taken place over a period of time. In Lesson 1 you read about pioneers and immigrants who came to settle in Michigan. From 1810 to 1850 Michigan's population grew rapidly. The line graph on this page shows how the population of Michigan grew during these years.

In order to read a line graph, first look at its title. Next read the label on the bottom of the graph. What information does this label give? Find the label on the left side of the graph. What information does this label give?

Now locate the year 1840 at the bottom of the graph. To find out the population of Michigan during the year

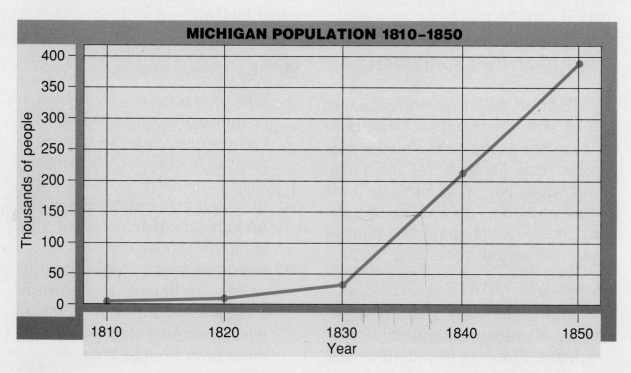

MICHIGAN POPULATION 1810–1850

1840, look at the dot above 1840. The dot is between the numbers 200 and 250 on the left side of the graph. Since the numbers 200 and 250 stand for thousands of people, the population of Michigan in 1840 was between 200,000 and 250,000. Notice that the dots for each year have been joined to make a line that rises on the graph as the population increases.

Reading a Circle Graph

Another kind of graph is a **circle graph**. This kind of graph shows how something can be divided into parts. Taken together, all the parts make up the whole. A circle graph is often called a pie graph because the parts look like slices of a pie.

The circle graph on this page shows the part of Michigan's population that was made up of immigrants in 1850. The graph also shows the part of Michigan's population that was born in the United States. Suppose that you wanted to compare the number of immigrants living in Michigan to the rest of Michigan's population. The circle graph can help you.

First read the title of the graph. The circle represents the total population of Michigan in 1850. Then note that the graph is divided into two sections, one representing those people who were born in another country and

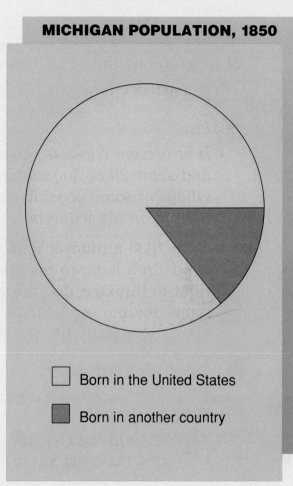

MICHIGAN POPULATION, 1850

☐ Born in the United States

■ Born in another country

those who were born in the United States. Which group of people made up the larger part of Michigan's population?

Reviewing the Skill

1. What does a line graph show? What does a circle graph show?
2. At which time did the population of Michigan reach more than 200,000?
3. Why is it useful to understand how to read graphs?

139

2 Life in Pioneer Michigan

READ TO LEARN

Key Vocabulary
subsistence farmer

Key Places
Vermontville

Read Aloud

It at present consists of some half-a-dozen log dwellings and some 20 or 30 [settlers] and bids fair to be a village of some considerable importance; but now it is literally in the wilderness.

In 1838 a pioneer named John Child wrote these words in a letter to his sister in New York. Child was right in thinking that the village—Lansing—would be of "considerable importance." In this lesson you will read about what daily life was like on the Michigan frontier.

Read for Purpose

1. **WHAT YOU KNOW:** What kinds of jobs or chores do you do at home?
2. **WHAT YOU WILL LEARN:** What was life in Michigan like during the early years of statehood?

A NEW HOME

In the last lesson, you read about the people who traveled west to settle in Michigan. In this lesson you will read a true story about one Yankee settlement in our state.

In 1836 a group of 22 families set out from Vermont for Michigan. After a three-week journey, the families arrived in Eaton County in southern Michigan. They named their new settlement Vermontville.

Eleven-year-old Tom Benton and his family arrived in Vermontville on a moonless October night in 1837. That night the Bentons slept in their wagon. At daylight they could see that every acre of their land was covered with huge trees. With winter just a few weeks away, there was no time to waste.

Tom started his frontier "education" that very day. His father had

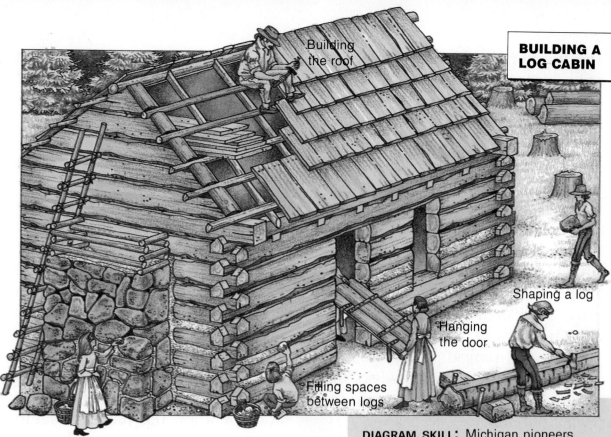

Building the roof

Shaping a log

Hanging the door

Filling spaces between logs

DIAGRAM SKILL: Michigan pioneers helped one another to build log cabins. What jobs were children given at the "cabin-raising"?

brought tools from Vermont, including a small ax made for a boy. Tom was given the job of chopping firewood from the pine trees his father cut down.

A CABIN-RAISING

Soon the other settlers arrived at the Bentons' for a cabin-raising. These neighbors had arrived in Vermontville months before the Bentons and had already built their own homes. Tom discovered that work was often turned into fun on the Michigan frontier. The cabin-raising was almost like a party, with everyone laughing, talking, and eating together. At the same time, everyone worked hard building a log cabin for the Bentons.

Tom's father already had cut down some trees and chopped them to the length needed for walls. The neighbors helped notch, or make deep cuts into, the logs and fit them together. Look at the diagram on this page to see how these notches fit together.

When the walls were up, Tom and his sister Rebecca filled in the spaces between the logs with grass and mud. Tiles of wood called "shake shingles" made up the roof. In order to keep the cabin warm during the winter, there were only one or two windows. Instead of using glass, which was scarce on the frontier, the Bentons stretched thin pieces of buckskin over the cabin windows.

THE BENTON HOME

The Benton house was small—about 20 feet (6 m) on each side. Try measuring your classroom to see just how small that is.

Tom's mother hung a curtain to divide the cabin into two parts. A fireplace took up much of the bigger part. This area was the center of the family's life. Here the Bentons cooked, ate, prayed, and read. The smaller area on the other side of the curtain served as a bedroom for Tom's parents.

As in most pioneer cabins, the children shared a sleeping loft up under the roof. The ceiling was very low. Lying on his straw-filled mattress, Tom could reach up and touch the roof without getting out of bed. When the first winter storm came in November, he and Rebecca

woke up to find the floor covered with 2 or 3 inches of snow that had drifted through cracks in the roof!

SCHOOL DAYS

The winter months meant school for the children of Vermontville. Most years they went to school for only about three months. Parents could not afford to pay the teacher for a longer period of time. And more important, the children were needed to help with the farm work once spring came.

Like the Benton home, the school was a one-room log cabin. Children who were eight years old or younger sat in the front. Ten-year-olds sat in the middle. Older children like Tom Benton sat in the back. Boys sat on one side of the room, and girls sat on the other.

There were no chalkboards, and paper was scarce. But schoolwork, too, could be turned into fun. Students and parents alike enjoyed going to the schoolhouse on Friday nights to compete in spelling bees.

Without chalkboards and paper, children had to memorize their lessons as they sat in a one-room log cabin school.

GAMES AND CHORES

Pioneer children had fun in other ways, too. They played games such as "chase" and "hide-and-seek." They also made cornhusk dolls, wooden whistles, and other toys.

However, the children had little time to play games—there were chores to be done! As they worked with their parents, they learned how to become good farmers, gardeners, and cooks.

To make the farm work easier, Tom repeated rhymes that his father had taught him. This short rhyme helped him to remember how many corn kernels to plant in each little mound of dirt.

> One for the blackbird, one for the crow,
> One for the cutworm and two to grow.

Tom also learned that the corn in the field should be "knee-high by the Fourth of July."

Tom's sister Rebecca learned by working with her mother. In the spring and summer she helped with the gardening. In the fall she and her mother dried the vegetables and fruits that they grew and stored them in the cellar for the winter.

Rebecca learned to make everything the family used, including clothes and soap. Families like the Bentons were **subsistence farmers**. This means that the family was able to provide for most of its own needs.

Pioneer children played with cornhusk dolls, marbles, and limber jacks.

PIONEER TOWNS GROW

Vermontville and other farm towns in Michigan were built by the courage and hard work of men, women, and children. In their new homes, they learned to depend upon one another for help, fun, and friendship. You will read a story about a pioneer friendship in the Legacy lesson on pages 144–149.

Check Your Reading

1. What was a cabin-raising?
2. How does your own classroom differ from Tom Benton's?
3. What did pioneer boys and girls do to help their families?
4. **THINKING SKILL:** List three questions that you would ask in order to find out more about Tom and Rebecca Benton's life on the Michigan frontier.

Legacy

READ TO LEARN

 Read for Purpose

1. **WHAT YOU KNOW:** Why did so many people move to Michigan from New England and western New York in the early 1800s?
2. **WHAT YOU WILL LEARN:** What was pioneer life like for children in Michigan?

A LETTER TO Grandma Ellis

by Joan W. Blos

In Lesson 1 you read that thousands of pioneers left their homes in New England and western New York to settle in Michigan during the early 1800s. Life in the new land was exciting. There were new places to explore, and new adventures to experience. But there was much work to be done, and it was also lonely at times. The following story tells what life in southern Michigan was like for one young pioneer girl in the 1840s.

On this loveliest of bright spring days, 12-year-old Hanna Carpenter stands at the door of the cabin that is her family's home. Enormous pine trees press against the cabin on all sides but the front. There, the area they hopefully call "the yard" stretches from the cabin to the narrow strip of road.

Back in New York State, where they used to live, the yard was carefully fenced. Hanna had played there when she was a little girl, and Grandma Ellis's roses had bloomed richly each June.

When Grandma Ellis was not much older than Hanna herself is now, she had arrived in New York State as a pioneer's bride. Remembering those bygone days, Grandma Ellis used to say that loneliness was the enemy. Being busy helped somewhat; finding a friend was better.

"And now I am the lonely one," Hanna thinks. Away in the distance her father and older brothers are working to clear the land. Behind her, in the cabin, her mother is hearing the lessons she has prepared for the younger children, Ben and little Sue.

Everyone else has someone else, it seems! And how can she hope for friendship when no other settlers live nearby and the village of Millfield is too far away? Hanna leans back against the heavy wooden frame surrounding the broad, slab door. The sun has warmed it pleasantly. She loosens the shawl she is wearing and tilts her face to the sun.

It was hardly a year ago, Hanna reminds herself, that her father and older brothers built the little cabin. And it was only last summer—when the cabin was complete—that Mama and Hanna, along with Ben and little Sue, had come to Michigan.

"Hanna?"

This is Mama calling, reminding Hanna that dreaming away in the sunshine brings no water to the house. Hanna had been sent to fetch a bucket of water. It is perfectly clear to her mother that she hasn't taken a step. Hanna, sighing, tightens her shawl again and picks up the homemade bucket.

Trillium and other wildflowers are coming up in the woods. Back in New York where they used to live, trillium bloomed plentifully in the woods near the Erie Canal. The canal had opened shortly before Hanna's birth, and sometimes the family called it "Hanna's Canal." Hanna used to play along its banks and watch the barges as they moved slowly by. In time she had come to recognize the men and they, in turn, knew her. There was red-bearded Captain Peterson, the tall and fair-haired Michael who looked after the horses, and the slender crewman she knew only as Dan.

Some of the barges were filled with crates and boxes; some carried well-dressed passengers who sat on

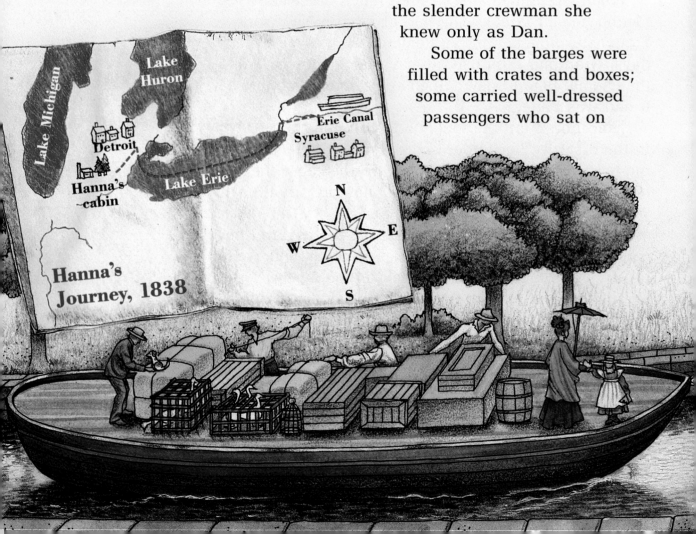

Lake Michigan

Lake Huron

Lake Erie

Detroit

Hanna's cabin

Erie Canal
Syracuse

N
E
W
S

Hanna's Journey, 1838

little folding chairs or strolled about the upper deck walking hand in hand. Hanna, when she watched them, had never guessed that her own family would move to Michigan or that her journey to the West would begin on the Erie Canal.

Sunlight sprinkles the forest floor with light; out of the wind, it is warm. Back home in New York, Hanna would have been in school on a day such as this! It would have filled her with longing to be outdoors. Now, in contrast, she wishes that she were in school with other students. But here, as yet, there is no village school. There is talk that the town will hire a teacher soon, but Hanna's father wonders if this is really so. "Comes to that," she has heard him say, "they'd rather spend a dollar for a road than a penny toward the school."

Now that she has come to the last turn in the path, she is almost at the creek.

Arriving there, Hanna can hardly believe what her eyes reveal! Across the stream there stands another girl. The new girl also carries a bucket of wood, is wrapped in a shawl against the coolish air, and wears her brown hair braided in a thick but single braid. The two girls stare at each other, silenced by surprise.

"I'm Hanna Carpenter," Hanna says at last, "living hereabouts."

"Laura Miller," the other girl replies. "We don't live anywhere as yet, but my father hears there's good land to be had and my ma, she likes a homesite that is not too far from town. Buffalo, is where we're from. . . ."

"We're New Yorkers, too," says Hanna, "but nearer to Syracuse." She pauses a moment, then adds, "I'm 12 years old this month."

Laura puts her bucket down and starts across the creek. Moving lightly from stone to stone, Hanna does the same. They meet in the middle of the stream, shakily balanced on large, flat stones.

"Oh," says Hanna, "Are you really here to stay? Millfield's about to have a proper school—everyone is saying that—and the railroad's coming too! I suppose your papa has already found the bank? There's a sawmill working and they say a mill for grain is promised."

Laura is half laughing. "You sound," she says, "like the booklet that made my father think this was the place to settle."

"It's only," says Hanna shyly, "that I so much want you to stay."

"Oh, I know," says Laura. "Think how we could walk to school together—that is, once they build a school—and help each other with sums. This," she adds, "is my very first time to come to the creek for water."

The water is splashing around their separate rocks. Their high-buttoned shoes are wet. Neither one wants to be the first to go; each knows she must not stay.

"You'll come again tomorrow?" Hanna asks.

"At just this time," says Laura.

The two of them carefully recross. Their paths rise quickly, leading away from the stream. "Good-bye, good-bye, good-bye," they call as the trees close in around them.

Going home now, Hanna's thoughts run on. Perhaps their mothers will become good friends and visit back and forth. If the Millers build a house, her father and brothers will help. It will be so different having another family nearby!

Her father has spoken often of all the work that must be done to tame this brave new land. "Hanna can help make Michigan grow," he has said. Now Hanna Carpenter, age 12, begins to feel the excited spirit of the pioneer.

When the family writes to Grandma Ellis the next time, Hanna will have much to tell her grandmother. "And," she tells herself happily, "Grandma Ellis will understand."

Check Your Reading

1. Where did Hanna Carpenter and her family live before coming to Michigan as pioneers?

2. Why does Hanna feel lonely in her new home?

3. **THINKING SKILL:** Compare and contrast Hanna's life in New York with her new life in Michigan.

149

Teacher OF THE Year

Katherine Afendoulis (ä fən dü′ ləs) is a third-grade teacher at Collins Elementary School in Grand Rapids. She cannot remember a time when she didn't think of herself as a teacher.

As a child I pretended to teach school and urged my friends to be my students. It became my dream to have my own classroom.

Before moving to the United States, Katherine Afendoulis's parents lived in Greece. There, poor children could not go to school but had to work to help their parents earn a living. When Katherine Afendoulis was very young, her parents taught her the importance of getting a good education.

After many years of schooling, Afendoulis's dream came true. She has been a teacher now for 18 years. In 1990 Katherine Afendoulis was named Michigan Teacher of the Year. She was chosen as the best example of an outstanding teacher.

One of Afendoulis's goals is to teach her students to have respect for themselves and for others.

Growing up with parents who were born in another country gave me an advantage. I grew up knowing two cultures. In my classroom I encourage my students to share their differences. This is what makes us all special.

To help her students learn about different cultures, Afendoulis reads fairy tales from around the world. The students then enjoy planning and giving a perfomance of some of these tales. Her students read *Yeh-shen*, a version of Cinderella from China. After making costumes and designing a castle for the stage, Afendoulis's class held an "Open Castle" night. They performed *Yeh-shen* and other tales.

Katherine Afendoulis loves being a teacher.

It gives me great pleasure to watch children grow. And when they come back to see me, I take pride in knowing that I helped them.

150

3 Timber, Copper, and Iron Ore

READ TO LEARN

Key Vocabulary
industry

Key People
Douglass
Houghton

Key Places
Muskegon
Saginaw
Keweenaw Peninsula

Read Aloud

Come listen, young fellows who follow the lakes
In iron ore vessels your living to make,
I shipped in Chicago, bid adieu [good-bye] to the shore,
Bound away to Escanaba for red iron ore.

These words are part of a song that Michigan sailors sang during the 1850s. The vessels, or ships, that they sang about carried iron ore from the Upper Peninsula to factory towns along the Great Lakes. In this lesson you will read how timber, copper, and iron ore helped to bring more settlers and new wealth to our young state.

Read for Purpose

1. **WHAT YOU KNOW:** Who were the first people to mine copper in our state?
2. **WHAT YOU WILL LEARN:** How did timber and mining become important to our state?

THE "GREEN GOLD RUSH"

During the 1830s Michigan was not the only state with a growing population. Pioneers also poured into Illinois, Indiana, and Iowa. These settlers needed wood to build houses, stores, and roads.

There were few trees growing in Illinois, Indiana, and Iowa. Most of the forests in the states farther east had been cut down. However, forests still covered most of our state. During the 1830s Michigan forests became the biggest source of lumber in the United States.

People began to call Michigan's trees "green gold." Thousands of people joined the "green gold rush"

151

Lumberjacks worked in teams to put towering piles of logs onto horse-drawn sleds. They used hammers like this to stamp the ends of each log.

to our state. Many came from Ireland, Sweden, Finland, or Norway. Some were Yankees who had cut timber in the Maine woods. Still others were African Americans who arrived in Michigan from the South in search of freedom and better pay.

TIMBER!

In the early days of Michigan's lumber boom, men called lumberjacks used axes to cut down the state's huge pine trees. Trees were chopped down during the winter because it was easier to move logs along the snowy, icy ground.

The lumberjacks hauled big sleds of logs down to the river banks. There they stacked the logs into piles and stamped the end of each log to show who owned it.

When spring came, the warm weather melted the ice and caused the rivers to flood. Lumberjacks

pushed their towering piles of logs into the rushing rivers. Then, men known as "river hogs" stood on the logs and guided them downstream to the sawmills. River hogs wore heavy spiked boots to keep from being thrown into the icy waters.

The loggers lived in camps which were built in clearings beside the timber. These camps were rough, noisy places. To pass the time, the loggers sang songs and told "tall tales." You read a tall tale about Paul Bunyan in the Traditions lesson on pages 46–50. One famous lumberjack named Silver Jack claimed that he had knocked over an ox with his bare fist!

NEW MICHIGAN INDUSTRIES

The lumber boom helped to create many other jobs and industries in Michigan. An industry is a company or group of companies that

makes a certain product or provides a certain service.

In towns such as Muskegon and Saginaw, Michiganians built huge sawmills to cut the logs into boards. By the 1850s, our state was criss-crossed by railroads carrying logs from the forests to the mills. In Grand Rapids, factory workers turned Michigan timber into world-famous furniture. Other factories produced everything from wooden pails to wooden railroad cars.

COPPER AND IRON FEVER

At the same time as the green gold rush began, discoveries in the Upper Peninsula brought Michigan fame as a mining state. The copper long known to Native Americans finally became big news to other Americans in 1841. That year, Douglass Houghton, a government scientist, reported that he had found large deposits of copper in the Keweenaw Peninsula.

Just a short time later, a survey-ing party in the Upper Peninsula made another discovery—iron ore. Soon Michigan became a leader in the mining of both copper and iron ore. Thousands of men from Europe and from other parts of the United States rushed into the Upper Penin-sula. Most of them had never worked in a mine before. Writer Angus Murdoch joked that these men were "ex-lawyers, ex-preachers, . . . ex-everything you can think of except expert miners."

Iron mining was hard work. Min-ers cleared the trees and bushes off the land. Then they used picks and hammers to dig out the ore. Later on they dug deep shafts into the earth to recover still more iron.

Copper mining was more com-plicated and dangerous. Miners first had to sink a shaft beside a de-posit of copper. From the shaft, men dug tunnels out at different levels.

Working within the tunnels, the miners drilled holes in the rock. Then they set off explosions in each hole that blew out chunks of rock and copper. These big chunks were then raised to the surface by a bucket. A mill near the shaft crushed the rock to free the copper chunks. The copper was then shipped to Detroit and other factory towns.

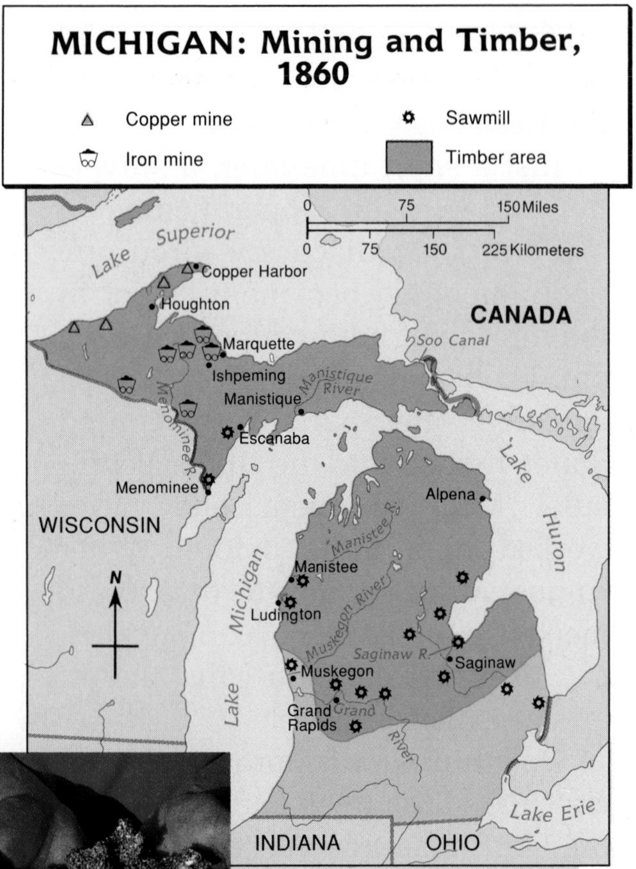
MICHIGAN: Mining and Timber, 1860
Copper mine
Sawmill
Iron mine
Timber area
0 75 150 Miles
0 75 150 225 Kilometers
Lake Superior
Copper Harbor
Houghton
CANADA
Soo Canal
Marquette
Ishpeming
Manistique River
Manistique
Menominee R.
Escanaba
Lake Huron
Menominee
Alpena
WISCONSIN
Manistee R.
Manistee
Lake Michigan
N
Ludington
Muskegon River
Saginaw R.
Saginaw
Muskegon
Grand Rapids
Grand River
Lake Erie
INDIANA
OHIO

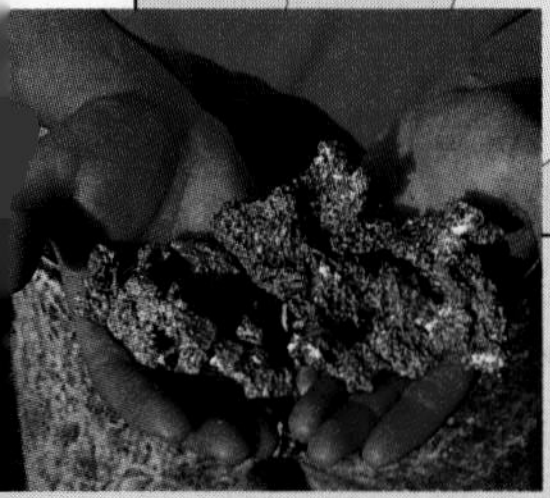

MAP SKILL: Large chunks of copper like this one were brought up from Michigan's mines. Which towns were located near copper mines?

THE SOO CANAL

In the early days of mining, transporting the ore was slow and difficult. Iron and copper had to be unloaded from boats at Sault Ste. Marie, loaded onto wagons, and carted to waiting ships below the falls in Lake Huron.

Then, in 1853, work began on the Soo Canal. For 2 years, more than 1,500 workers labored to dig and blast the canal through solid rock. Progress was slow. During the long winters, the workers suffered through temperatures as low as −40°F. (−40°C)!

The opening of the canal in 1855 made transporting copper and iron much easier. Look at the map on this page to see the location of the Soo Canal. Mining companies could now ship ore directly from the mines of the Upper Peninsula to factories located in Detroit, Cleveland, and other Great Lakes cities.

NEW RICHES

In the 1830s Michigan was made up of small farming communities like Vermontville, which you read about in the last lesson. By the 1840s, however, Michigan was becoming one of the busiest and fastest-growing states in the entire country. Lumber, iron, and copper brought new people and new riches to the Wolverine State.

Check Your Reading

1. Why did Michigan lumber become so important by the 1840s?
2. How did the Soo Canal help the copper and iron industries?
3. **GEOGRAPHY SKILL:** Why did the lumberjacks first cut down the forests located near the rivers?
4. **THINKING SKILL:** Compare and contrast the ways in which the timber and mining industries helped our state to grow.

REVIEWING VOCABULARY

immigrant   subsistence farming
industry   surveyor

Number a sheet of paper from 1 to 4. Beside each number write the word or term from the list above that best completes the sentence.

1. The family could provide most of its own needs; they practiced ____.
2. The ____ came from another country to live in the United States.
3. The lumber ____ makes products from logs.
4. The ____ measured the land and marked off the boundaries.

REVIEWING FACTS

Number a sheet of paper from 1 to 5. Beside each number write the letter of the choice that best completes each sentence.

1. Many pioneers traveled to Michigan
   a. from Italy and Spain.
   b. along routes of Indian trails.
   c. from the western territories.
2. Water transportation was improved
   a. by the building of the Erie Canal.
   b. by the invention of motorboats.
   c. by the building of corduroy roads.
3. Pioneer children
   a. attended school all summer.
   b. learned skills from their parents.
   c. played games very often.
4. Green gold was
   a. another name for the large amount of timber in Michigan.
   b. a metal mined in Michigan.
   c. a character in a tall tale.
5. Iron mining in Michigan
   a. was never an important industry.
   b. began when Douglass Houghton discovered iron ore.
   c. was helped by the Soo Canal.

WRITING ABOUT MAIN IDEAS

1. **Writing a Letter:** Imagine that you could send a letter to a ten-year-old pioneer living in Michigan in 1840. Write a letter telling how your life compares to his or hers.
2. **Writing a Summary:** Write a paragraph summarizing the material found in Lesson 2 under the heading "Games and Chores."

BUILDING SKILLS: READING LINE AND CIRCLE GRAPHS

Use the graphs on pages 138–139 to answer these questions.

1. What is a line graph? A circle graph?
2. What was the population of Michigan in 1830?
3. To graph the amount of iron ore mined between 1840 and 1850, which kind of graph would you use? Why?

CHAPTER 7

MICHIGAN AND THE CIVIL WAR

FOCUS

Dr. Thomas's house was used as a hiding place for people escaping from slavery. It makes me feel proud to know that people in my town helped slaves escape to freedom.

Luke Parker lives near the Nathan Thomas house in Schoolcraft. In this chapter you will read about the brave people of our state who helped to end slavery.

1 Slavery and Freedom

READ TO LEARN

Key Vocabulary

abolitionist
Underground
  Railroad

Key People

Elizabeth Chandler
Sojourner Truth
George de Baptiste
Laura Haviland

Key Places

Cassopolis

Read Aloud

When the sun comes back and the first quail calls,
Follow the drinkin' gourd.
Then the Old Man is a-waitin' for to carry you to freedom
Follow the drinkin' gourd.

This is a song about people escaping from slavery to freedom. The drinking gourd is what African Americans called the Big Dipper. The two front stars of the Big Dipper point toward the North Star. These stars guided slaves on their journey north. In this lesson you will read about how Michiganians helped slaves reach freedom.

Read for Purpose

1. **WHAT YOU KNOW:** How and when did the practice of slavery begin in the United States?
2. **WHAT YOU WILL LEARN:** What role did Michiganians play in the fight against slavery?

SLAVERY IN THE UNITED STATES

In Chapter 4 you read about how thousands of enslaved Africans were brought to the American colonies during the 1600s. This practice continued throughout the 1700s. At first, enslaved people worked in towns and farms throughout the United States. However, slavery gradually became less common in the northern states. By the early 1800s, most northern states had passed laws that made slavery illegal.

Sojourner Truth (*left*) and Elizabeth Chandler (*right*) were two important abolitionists. They fought to end slavery in the South.

Meanwhile, more and more enslaved Africans were forced to work on the plantations of the southern states. A plantation is a very large farm that usually grows only a single crop, such as cotton or tobacco. Many workers were needed to grow these crops.

As you read in Chapter 5, the Northwest Ordinance made slavery illegal in the Northwest Territory. However, as new states were formed out of the Territory, each state decided whether slavery should be allowed within its own borders. When Michigan became the twenty-sixth state in 1837, its constitution outlawed slavery forever.

ABOLITIONISTS IN MICHIGAN

Some people in Michigan were abolitionists (ab ə lish′ ə nists). Abolitionists wanted to abolish, or end, slavery everywhere in the United States. Many of them were members of religious groups. The first antislavery group in Michigan was started by a young Quaker named Elizabeth Chandler. Quakers are members of the Christian religion. They believed that it was against God's will for one person to be owned by another.

In Detroit, African-American residents founded the Second Baptist Church, the first African-American church in Michigan. The members of this church banded together to fight against slavery.

Stories about the cruel treatment of slaves angered black and white Michiganians alike. Many fugitives (fū′ ji tivz), or people who escaped from slavery, came north and told about having to watch while their children were sold and taken away forever. They also told about being whipped and put in chains.

158

Henry Bibb, a fugitive who escaped to Michigan, wrote to his former owner to explain why he had run away:

> . . . to stand by and see you whip and slash my wife without mercy, when I could afford her no protection . . . was more than I felt it to be the duty of a slave husband to endure [experience].

Sojourner Truth was another African American who made her way to Michigan after gaining her freedom. Truth and her family were enslaved in New York until 1827. Then a new law made slavery illegal in the state. However, Truth's son had already been sold to a plantation owner in Alabama. With the help of an abolitionist couple, she went to court and won her son's freedom. Truth settled in Battle Creek, Michigan in the 1850s. She became famous for her powerful speeches. She spoke to groups of abolitionists throughout the country about her experiences as a slave.

FREEDOM TRAIN

Enslaved African Americans like Henry Bibb risked their lives by escaping from their owners. Many slipped away from plantations at night and ran as far away as possible before morning came. Still, the route to freedom was a long and dangerous one.

More and more abolitionists, including many Michiganians, decided that they must help those slaves who fled from the South. Together, blacks and whites organized the **Underground Railroad** to help the fugitives. The Underground Railroad was not really a railroad. The movement got its name in the early 1830s when railroads first became popular. The term *Underground Railroad* stood for a system

Michiganians helped people escape from slavery to freedom along the **Underground Railroad**.

of secret routes that escaping slaves followed to freedom. The routes were secret because it was against the law to help a slave escape.

Workers on the Underground Railroad used railroad terms as a secret code. The men and women who helped escaping slaves were called "conductors." Slave "passengers" were hidden in wagons loaded with hay, wheat, or other goods.

They traveled from one "station," or hiding place, to another.

Michigan was a very important part of the Underground Railroad. The map on this page shows the two main routes across Michigan. The Central Michigan Line began at Cassopolis. Where did it end?

A second route was called the Southern Line. It started in Michigan City, Indiana and ended in Detroit. Detroit was the last stop for most fugitives before they escaped across the border into Canada.

Sometimes Southern slave owners paid men known as "slave catchers" to stand watch in Detroit. If the conductors learned that these men had been seen, they took their passengers to Mount Clemens or Port Huron instead. From there they were rowed across the St. Clair River to Canada. Slave catchers were not allowed to bring fugitive slaves back from Canada.

MAP SKILL: Which cities on the Underground Railroad in Michigan were stops on both the Central Michigan Line and the Southern Line?

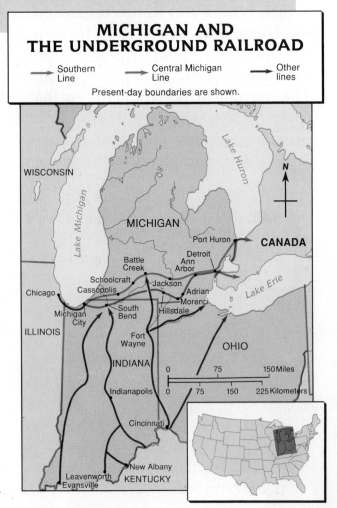

THE MICHIGAN CONDUCTORS

Serving as an Underground Railroad conductor was a dangerous job. Some conductors were free African Americans. They risked being captured and sold into slavery if they were caught in the South. George de Baptiste was one of the most important of these conductors. As a boy he had helped a slave escape from Virginia. In the 1840s Baptiste ran a station for the Underground Railroad in Indiana. From

160

there he moved to Detroit, where he worked as a barber and helped many other African Americans to escape from slavery.

Laura Haviland was one Michigan woman who was very active in the Underground Railroad. Like many conductors, she was a Quaker. Haviland led fugitives to Canada along the Underground Railroad through Ohio, Indiana, and Michigan. Southern slave owners offered a $3,000 reward for her capture, but she was never caught.

Laura Haviland was an important "conductor" on Michigan's Underground Railroad.

SLAVE CATCHERS

Because of its role in the Underground Railroad, Michigan became an unpopular place among Southern slave owners. These Southerners often sent slave catchers to free states in search of their "property." Free states were Northern states in which slavery was illegal.

How could slave catchers legally capture African Americans in a free state? According to United States law, escaped slaves remained the property of their owners, even if the fugitives had traveled to a free state. They had to be returned, just as a farmer's horse would have to be returned if it ran away.

In free states like Michigan, more and more people began to dislike this law. They did not want to protect slave owners and cooperate in the capture of fugitives. This made Southerners even more angry.

THE ISSUE OF SLAVERY

By the 1850s more and more African Americans began to flee from slavery. People in Michigan helped them to ride the Underground Railroad to freedom in Canada. Slavery had become an issue that divided the people in the North from the people in the South.

Check Your Reading

1. Why was slavery more common in the South than in the North?
2. What was the goal of the abolitionists?
3. Who was Laura Haviland and why was she important?
4. **THINKING SKILL:** List three questions that you could ask in order to find out more about the Underground Railroad.

Identifying Fact and Opinion

Key Vocabulary

fact   opinion

Imagine that you and a friend are reviewing some of the material you read in the previous lesson in preparation for a quiz. Your friend tells you that Sojourner Truth's real name was Isabella Baumfree. This statement is a **fact**. You can check it in an encyclopedia or a history book to see if it is true. A fact is a statement that can be proved true.

Your friend then tells you that Sojourner Truth was the most important abolitionist in Michigan. This statement cannot be proved. It is your friend's **opinion**. An opinion is a belief or feeling that a person has about something. Another person may have the opinion that George de Baptiste was the most important abolitionist.

It is important to be able to tell the difference between fact and opinion. Otherwise, you may accept someone's opinion as fact.

Trying the Skill

Tell whether each of the following statements is a fact or an opinion.

1. Sojourner Truth visited Abraham Lincoln in the White House in 1864.
2. Sojourner Truth should not have left New York after slavery became illegal there.

HELPING YOURSELF

The steps on the left are one way to tell the difference between facts and opinions. The example on the right shows how to use these steps to recognize which statements about Sojourner Truth are facts and which are opinions.

One Way to Recognize Fact and Opinion	Example
1. Ask yourself if the statement can be proved true.	Could you prove that Sojourner Truth visited Abraham Lincoln in the White House?
2. If the answer is yes, ask yourself how it could be proved true.	How could you check to see if she went to the White House? You could look up this information in a history book or in an encyclopedia.
3. If you do not think a statement can be proved true, ask yourself if it gives someone's beliefs or feelings. Look for word clues such as *the best*, *should*, or *I think*.	Is the statement that Sojourner Truth should not have left New York someone's belief? The word *should* is a clue that the statement is an opinion.

Applying the Skill

Now apply what you have learned. Tell whether each statement below about the events in Sojourner Truth's life is a fact or an opinion.

1. Sojourner Truth was not the only abolitionist to speak out against slavery in Michigan.
2. I think Michiganians should celebrate Sojourner Truth Day.
3. Sojourner Truth's son had been sold to a family in Alabama.

Now check yourself by answering the following questions.

1. How do you know that Statement 1 is a fact?
   a. It is someone's belief or feeling.
   b. It has word clues.
   c. It can be proved true.
2. How do you know that Statement 2 is an opinion?
   a. It can be proved true.
   b. It uses a word clue—I think— that tells you that the writer is giving his or her personal belief.
   c. Everyone would agree with it.

Reviewing the Skill

1. What is a fact? What is an opinion?
2. Which word clues can help you to tell the difference between a fact and an opinion?
3. When is it helpful to know the difference between a fact and an opinion?

163

1847—Should Michiganians Have Obeyed the Fugitive Slave Law?

As you read in the last lesson, Michigan abolitionists worked hard to help enslaved African Americans escape to freedom. One famous fugitive family was the Crosswhites. In 1844 Adam Crosswhite of Kentucky was able to escape with his family from a slave owner named Francis Giltner. With the help of some abolitionists, the Crosswhites traveled along the Underground Railroad. They settled in Marshall, Michigan, as free people. However, many slave owners, like Giltner, knew that fugitive slaves settled throughout the North. These owners often sent slave catchers to arrest former slaves.

The Crosswhites had lived safely in Marshall for three years. But one day Giltner found out that the Crosswhites were living there. He sent Francis Troutman to bring the Crosswhites back to Kentucky. He did this because the United States Fugitive Slave Law stated that fugitive slaves could be arrested and taken back to their owners in the South.

When Troutman came to Marshall, the townspeople refused to let him arrest the Crosswhites. The townspeople did not believe that the Fugitive Slave Law was fair. Instead, they helped the Crosswhites to escape to Canada.

Two DIFFERENT Viewpoints

Michiganians Should Have Obeyed the Fugitive Slave Law

Slave catcher Francis Troutman believed that it was right to arrest the Crosswhites because he was obeying the Fugitive Slave Law. The Fugitive Slave Law said:

When a person held to [slavery] in any of the United States . . . shall escape . . . the master . . . is hereby empowered [given the right] to arrest such fugitive . . . and to remove the fugitive . . . to the state or territory from which he or she fled.

Troutman told the people of Marshall that because the Crosswhites broke the law by running away from slavery, they had to be arrested and returned to their owner.

I . . . should be permitted peaceably to take the family of Crosswhite before a judge, that I may make proof of property in the slaves, and take them to Kentucky.

● According to the Fugitive Slave Law, how were slaves to be treated?

Michiganians Should Not Have Obeyed the Fugitive Slave Law

The people of Marshall, like many other Michiganians, believed that slavery was wrong and should be ended. They thought that the Fugitive Slave Law was not a fair law. They believed that they should not follow a law that would take away the rights of others. When Troutman came to arrest the Crosswhites, a crowd gathered. Charles T. Gorham, a leading Marshall banker, stepped forward and spoke to Troutman on behalf of the crowd.

You have come here after some of our citizens. You can't have them, or take them; this is a free country, and these are free persons. . . . These Kentuckians shall not take the Crosswhite family by virtue of moral [true], physical, or legal force.

● How did the people of Marshall feel about the Crosswhites?

BUILDING CITIZENSHIP

1. Why did Francis Troutman believe that Michiganians should obey the Fugitive Slave Law? Do you think that he believed slavery was wrong?
2. Why did the people of Marshall help the Crosswhites?
3. Which side do you think made the stronger case? Why?

2 A Divided Nation

READltr READ TO LEARN

Key Vocabulary

secede
Union
Confederacy

Key People

Abraham Lincoln

Read Aloud

I am pleading that my people
May have their rights restored,
For they have long been toiling
And yet have no reward.

Sojourner Truth, whom you read about in the last lesson, wrote this poem about enslaved African Americans. In this lesson, you will read how disagreements about slavery divided our country.

Read for Purpose

1. **WHAT YOU KNOW:** How did people in the North work to abolish slavery?
2. **WHAT YOU WILL LEARN:** Which events led to the Civil War?

THE REPUBLICAN PARTY

You have read about abolitionists who helped African Americans to escape from slavery. But many Americans felt that slavery should be allowed in the South, where plantations needed workers. For this reason, the government divided the country into slave states in the South and free states in the North.

During this time many new territories, like Kansas and Nebraska, were being formed in the West. When slave owners wanted to take their slaves to the new territories, many Northerners became angry. They did not think slavery should spread to new parts of the United States. But many Southerners believed in states' rights, or the right of every state to make its own decisions about most issues. Some

Southerners also worried that they would lose political power if no new slave states were formed in the West.

Michigan was one of the Northern states where most people were opposed to the spread of slavery. Michiganians met in Jackson in 1854 to form the Republican party. They planned to elect Republicans to state and national offices. Then these Republican officials could work to prevent the spread of slavery to the West.

A lawyer from Illinois named Abraham Lincoln spoke for the new party. In 1860 the Republicans chose Lincoln to run for President. Southerners feared the Republican party. They worried that slavery would be abolished if Lincoln were to win.

LINCOLN BECOMES PRESIDENT

On March 4, 1861, church bells rang wildly in Monroe, Marshall, Battle Creek, and other towns all across Michigan. Along with many others in the North, Michiganians were celebrating because Abraham Lincoln had been officially declared the sixteenth President that day.

In the South the scene was very different. Few people celebrated. Many people took down their American flags. They were upset and angry that Lincoln was now President. He was one of the Northerners who thought that it was wrong to buy and sell human beings.

THE SOUTH BREAKS AWAY

As soon as Lincoln was elected, Southern leaders decided to set up their own country. If the Southern states were no longer part of the United States, President Lincoln would be unable to control the practice of slavery.

South Carolina became the first state to secede, or leave the Union. At that time, many people called the United States the *Union* because it was a "union" that joined together all the different states.

Ten more slave states soon joined South Carolina to form a new government. Southerners called their country the Confederate States of America, or the Confederacy (kən fed′ ər ə sē). They had their

The Republican party was founded in Michigan in 1854. In 1861 Abraham Lincoln became the first Republican President.

The Granger Collection

LATEST NEWS
BY TELEGRAPH.
THE ELECTION.
THE NORTHERN STATES
ALL FOR LINCOLN.
HIS ELECTION BY THE PEOPLE.

MICHIGAN.
Ypsilanti city, republican majority 40 over all. Marshall city, 50 majority for Lincoln; 41 for Crane, Sheriff. Marshall township, 97 majority for Lincoln. Eckford township, 100 republican majority. Ypsilanti township, 95 republican majority. Grass Lake town, 23 majority for Lincoln; 19 for Granger; 15 for Blair. Jackson city, Lincoln 30 majority; Granger 20 majority.
Holly, national, State, and county tickets, with exception of Register and Sheriff, average democratic majority 7—republican gain 60 to 70; Sheriff and Register, democratic majority 40. Royal Oak, national, State, and county tickets, except Sheriff, 68 republican majority—gain of 30 to 35.

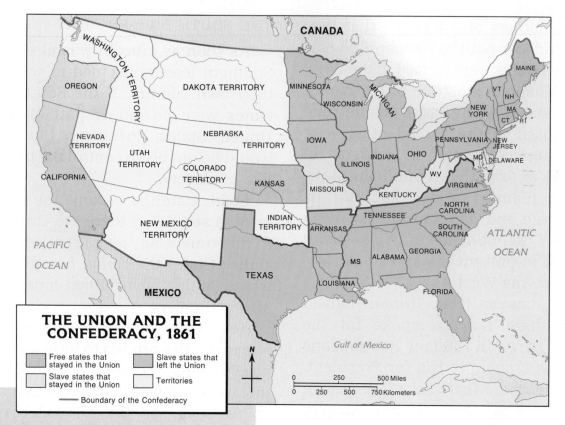

THE UNION AND THE CONFEDERACY, 1861

Free states that stayed in the Union

Slave states that stayed in the Union

Slave states that left the Union

Territories

Boundary of the Confederacy

MAP SKILL: In 1861 Southern states seceded from the Union. How many states made up the Confederacy?

own flag, their own president, and their own capital.

This news made many Northerners angry. Even those who did not object to slavery thought that the South had no right to break up the Union. Michigan's Governor, Austin Blair, announced that men from his state would join the fight to save the Union. Still, almost everyone in the North hoped that there would not be a war between the states.

THE FIGHTING STARTS

Early in the morning on April 12, 1861, Confederate troops attacked Fort Sumter, a Union fort off the coast of South Carolina. With this battle, the Civil War between the North and the South began. Boys and girls who were 10 years old when the first shots were fired at Fort Sumter would be 14 before the war finally came to an end in 1865.

Check Your Reading

1. Why did some Southerners dislike the Republican party?
2. What does *secede* mean?
3. **GEOGRAPHY SKILL:** Use the map on this page to name the slave states that left the Union.
4. **THINKING SKILL:** What opinions did Northerners hold about slavery in the West?

3 Michigan and the Civil War

READ TO LEARN

Key Vocabulary

Emancipation
Proclamation

Key People

George Custer
Sara Emma Edmonds

Read Aloud

You think slavery is right and ought to be extended; while we think it is wrong and ought to be restricted [limited]. That I suppose is the rub [problem].

Shortly before he was elected President, Abraham Lincoln wrote these words to an old friend from the South. In this lesson you will read how this "rub" between the North and the South led to the bloodiest war in our nation's history.

Read for Purpose:

1. **WHAT YOU KNOW:** What important role did the people of Michigan play in the fight to abolish slavery?
2. **WHAT YOU WILL LEARN:** How did the Civil War change the lives of the people of Michigan?

THE WAR BEGINS

As soon as they read the Detroit *Free Press* headline, "WAR! WAR! WAR!" many Michiganians rushed off to join the Union army. The first 798 Michigan soldiers arrived in Washington, D.C., just 3 weeks after the attack on Fort Sumter. President Lincoln was so happy to see them that he exclaimed, "Thank God for Michigan." Over the course of the war, more than 90,000 men from Michigan served in the Union army and navy.

SOLDIERS FROM MICHIGAN

Michiganians from many different backgrounds fought in the Union army. Most of the soldiers from Michigan had been born in the state, or had come from New York or New England. But many of them

Thousands of Michigan soldiers, including Sara Emma Edmonds (*left*) and George Custer (*right*), fought for the Union army.

were immigrants who had recently arrived from Ireland, Germany, and other countries.

A total of 1,673 African Americans from Michigan also fought for the Union. Most of these African Americans served in the First Michigan Colored Infantry Regiment. You will read about this group in the Legacy lesson on pages 173–176. From the area around Petoskey came the Sharpshooters, a group of 145 Native Americans who were expert riflemen.

George Custer, a 23-year-old general from Monroe, became famous as the leader of the Michigan Cavalry Brigade. The Cavalry Brigade rode horses in battle. Custer's men would follow him by watching for his long blond hair flying wildly from under his hat. Some soldiers said that he looked like a "circus rider gone mad."

Although women were not allowed to join the army, one Michigan woman managed to do so. Sara Emma Edmonds from Flint wanted to help the North. She disguised herself as a man and took part in several battles.

MICHIGANIANS IN BATTLE

Michigan soldiers fought in many important battles. One group, the Twenty-fourth Michigan Infantry, was part of the famous Iron Brigade. In 1863 these men fought "with the strength of iron" at the Battle of Gettysburg, in Pennsylvania. They suffered severe losses. Eight out of every ten men were killed or wounded.

Soldiers often went off to the war excited about the adventure that lay ahead of them. But after many months away from home, almost all of the men became tired and lonely. Many died of diseases that spread quickly through the rough, muddy camps. One Michigan soldier, Orlando Carpenter, wrote the following passage in his diary.

The weather [is] cold, cloudy and rainy. I am about sick with cold, blues and other ills too numerous to mention.

LIFE IN WARTIME MICHIGAN

Back home in Michigan, people worked hard to help the Union cause. Children did extra farm chores in place of their fathers or big brothers. Miners worked day and night digging iron and copper. The Union army needed Michigan's iron ore to build train cars, rails, and ship engines. Michigan's copper mines provided copper for telegraph wires, bullets, and even for the buttons on soldiers' uniforms. Ships loaded with copper and iron ore traveled through the new Soo Canal to factories in Detroit, Cleveland and other ports. Michigan loggers cut thousands of trees for army wagons, gun handles, and other war supplies.

The war caused shortages of food, fuel, and other supplies at home. People became anxious for these hard times to end. Some Northerners began to blame African Americans for causing the war.

In 1863 this bad feeling led to a riot in Detroit. Some people started a rumor that an African American named William Faulkner had attacked two girls. Although there was no truth to this rumor, a mob attacked Faulkner's neighborhood and burned 30 homes. People were beaten and one man died. Sometimes life was as difficult and violent for the people at home as it was for the soldiers at war.

Other events made Michigan's African Americans more hopeful. In January 1863 a crowd gathered in the Second Baptist Church of Detroit. They had come to hear the **Emancipation Proclamation**. This proclamation, written by President Lincoln, declared an end to slavery in the 11 states of the Confederacy.

The **Emancipation Proclamation** was read at the Second Baptist Church, a center of Detroit's African-American community.

The Granger Collection

Michiganians celebrated the end of the Civil War in Detroit in 1865.

People celebrated throughout the North. But many of the slaves in the South did not learn of their freedom for more than two years. In both the North and the South, African Americans still did not have the same rights and freedoms that other Americans had.

THE WAR ENDS

The South had a smaller army, fewer factories and railroads, and less money than the North. Slowly the tide of the war turned in favor of the Union. Finally, on April 9, 1865, the Confederate army surrendered. The South gave up the hope of becoming a separate country. The long Civil War was over at last.

Then on April 14, 1865, another tragedy occurred. As Abraham Lincoln watched a play in Washington, D.C., he was shot by John Wilkes Booth, a man who was upset about the Confederate defeat. Lincoln died early the next morning.

A SAD NATION UNITED

As they had on the day that Lincoln became President, church bells once again sounded in Michigan towns and across our nation. But this time they rang slowly. People were sad about Lincoln's death. They were also sad because so many people from both the North and South had died during the war. It would take many years to heal the country's wounds. However, all the states were again united and slavery was ended.

Check Your Reading

1. How did people in Michigan help the Union?
2. What was important about the Emancipation Proclamation?
3. Why did the Confederacy lose the war?
4. **THINKING SKILL:** Predict what might have happened if Confederate soldiers had destroyed the Soo Canal.

READ TO LEARN

 Key Vocabulary   **Key People**

regiment   Kinchen Artis

 Read for Purpose

1. **WHAT YOU KNOW:** Why was the Civil War an important struggle for African Americans?
2. **WHAT YOU WILL LEARN:** How did African Americans from Michigan help in the war effort?

A Civil War Regiment
by Norman McCrae

In this lesson you will read about Kinchen Artis, *pictured at right, and other Michiganians who served in an all-African American* regiment *(rej' ə mənt) during the Civil War. A regiment is a military unit. Most of the regiment's soldiers were former slaves. If they had been captured in battle, they could have been forced into slavery once again. So, while all soldiers risked their lives in the war, African American soldiers also risked their freedom in the struggle to end slavery in America.*

Kinchen Artis

A SPECIAL PARADE

 t was a chilly October afternoon in 1863. The sun shone brightly, but it provided little warmth for the crowd of people who were lined up eagerly along the streets of downtown Detroit. Children hopped up and down as much from the cold as from their excitement.

The people of Detroit had seen many parades go by on these streets since the Civil War had started, but this day's parade was special. It honored Michigan's first African-American regiment, the First Michigan Colored Regiment. Only recently had the government of Michigan allowed African Americans to form a regiment to fight in the Civil War.

Suddenly, a loud cheer rose up from the crowd as the regiment came into sight. For many people in the crowd and in the regiment, this was one of the proudest moments of their lives.

EXCITEMENT AND DISAPPOINTMENTS

Soon the parade was over, but this was only the beginning of many exciting times for the regiment. In November, the abolitionist Sojourner Truth brought the soldiers gifts and food from the people of Battle Creek. In December the regiment was sent on a ten-day trip through southern Michigan.

During this trip the regiment followed one of the routes of the Underground Railroad in Michigan. Many soldiers in the regiment had made their way to freedom along this very path just a few years earlier.

In Ypsilanti, Ann Arbor, Kalamazoo, Niles, and Cassopolis, the troops were met by excited supporters. At Jackson, Governor Austin Blair viewed their parade and told the troops, "I am very proud of your general bearing. Take courage, and do your duty nobly." Men signed up to join the regiment in each town along the way.

One of the soldiers who signed up in Battle Creek was 37-year-old Kinchen Artis, whose photograph appears on page 173. Artis, born in Cassopolis, was the son of a man who had escaped to freedom along the Underground Railroad. He was one of six Artises who volunteered to serve in the Michigan regiment.

The ten-day trip through southern Michigan was declared a great success by all who took part in it. But when the soldiers returned to Detroit, their excitement turned to bitter disappointment.

Camp Ward, their new home, was a mess. The roofs leaked and the walls had huge cracks that let in piles of snow. Little was done to improve the living conditions at Camp Ward, which remained the regiment's base for three long winter months.

THE 102D AT WAR

In March 1864 the regiment's 1,673 men prepared to go to battle in the South. At first the Michigan soldiers were sent to Annapolis, Maryland. There the regiment's name was changed to the 102d United States Colored Troops. By the end of 1864, the soldiers of "the 102d" were veterans of several battles with Confederate troops.

The 102d's most difficult battle took place at Gorhanville, South Carolina, in November 1864. A newspaper reporter later wrote, "In this affair the 102d covered themselves with glory. . . . I never before saw men exhibit such never-ending bravery in battle."

> Never before have I known men to fight on after being severely wounded, and anxious to return to the field as soon as their wounds were dressed [cared for]. After having been 3½ years in the field, I never before saw men exhibit such unyielding bravery in battle.

A PROUD REGIMENT

he 102d served bravely in South Carolina until the end of the Civil War in 1865. The soldiers were proud that they had helped to bring an end to the Civil War and slavery in the United States. But although the war had ended, the soldiers of the 102d knew that their struggle for equality would continue.

 Check Your Reading

1. Why was the regiment's trip through southern Michigan familiar to many of the soldiers?
2. Why do you think that the soldiers' struggle for equality would continue after the war's end?
3. THINKING SKILL: Look at the newspaper reporter's quote above. List one fact and one opinion.

4 A Changing State

READ TO LEARN

Key Vocabulary
technology
cash crops

Key People
Thomas Alva Edison
Elijah McCoy

Read Aloud

About 150 ladies and gentlemen assembled [met] last evening at the rooms of the Detroit Club to listen to the first exhibition of the telephone.

This article in the Detroit *Free Press* of March 7, 1877, amazed readers. It explained how the "ladies and gentlemen" in Detroit had listened over the telephone as an orchestra played in Chicago—284 miles (547 km) away!

Read for Purpose

1. **WHAT YOU KNOW:** How is your life different from the lives of the Michigan pioneers?
2. **WHAT YOU WILL LEARN:** How did life change for the people of Michigan during the late 1800s?

A TIME OF CHANGE

In the summer of 1865, many Michigan soldiers began returning home from the Civil War. During the years that they were gone, the soldiers had often sat around their campfires, singing this song.

Home of my heart, I sing to thee!
Michigan, my Michigan.
Thy lake-bound shores I long to see,
Michigan, my Michigan.

But when these soldiers came home to the "lake-bound shores," they found that their state was changing in many ways.

CHANGES ON THE FARM

One area of great change in our state and nation was agriculture. During the war there were fewer men to work the fields. The farmers who had stayed behind began to use more technology (tek nol′ ə jē)

turn to p. 6 177

to help get their work done. Technology is the use of new ideas and tools to meet people's needs.

Many farmers had stopped cutting grain by hand. Instead, horse-drawn reapers and mowers now moved through fields with remarkable speed. Rather than planting kernels of corn in little hills by hand, farmers now used "seed-drill" machines to plant the seeds. These new kinds of equipment made farm work easier and faster.

Because farming with new technology required fewer workers and produced more crops, some farmers shifted to raising **cash crops**. Cash crops are crops, such as wheat, that farmers raise to sell for profit.

During this time many farm families began to form organizations for sharing their problems and helping each other. One of these groups was known as the Grange. Men and women throughout Michigan met in local schoolhouses or in buildings known as Grange halls. There, they talked about new inventions and new ideas.

NEW TRANSPORTATION

Farmers, lumber companies, and mining companies all needed railroads to ship their products to market. Congress gave Michigan nearly 4 million acres (1.6 million ha) of land to offer to companies that would build railroads.

Many companies took up this offer of land. In the years after the Civil War, railroads spread across the state like webs. Miles of track soon connected the Upper Peninsula with Chicago and Milwaukee. Ferries carried railroad cars across the Straits of Mackinac. A train tunnel was built to connect Port Huron, Michigan, and Sarnia, Ontario.

In 1860 Michigan had less than 800 miles (1,287 km) of railroad track. By 1900 more than 10,000 miles (16,090 km) of track crisscrossed the state, with passenger and freight trains running day and night. Look at the map on page 179 to see the growth of railroads.

New **technology** changed the way in which hay and other crops were harvested in Michigan.

NEW FACTORIES AND NEW IDEAS

These new railroads also helped many new factories to start in Michigan. Soon factories in our state made everything from iron stoves to fancy shoes. These products were then shipped by rail and sold in all parts of the country.

All of these changes led many Michiganians to think of new products and new technology. **Thomas Alva Edison** worked as a newsboy on the train that ran from his hometown of Port Huron to Detroit. Soon he learned how to operate the telegraph that connected the two stations. Edison went on to invent both the light bulb and the record player. **Elijah McCoy**, from Detroit, invented a product called an "oil cup." This special machine helped trains to run more smoothly along the tracks. Customers who wanted to make sure they were buying McCoy's product would often ask, "Is this the real McCoy?"

NEW IMMIGRANTS

Between 1860 and 1900 about 700,000 newcomers arrived in Michigan. Most of these people came from other countries. By 1890 one out of every four people in Michigan had been born in a foreign land. Many came to work as farmers, miners, or loggers. Others found jobs in the small factories that were opening in our state.

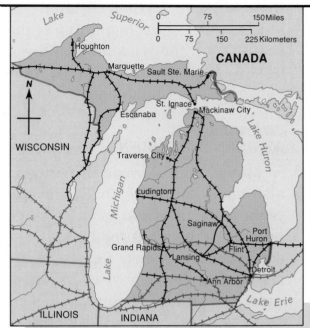

RAILROADS IN MICHIGAN, 1900

-+-+- Railroads before 1860   -+-+- Railroads 1860–1900

MAP SKILL: Thomas Edison (*left*) lived in Port Huron and Elijah McCoy (*right*) lived in Detroit. Why were these two cities important to Michigan's railroads?

Most of these newcomers came from European countries such as Germany, Great Britain, Ireland, the Netherlands, and Finland. Many others came to Michigan from

179

Canada. In a one-room school in the Upper Peninsula, German, Finnish, Swedish, and Italian children sat side by side. At the beginning of the school year, the students could not talk to each other, because they spoke different languages!

CHANGES FOR AFRICAN AMERICANS

Many more African Americans also came to Michigan during the years after the Civil War. A large number of them returned from Canada, where they had fled to safety before the war. For years African-American children had to go to separate schools. However, the Michigan legislature passed a law in 1867 declaring that all children had an equal right to attend any of the state's schools. Three years later,

two African-American students enrolled at the Duffield Union School. Black children and white children were together in a public-school class in Michigan for the first time.

In 1870, the state constitution was changed to allow African-American men to vote. However, both black women and white women were still not permitted to vote. And all of Michigan's African Americans, both men and women, were still denied many of the rights that white Americans had.

A CENTURY OF CHANGE

By 1900 the population of Michigan had grown to more than 2,000,000. New immigrants were arriving every day. New technology changed life on farms and in cities. Roads and railroads crisscrossed the state. Still, more changes lay ahead for the people of our state.

In 1870, African-American men could vote in Michigan for the first time.

The Granger Collection

Check Your Reading

1. Which changes had come to Michigan's farms in the years after the Civil War?
2. Where did many of Michigan's new immigrants come from at the end of the 1800s?
3. **GEOGRAPHY SKILL:** Identify some ways in which railroads changed life in our state.
4. **THINKING SKILL:** What are some reasons that Europeans may have decided to come to Michigan to live?

REVIEWING VOCABULARY

abolitionist   technology
Confederacy   Union
secede

Number a sheet of paper from 1 to 5. Beside each number write the word from the list above that best completes the sentence.

1. The ____ made speeches against slavery.
2. During the Civil War, the Northern states were also known as the ____.
3. The Southern states formed a new country known as the ____.
4. Reapers, mowers, and railroads are examples of ____.
5. After Lincoln was elected President, some Southern states decided to ____ from the Union.

REVIEWING FACTS

Number a sheet of paper from 1 to 5. Beside each number write **T** if the statement is true. If it is false, rewrite the statement to make it true.

1. Elizabeth Chandler was one of the few women who actually fought in the Civil War.
2. The Underground Railroad was one of Detroit's earliest subways.
3. Abraham Lincoln's election led to the creation of the Confederate States of America.
4. The Emancipation Proclamation gave all African Americans the right to vote.
5. By 1900 Michigan was crisscrossed by thousands of miles of railroad tracks.

WRITING ABOUT MAIN IDEAS

1. **Writing a Paragraph:** Write a paragraph that answers the following question. Why do you think that Michigan became an important part of the Underground Railroad?
2. **Making a List:** Make a list of the ways in which Michiganians helped the Union during the Civil War. Include at least five items on your list.

BUILDING SKILLS: IDENTIFYING FACT AND OPINION

1. What is the difference between a fact and an opinion?
2. Which steps should you follow to decide if a statement is a fact or an opinion?
3. Look through the chapter and find one statement of fact. Write a statement of opinion about the same subject.
4. Why is it helpful to know the difference between facts and opinions?

REVIEWING VOCABULARY

abolitionist
constitution
frontier
immigrant
industry
legislature
secede
subsistence farmer
tax
technology

Number a sheet of paper from 1 to 10. Beside each number write the word or term from the list above that best matches the definition.

1. A plan of government
2. Companies that make a product or provide a service
3. A group of people who have the power to make laws
4. The money that people pay to support their government
5. A person who wanted to end slavery in the United States
6. A person who comes to another country to live
7. A person who is able to grow most of his or her own food and provide for most of his or her own needs
8. To withdraw from a country
9. The use of new ideas and tools to meet people's needs
10. The settled land at the edge of an unsettled area

◀▶ WRITING ABOUT THE UNIT

1. **Writing an Opinion Paragraph:** You have read about three of Michigan's governors—William Hull, Lewis Cass, and Stevens T. Mason. Which governor do you think did the most to help Michigan? Write a paragraph about the governor you chose, and give the reasons for your choice.
2. **Writing a Description:** Study the diagram of pioneer life that is shown on page 141. Write a paragraph describing pioneer life, using the information in the diagram.

ACTIVITIES

1. **Making a Time Line:** Review the events discussed in this unit. Then make a time line that includes the main events.
2. **Making a Model:** Make a model of the Erie Canal, a log cabin, or a copper mine. You might want to use an encyclopedia or other source to get more information. Try to make the model as realistic as possible. Display your model for the class to see.
3. **Researching:** Find out more about Lewis Cass's exploration of Michigan. Where did he travel? Who went with him? What did they see? How do we know about the expedition? Prepare a written report about what you found out.

BUILDING SKILLS: IDENTIFYING FACT AND OPINION

1. What is a fact? What is an opinion?
2. Tell whether each of the following statements is a fact or an opinion.
   a. George de Baptiste was one of the most important conductors on the Underground Railroad.
   b. Sara Emma Edmonds disguised herself as a man in order to help the North during the Civil War.
   c. Abraham Lincoln acted correctly when he issued the Emancipation Proclamation.
3. Why is it helpful to be able to tell the difference between facts and opinions?

 **LINKING PAST, PRESENT, AND FUTURE**

The early population of Michigan was made up of many different groups—Yankees, European immigrants, African Americans, and Native Americans. What evidence of these groups remains today in your area? Make a list of place names, customs, or other examples of the background of Michigan's people.

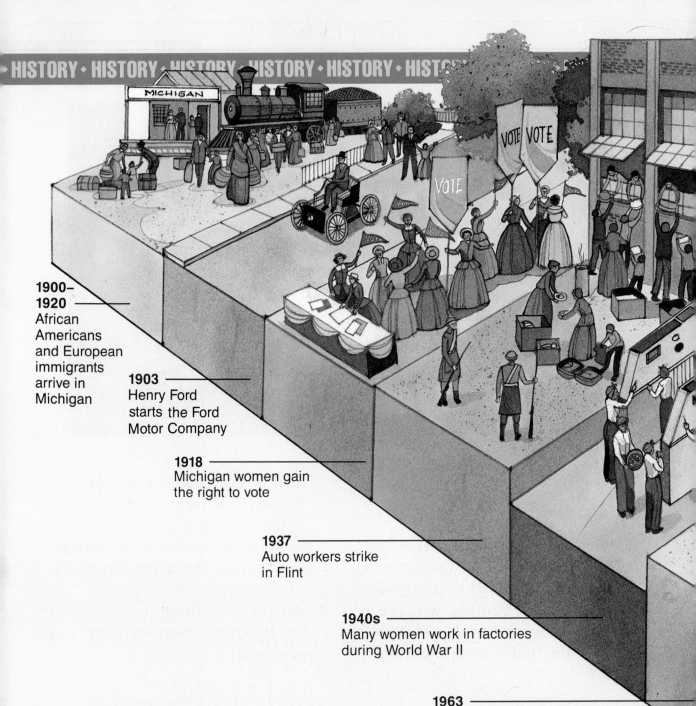

1900– 1920
African Americans and European immigrants arrive in Michigan

1903
Henry Ford starts the Ford Motor Company

1918
Michigan women gain the right to vote

1937
Auto workers strike in Flint

1940s
Many women work in factories during World War II

1963
Michiganians march for civil rights

1987
Michigan celebrates 150 years of statehood

WHAT HAPPENED

At the start of the 1900s, Michigan was growing and changing faster than ever before. In this unit you will read about the new people and new ideas that brought changes to our state. You will also read about the people who worked to bring equal rights to all Michiganians.

UNIT 4

MICHIGAN GROWS

CHAPTER 8

MICHIGAN AND THE NEW CENTURY

FOCUS

Riding in these cars must have been very different from cars today. The old cars didn't have roofs, so you couldn't drive them on rainy days.

Lyndsay Dusek, from Farmington, visited the Henry Ford Museum in Dearborn. She saw some of the very first cars that were built in Michigan. In this chapter you will read about how the automobile changed life in our state.

1 A Growing Population

READ TO LEARN

Key Vocabulary
discrimination
economy

Key Places
Dearborn   Black Bottom
Hamtramck

Read Aloud

Here in America you don't have to go without work if you want to do something. . . . There certainly is a difference between here and Sweden, where you have to bow and be humble and ask everywhere and still don't get any work.

These words come from a letter written by George Erickson in 1910. Erickson had recently emigrated from Sweden to Stambaugh (stam' bô), a town in the Upper Peninsula. In this lesson you will read about the many immigrants who arrived in Michigan in the early 1900s.

Read for Purpose

1. **WHAT YOU KNOW:** Did you or someone you know move to Michigan from another place?
2. **WHAT YOU WILL LEARN:** Why did so many immigrants come to Michigan during the early 1900s, and what kind of life did they find here?

NEW IMMIGRATION

As you have read in Chapter 7, a flood of immigrants began to arrive in Michigan after the Civil War. After 1900 many more immigrants came to our state. These new Michiganians differed from earlier immigrants in several ways. For one thing, many of them came from countries in southern and eastern Europe. In addition, most of these new immigrants did not come to Michigan to farm or to work as miners or loggers. Instead, they searched for jobs in factories.

NEW MICHIGANIANS

Why did these immigrants leave their homes? Many left to escape poverty in their own countries. Others came to Michigan in search of religious or political freedom.

In faraway cities such as Budapest, Hungary, and Belgrade, Yugoslavia, people heard stories about Michigan. In Michigan, they were told, as many as 14,000 people worked in a single factory! The promise of jobs brought thousands of immigrants to our state.

Many Germans continued to come to Michigan. The largest group of new immigrants came from Poland. By 1920 100,000 Poles had made the trip to Michigan. Other large groups included Russians, Jews, Italians, Yugoslavians, Hungarians, and Greeks. Look at the chart on page 189. How many Italians lived in Michigan by 1920?

Europeans were not the only immigrants who crossed the Atlantic Ocean to reach Michigan. Arab families from Middle Eastern countries, such as Lebanon and Syria, arrived during these years. Look at the Atlas map on pages 294–295 to locate these countries. Dearborn became one of the first cities in the United States with an Arab-American community. Arab Americans in Dearborn built one of our country's first mosques (mosks). A mosque is a house of worship for people who practice Islam.

(*above*) This immigrant family from Russia arrived in Michigan around 1900. (*below*) Arab immigrants started a newspaper and built one of our country's first mosques.

THE "GREAT MIGRATION"

In Michigan, newcomers like Charles Denby found reason for both hope and disappointment. The early 1900s were good years for Michigan's economy (i kon′ ə mē). An economy is the way in which a state or a country uses its resources to meet people's needs and wants. As Michigan's economy boomed, thousands of jobs became available to African Americans. But many of the newcomers to Michigan suffered from unequal treatment at work and in other parts of their lives.

In the years following 1900, African Americans also began settling here in large numbers. In 1880 around 15,000 African Americans lived in Michigan. By 1930 Michigan's African American population had reached almost 170,000!

Many African Americans moved north to Michigan from states in the South. They had faced much discrimination (di skrim′ ə nā′ shən) in the South. Discrimination is an unfair difference in the treatment of people. Southern governments did not allow black Southerners to vote. Because of discrimination, African Americans were denied the right to work at high paying jobs. They were not allowed to go to school with whites. Schools for blacks had old books and were badly rundown.

Hoping to find both freedom and jobs, many African Americans headed north during the early 1900s. So many African Americans joined this journey that it came to be called the "Great Migration."

MICHIGAN IMMIGRANTS, 1920	
Country of Origin →	Population
Poland	104,000
Germany	86,000
Scandinavia	69,000
Great Britain	60,000
Russia	51,000
Netherlands	33,000
Italy	30,000
Hungary	23,000
Austria	22,000
Ireland	17,000
Czechoslovakia	11,000

CHART SKILL: How many Hungarians had arrived in Michigan by 1920?

HOPES AND DISAPPOINTMENTS

The Great Migration gave new hope to many African Americans. Charles Denby, an African-American farmer, left Tennessee to settle in Detroit. Denby said that he and his friends had imagined Detroit to be a land of "milk and honey. . . . We didn't want to believe [there was] discrimination up North."

But African Americans discovered that there was discrimination in Michigan, too. In many factories they were given the hardest jobs. Often, white workers refused to work with black workers. Also, African Americans were not welcome in many white neighborhoods.

189

THE "PATCHWORK" OF DETROIT

Have you ever seen a patchwork quilt? This type of quilt is made by sewing together many squares of different-colored material. By 1904 the map of Detroit looked something like a patchwork quilt. The different groups who had settled in the city each lived in separate neighborhoods. Look at the map on this page to study the "quilt" of neighborhoods in Detroit.

Within most of Detroit's neighborhoods, almost everyone came from the same country, spoke the same language, and celebrated the same holidays. For example, you could walk down a crowded street on Detroit's East Side in 1910 and hear everyone speaking Polish. Across town on the West Side, there were neighborhoods where everyone spoke Hungarian.

These crowded neighborhoods could be great fun for children. One Polish American man named Robert Kozaren later became mayor of Hamtramck (ham tram' ik). He remembered his Detroit childhood in this way.

There was always somebody to play with. You were never lonely. You could just go out in the street and whistle and other kids would show up!

MAP SKILL: In 1904, Detroit looked like a patchwork quilt of different neighborhoods. In which part of Detroit did many Belgians live?

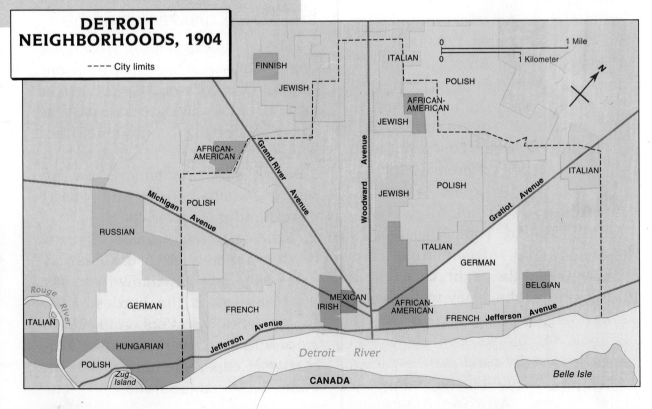

DETROIT NEIGHBORHOODS, 1904

---- City limits

AFRICAN AMERICANS IN DETROIT

Detroit's African American community was located on the east side of the city, between the Detroit River and Gratiot Avenue. During the late 1800s and early 1900s, some of Detroit's most well-known African Americans made their homes in this community. One was Benjamin Pelham, who published an African-American newspaper called the *Plaindealer*. Another was Fannie Richards. Richards was the first African-American teacher in Detroit's public school system.

Faced with a shortage of apartments and houses, African Americans crowded more tightly into the blocks on the east side of Woodward Avenue. This area was often called Black Bottom.

Black Bottom became a city within a city. Its houses were old and run down. Many lacked windows or running water. But African Americans worked hard to make good lives for themselves in Black Bottom. They built churches, stores, and restaurants. Hastings Street became famous throughout the country for its jazz music clubs.

WORK AND FREEDOM

You have read about the arrival of thousands of new Michiganians during the early 1900s. European immigrants and African Americans moved to our state in

This community center in Black Bottom was an important meeting place for Detroit's African Americans.

enormous numbers. These different groups did not speak the same language, worship in the same way, or look the same. But they all shared the same dream: to find work and freedom in their new home.

Check Your Reading

1. From which parts of Europe did most immigrants come during the early 1900s?
2. What was the Great Migration?
3. In what way does the map of Detroit in 1904 look like a patchwork quilt?
4. **THINKING SKILL:** What are some of the reasons that many African Americans decided to move to Michigan?

Writing an Outline

Key Vocabulary
outline

Suppose that you have to write a report about immigrants who came to live in Michigan. First you will need to decide on a specific topic. You might choose to do your report on Polish immigrants who came to live in Michigan.

Then make a list of at least three things you want to find out about your topic—Polish immigrants in Michigan. You might ask these questions: Why did Polish immigrants come to Michi-

gan? What was an early Polish community like in Michigan? How did Robert Kozaren, a Polish American, remember his childhood in Hamtramck?

Next, read about Polish immigrants and take notes to answer your questions. The example below shows you one way to take notes.

After reading and taking notes, you need to write an outline. An outline is a plan that lets you organize what you want to say about a subject. It presents all your thoughts and ideas in an organized way.

- searched for jobs in the factories and in big cities (I)
- Kozaren remembers playing with lots of children (III)
- came to Michigan in search of political and religious freedom (I)
- Kozaren was never lonely as a child (III)
- In 1920 Polish immigrants were the largest group of immigrants to come to Michigan (I)
- Everyone spoke the same language and celebrated the same holidays (II)
- grocery stores, bakeries, and meat markets were owned by Polish immigrants (II)

Choosing Your Main Ideas

An outline is made up of main ideas and supporting details. You can use the three questions that are listed on page 192 as the main ideas in your outline. Label each main idea with a Roman numeral. Your outline should look like the one below.

I. Why did Polish immigrants come to Michigan?

II. What was an early Polish community like in Michigan?

III. How did Robert Kozaren, a Polish American, remember his childhood in Hamtramck?

Adding Supporting Details

Look at your notes. Your notes are the supporting details for your outline. You need at least two supporting details for each main idea. As you read your notes, decide which question each note answers.

For example, suppose that you have written down several facts about Polish immigrants. Next to each fact write the Roman numeral of the question that it answers.

Putting the Outline Together

Now put each fact, or supporting detail, under the correct main idea in the outline. Label each supporting detail with a capital letter and a period. Write a title at the top. Your outline should look like the one that appears in the next column.

Polish Immigrants in Michigan

I. Polish immigrants came to Michigan
   A. in search of political and religious freedom.
   B. in search of jobs in the factories and in big cities.
   C. and were the largest immigrant group to come in 1920.

II. Early Polish communities
   A. were like small towns in which everyone spoke the same language and celebrated the same holidays.
   B. had their own grocery stores, bakeries, and meat markets.

III. In speaking about his childhood, Robert Kozaren remembered that
   A. there was always another child to play with.
   B. he was never lonely as a child.

Reviewing the Skill

1. What is an outline?
2. Reread the part of Lesson 1 that tells about the Great Migration. Take notes to answer the question, "What were the hopes of African Americans who came to settle in Michigan, and in what ways were they disappointed?"
3. Write an outline based on the information you found in question 2.
4. Why is it important to make an outline before writing a report?

2 The Progressive Era

READ TO LEARN

Key Vocabulary

Progressive
reform
suffrage

Key People

Hazen Pingree
Caroline Bartlett Crane
Anna Howard Shaw

Read Aloud

I have too much respect for myself to [join] any political party until my vote is valuable enough to be counted in the ballot box.

These words were written by Dr. Anna Howard Shaw in the early 1900s, when women were not allowed to vote in Michigan or in most places in the United States. Shaw, like many Michiganians, worked hard to bring more rights and opportunities to all of the people of our state.

Read for Purpose

1. **WHAT YOU KNOW:** Which immigrant groups had come to Michigan during the early 1900s?
2. **WHAT YOU WILL LEARN:** How did the Progressive Movement change the lives of many Michiganians?

THE HIGH COST OF LIVING

The immigrants who arrived in Michigan during the early 1900s found a changing state. For the first time, some Michiganians could enjoy gas heat, electric lights, and running water. Instead of walking to work, thousands of people now traveled on electric streetcars.

Many of the companies that provided these services charged high prices for them. In Detroit people had to pay almost twice as much for electricity and gas as people did in Grand Rapids. Detroiters paid 5 cents to ride on the streetcar. At the time, however, most working women earned less than 10 cents a day! These high prices made life hard for workers who did not earn much money.

HAZEN "POTATO" PINGREE

Hazen Pingree was one Detroiter who decided to fight for the city's working people. Pingree ran for mayor of Detroit in 1889. He was elected and served as mayor for the next eight years. During that time, he fought hard to make life easier by making services more affordable for working people. Pingree forced the Detroit Gas Company to cut its prices in half and lowered the streetcar fare to 3 cents.

In 1893 the United States economy suddenly slowed down. Many people lost their jobs. Pingree offered Detroit families the use of empty lots in the city to grow potatoes and other vegetables. He even sold his favorite horse and gave the money to poor people so that they could buy seeds! Soon newspapers around the country were praising Detroit's mayor—"Potato" Pingree.

Pingree was elected governor of Michigan in 1896. He tried to pass laws to improve work conditions and schools, but rarely succeeded. However, leaders in other states began calling for similar laws. These leaders became known as Progressives (prə gres' ivz). Progressives tried to improve the quality of life.

Later, several Michigan governors succeeded in passing laws to

Hazen Pingree was an important Progressive from Michigan. He worked to lower streetcar fares in Detroit.

regulate railroads, telephone, and insurance companies. They also won a shorter work week for people under 18. New laws made elections more democratic.

WOMEN IN THE PROGRESSIVE MOVEMENT

In the Progressive Movement several Michigan women brought about important reforms. A reform is a change or improvement.

In Kalamazoo Caroline Bartlett Crane fought for better health conditions. She talked and wrote about the unclean conditions in meat-packing plants. After listening to her arguments for reform, the state legislature passed a law requiring that all meat be inspected.

In the early 1900s, many women in Grand Rapids joined the struggle for women's suffrage.

One important reform was women's **suffrage** (suf′ rij). *Suffrage* means "the right to vote." Beginning in the 1840s, a growing number of women and men worked to change the laws of the United States so that women could vote. **Anna Howard Shaw**, whom you met in the Read Aloud, was an important leader in this fight. Shaw grew up in Big Rapids, in Mecosta County, and went to school to become both a doctor and a minister. To convince people that women should have the right to vote, Shaw gave thousands of speeches all over the country.

Through the efforts of Shaw and other Progressives, the Michigan Constitution was changed in 1918. Finally, women in our state were allowed to vote. Two years later, the Nineteenth Amendment was added to the United States Constitution. This new amendment gave women throughout the United States the right to vote.

THE REFORM EFFORT

During the early 1900s, Hazen Pingree, Anna Howard Shaw, and other Progressives brought much-needed reforms to Michigan. They fought for laws that would make it possible for working people to have a better life. By fighting for the vote for women, they also won Michiganians a greater voice in their own government.

Check Your Reading

1. Why were many Michiganians without electric lights or running water in the early 1900s?
2. Name two reforms that Hazen Pingree brought to Detroit.
3. How did Anna Howard Shaw help to improve life in our state and in our country?
4. **THINKING SKILL:** List three questions that you might have asked Hazen Pingree in order to learn more about the Progressive Era.

3 The Birth of the Automobile

READ TO LEARN

Key Vocabulary

mass production
assembly line

Key People

Ransom E. Olds
Henry Ford

Read Aloud

The darned thing ran!

After months of tinkering in his workshop, Henry Ford finished building his first car. On June 4, 1896, he drove the car through the streets of Detroit. As his words above show, he was surprised that his invention actually worked! Soon Henry Ford would own the largest factory in the world, and Michigan would be famous for its automobile manufacturing.

Read for Purpose

1. **WHAT YOU KNOW:** What are the most important kinds of transportation in your community?
2. **WHAT YOU WILL LEARN:** How did the automobile change life in Michigan and across the country?

HORSE-AND-CARRIAGE DAYS

How many trips have you made in a car or bus during the last week? Did you come to school on a bus this morning? Life in your community would be very different if there were no cars, trucks, or buses. Only 90 years ago, however, people still traveled around Michigan by horse and carriage. Back then, a trip from Flint to Grand Rapids might have taken as long as 10 hours! Today you can make this same trip in 2 hours by car.

HENRY FORD

By the end of the 1800s, many people were trying to build "horseless carriages." A German inventor attached a gasoline engine to a bicycle in 1885. Two years later, a French inventor completed a three-wheeled, steam-powered car.

197

However, many of the earliest cars were built here in Michigan. Ransom E. Olds of Lansing started the world's first automobile factory in 1899. But it was Henry Ford who became the most famous automaker in the world.

THE "TIN LIZZIE"

Henry Ford founded the Ford Motor Company in 1903. This young inventor had some special ideas in mind for his company. He planned to build a car that would meet the needs of people everywhere—those living in cities, small towns, and on farms. Ford also wanted to make his cars simple enough so that anyone with a screwdriver and a pair of pliers could repair them.

By 1908 he began producing this special car. Ford called it the Model T, and in one year he sold 25,000. Often people called the lightweight Model T the "Tin Lizzie."

Henry Ford's Model T was used by Michigan farmers for hauling hay and other crops.

The Tin Lizzie became the most popular car in history. Owners across the country wrote to Ford telling him of his car's many uses. One used it for hauling his hayrack from the fields. A man from Texas wrote that he used the Model T to pull tree stumps from his field!

THE PRODUCTION LINE

In 1908 the Model T sold for $850. This amount was more money than most people earned in a year. Soon, however, the price started to drop. By 1916 the Model T sold for only $360!

Why did the Model T become cheaper? One reason was Ford's new methods of mass production. *Mass production* means "making large numbers of one particular product, and making them quickly and cheaply."

Ford mass-produced the Model T by using an assembly line. In the Ford factory in Highland Park, workers stood alongside a moving belt. As the belt carried the cars through the factory, each worker did one task. One worker might attach the gas tank. Another might polish the fenders. As a result of this system, the amount of time it took to build a car dropped from 14 hours to 93 minutes. Look at the diagram on page 199 to see how Ford's assembly line worked.

Of course, every car built on the assembly line was exactly alike.

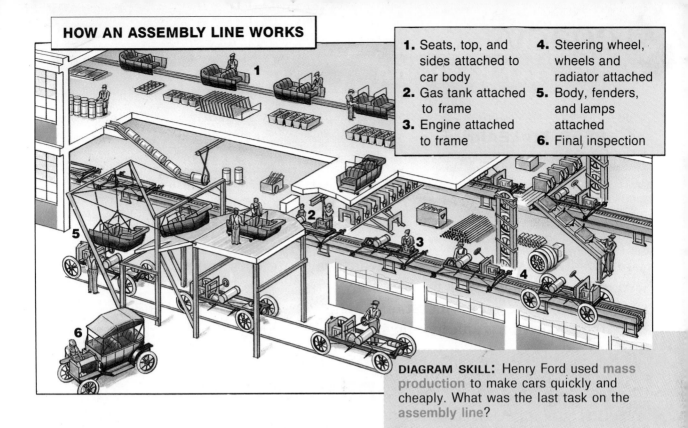

HOW AN ASSEMBLY LINE WORKS

1. Seats, top, and sides attached to car body
2. Gas tank attached to frame
3. Engine attached to frame
4. Steering wheel, wheels and radiator attached
5. Body, fenders, and lamps attached
6. Final inspection

DIAGRAM SKILL: Henry Ford used mass production to make cars quickly and cheaply. What was the last task on the assembly line?

Ford joked that his Model T was available in "any color the customer wants, as long as it's black." But by making his cars cheaply, Ford was able to sell them at low prices.

Ford changed the world of manufacturing in other ways, too. In 1914 he announced that he would pay workers $5.00 a day! At that time, most factories were paying no more than $2.75 a day. Other companies soon began using Ford's methods and paying higher wages. As more and more automobile factories opened up for business, people everywhere began calling Detroit the "Motor City."

A CHANGED STATE

During the years following 1900, Michiganians like Henry Ford made the automobile an important part of life in our state and country. Detroit soon became the center of the auto industry. Millions of Tin Lizzies drove over American roads. The United States and the world would never be the same again.

Check Your Reading

1. What made the Model T the most popular car in history?
2. How did mass production allow Henry Ford to lower prices?
3. How did the assembly line change the way in which workers did their jobs?
4. **THINKING SKILL:** State three facts about the auto industry that were mentioned in this lesson.

READ TO LEARN

 Key Places

Jackson

 Read for Purpose

1. **WHAT YOU KNOW:** In what ways are cars important to you and your family today?
2. **WHAT YOU WILL LEARN:** What was it like to own and drive an automobile in the early 1900s?

BRINGING THE JACKSON HOME — BY JOAN W. BLOS

In the last lesson you read about the beginning of the automobile industry in Michigan. In the following story you will read one grandfather's memories of the excitement that a new automobile brought to his family back in 1908, when he was a boy.

A TRIP TO JACKSON

ncle Ed, my father, and I were to go and get our new car. It would not be the very first in town, not even the first on our block. But cars were still unusual then and, if the pictures that Father had shown us were right, ours was going to be a beauty.

The car was called a "Jackson" because it was made in **Jackson**, Michigan, and that is where we would get it. Uncle Ed would go because he knew how to drive.

My father was the purchaser. And I, after weeks of talking of nothing else, had wearied and worried my parents so much that they finally gave in.

To get to the factory where the car would be waiting for us required a 90-minute trip by trolley. We rode the trolley often enough in town. Today, though, everything seemed new and exciting. I was filled with the joyful, wonderful purpose of our expedition. I felt sure that everyone passing by could guess where we were going. Certainly I had told enough of my classmates to spread the word!

After we boarded the trolley, I amused myself by keeping a good watch on the passing landscape. I found the trip so enjoyable that I even began to wish that it would never end. Then I remembered the reason for our journey and became impatient!

THE JACKSON

The Jackson was waiting on the delivery platform. It was all that I'd imagined and maybe a little bit more. The body was finished in a glorious bright red. Side lamps, headlamps, and radiator cap were all of gleaming brass. As a surprise for my mother, my father had ordered an additional horn for her side of the car. Its bulb was of shiny black rubber and the horn was brass.

"Louisa doesn't trust me," my father explained to Uncle Ed, who shook his head and laughed.

There were papers to sign and instructions to be given. A man in a tan smock reminded my father sternly to keep the grease caps filled. He also suggested that if we were to carry more than 3 passengers, they should be seated in a way that would balance the weight. Then he handed the crank to my father, who went around to the front of the car, placed the crank correctly, and gave it a few strong turns.

Uncle Ed had already seated himself in the driver's seat. I was in back. When my father was sure that the engine was running steadily, he put the crank away, walked around to his side of the car, and climbed in.

While we watched, Uncle Ed gently released the brake and eased the car into motion. Then, with a skillful shifting of gears, Uncle Ed backed up, turned left, and headed for the gate.

ON THE ROAD

We started out slowly, for we were still in town. Soon, though, the Jackson picked up speed: 12, 15, 20! Once the engine was broken in, we could go even faster. No wonder they'd passed a law for the state setting the speed limit at 8 miles an hour in cities and towns, 25 on the open road.

"Tell you what, Charlie," Uncle Ed said to my father. "If you did a bit of driving now, to get the hang of it, we could swap places before getting home. Wouldn't that tickle Louisa, you driving up to the house!"

At first my father wasn't sure about Uncle Ed's idea.

"Come on, Charlie," my Uncle Ed encouraged, "that's the beauty of these machines! They don't get scared as horses do and they don't run away. And with this car here, you could turn around on a dime and still leave nine cents showing!"

My father had to laugh at this, and while my father was laughing, Uncle Ed slowed the Jackson down and brought her to a halt. He left the motor running while my father left his seat on the passenger's side of the car and went around to Uncle Ed's.

Then Uncle Ed climbed in on the passenger's side and shut the door behind him with a satisfying thump.

"Okay, Charlie, now just let go of the brake and let her begin to roll."

Uncle Ed's voice was soothing but my father, in his excitement, caused the car to start with a jump.

"Easy does it," I heard my uncle say, for the first of many times.

After a while, though, my father did much better. Barns and houses sped by as we passed; women hanging out the clothes paused to watch us go by. Instead

of yelling "Get a horse!"
—as we did in Ann Arbor—
children waved from doorways.

COMING HOME

All too soon we found ourselves close to home. The road began to be crowded with wagons, buggies, and an occasional motorcar. My father changed places with Uncle Ed, letting him take the wheel. Meanwhile my thoughts turned to Conroy, who was my good friend. I sorely hoped that he'd be on the street as we came driving by. It wasn't every day, after all, that a fellow's family got a brand-new car.

Luck was with me all the way.

My father and my Uncle Ed had just changed places once again when Conroy came up the street. The look on his face, being one part envy and two parts joy, was all a friend could ask.

"That you, Tom?" he managed to call out. "Why don'tcha get a horse?"

 Check Your Reading

1. Why did Uncle Ed also go to pick up the Jackson?
2. How did Tom's father start the car?
3. Why do you think that Tom and his friends yelled "Get a horse!" at passing automobiles?
4. THINKING SKILL: Compare and contrast the ways the Jackson operated with the way cars operate today.

4 War and Prosperity

READ TO LEARN

Key Vocabulary

World War I
Prohibition

Key People

Woodrow Wilson
Charles Lindbergh

Read Aloud

Each night a group of boys and girls stayed after school to work. . . . Every week we had tape to cut in strips, then these were placed in piles of sixes and put in small envelopes.

Alma Gilbert from Saginaw wrote these words about her experiences cutting tape for bandages during World War I. In this lesson you will read about Michiganians like Alma who worked together to help the war effort.

Read for Purpose

1. **WHAT YOU KNOW:** What are some of the ways in which your own community has changed during your lifetime?
2. **WHAT YOU WILL LEARN:** What changes did World War I and the "Roaring Twenties" bring to Michigan?

WORLD WAR I

In 1914 many European countries became involved in a bitter war called World War I. The Central Powers of Germany, Turkey, and Austria-Hungary fought against the Allied Powers of Great Britain, France, and Russia.

At first, most Americans wanted to stay out of this new war. But in 1917, German submarines attacked American ships sailing to Europe. Before long, President Woodrow Wilson said that the United States must help the Allied Powers "make the world safe for democracy." He meant that Americans would fight so that people of other countries could have the right to choose their leaders. On April 6, 1917, Congress

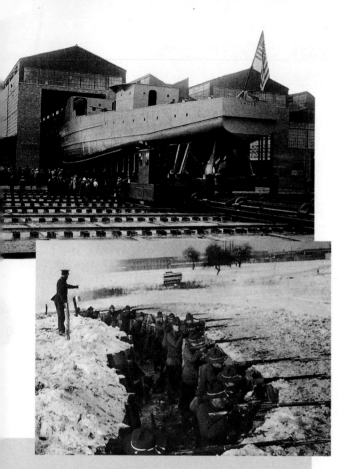

(top) Many Michigan auto factories built boats during **World War I**.
(bottom) Michigan soldiers trained for battle at Fort Custer near Battle Creek.

Leo Beslock returned safely to his home in Detroit. But more than 5,000 Michiganians died in Europe.

THE HOME FRONT

The people who remained at home in Michigan worked hard to support the war effort. Michigan's miners broke all records in providing iron and copper for military supplies. Automobile factories in Michigan switched to making tanks, airplanes, and boats. Because many farm workers were fighting in Europe, schoolchildren were given special holidays to help harvest crops.

Finally, in November 1918, Germany and the other Central Powers surrendered. As thousands of soldiers returned home to our state, people hoped that this terrible war had been "the war to end all wars."

voted to declare war on Germany and the other Central Powers.

Michigan sent 175,000 soldiers to fight with the Allied forces in Europe. These young soldiers faced many deadly new weapons such as poison gas, tanks, and airplanes. One Michigan soldier, Leo Beslock, wrote home to his family.

> *Most of the time the roar of the guns do not let you fall asleep. We used to have frequent gas alarms at night, but I have never been through the gas so far.*

THE "ROARING TWENTIES"

After the war a mood of excitement spread among many Americans. People called the 1920s the "Roaring Twenties." New inventions, like the radio and the telephone, changed the way people lived. Many Michiganians bought cars and now had the freedom to travel to different places.

These changing times affected Michiganians in every part of our state. In farming communities, many farmers had received loans from the government during the war to buy tractors. These new tractors allowed them to farm much more land with fewer workers.

By 1920 nearly half of all farmhouses had telephones. Also, farm families could now order products from catalogs for the first time. The letter carrier could deliver everything from shoes to lace curtains.

In cities life was changing just as fast. People rushed to buy new products and enjoy new forms of entertainment. Many factory workers now could afford electric refrigerators, washing machines, vacuum cleaners, and wristwatches. On Saturday nights people went to see silent movies. In 1927 the "talkies," or films with sound, appeared for the first time.

Every family that could afford to bought a radio. One of the world's first radio stations went on the air in Detroit in 1920. People tuned in to WWJ on their big, boxy radios to hear news reports, sporting events, and detective stories.

NEW TRANSPORTATION

Almost everybody was eager to buy an automobile. Many workers could afford inexpensive cars like the Chevrolet and the Model T. People with more money began buying the new, fancier cars like the Cadillac and Chrysler. In 1929, only 30 years after Ransom E. Olds opened Michigan's first car factory, over 1 million Michiganians owned their own automobiles.

New cars required new roads. The country's first "superhighway," a divided road with eight lanes, soon connected Detroit with Pontiac. By 1930 both the Ambassador Bridge and the Detroit-Windsor Tunnel made it possible for people to travel by car to Canada.

Michigan factories continued to produce airplanes after World War I ended. Few people dared to fly, and

During the 1920s, people in Michigan began to use radios, vacuum cleaners, toasters, and refrigerators for the first time.

Charles Lindbergh, who was born in Detroit, was the first pilot to fly alone across the Atlantic Ocean. His plane was named the *Spirit of St. Louis.*

most could not afford to. But Michigan residents were especially proud of Charles Lindbergh of Detroit. In 1927 he landed his shiny aluminum plane, the *Spirit of St. Louis*, in Paris, France. Lindbergh was the first pilot to fly alone across the Atlantic Ocean. The Detroit *Free Press* headline cheered, "HE'S OUR BOY!"

PROHIBITION AND CRIME

Another change during the 1920s was Prohibition (prō ə bish′ ən). Prohibition made the manufacturing, selling, and drinking of alcoholic beverages against the law. Michigan voters decided to approve Prohibition in 1918. A year later drinking was made illegal everywhere in the country.

Some people broke the law and brought liquor into Michigan from nearby Canada. Others made liquor in their basements and sheds. Criminal gangs controlled much of this illegal activity. These gangs brought violence and crime to Detroit and to other parts of Michigan. In 1933, however, Prohibition was ended. People hoped that this would help to decrease crime.

YEARS OF CHANGE

During the 1920s life in Michigan seemed to offer opportunity, promise, and excitement. People throughout our state enjoyed new inventions and more free time. But some people began to worry that the Roaring Twenties seemed too good to last. Just as the 1920s were ending, in the autumn of 1929, worries about our state's future became very real. You will read about these problems in the next chapter.

Check Your Reading

1. How did Michiganians help the country during World War I?
2. What were some of the new items that people were buying in the 1920s?
3. GEOGRAPHY SKILL: What new changes made it easier for people in Michigan to visit Canada?
4. THINKING SKILL: Compare the ways in which life changed for city people and country people during the Roaring Twenties.

REVIEWING VOCABULARY

discrimination   reform
economy   suffrage
mass production

Number a sheet of paper from 1 to 5. Beside each number write the word or term from the list above that best matches the definition.

1. The right to vote
2. A change or an improvement
3. The ways in which a state or country produces and uses money, goods, and natural resources
4. The making of large numbers of a certain product quickly and cheaply
5. An unfair difference in the treatment of people

REVIEWING FACTS

1. Name three countries from which large numbers of immigrants came to Michigan in the early 1900s.
2. Why did many African Americans come to Michigan during the early 1900s?
3. What were two ways in which Hazen Pingree tried to improve life in Detroit?
4. For which reform did Caroline Bartlett Crane work? For which reform did Anna Howard Shaw work?
5. Name three ways in which life changed for Michiganians during the Roaring Twenties.

WRITING ABOUT MAIN IDEAS

1. **Writing a Description:** Think of a simple task, such as making a sandwich or getting ready for school. Imagine how this task would be quickened by using an assembly line. Write a paragraph describing how you could complete the task using an assembly-line method.
2. **Finding the Main Idea:** Review the material about women Progressives on pages 195–196. Write a paragraph based on the information. State the main idea in your topic sentence. Then add two or three details to support the main idea.

BUILDING SKILLS: WRITING AN OUTLINE

1. Suppose you were writing a report about the Roaring Twenties. You want to answer these questions: What did people do during their leisure time? How did life change for farmers? How did Prohibition affect life in Michigan? Take notes about the Roaring Twenties from the material on pages 206–207. Then make an outline for your report.
2. Why should you make an outline before writing a report?

CHAPTER 9

DEPRESSION, WORLD WAR, AND RECOVERY

FOCUS

I think the Museum of African American History is great! It makes me feel proud to know that African Americans had a great role in our community.

Nyamekye Smith lives in Detroit, the home of the Museum of African American History. When Nyamekye visits the museum, he looks at paintings and sculptures of important African Americans. In this chapter you will read about some of these leaders who brought changes to our state.

1 The Great Depression

READ TO LEARN

Key Vocabulary
stocks
Great Depression
New Deal

Key People
Franklin D. Roosevelt
Joe Louis

Key Places
Inkster

Read Aloud

Dad isn't working since I last saw you and we must pay for the house, gas, electric, water and tax bills, of course grocery, and we don't know from where we shall get the money.

In 1931 a Michigan teenager, Stella Ladoska, wrote these words in a letter to the mayor of Detroit. The 1930s were a very difficult time for Stella's family and for families throughout Michigan. In this lesson you will read how Michiganians struggled through this time.

Read for Purpose

1. **WHAT YOU KNOW:** What are some ways in which people in your community earn a living?
2. **WHAT YOU WILL LEARN:** What was the Great Depression, and how did it affect the people of Michigan?

THE GREAT DEPRESSION

In the 1920s it seemed as if the good times would go on and on. But in 1929 these good times came to an end. During the autumn of 1929, the prices for stocks began to drop. Stocks are shares of ownership in a company. During the 1920s many people had bought stocks, hoping to earn money as the economy boomed and stock prices went up. But now many stockholders grew worried as prices began to fall.

On October 29, as people across the country rushed to sell their stocks, prices dropped even further. By the end of the day, the stock market had "crashed."

The stock market crash caused many problems in the economy. Trouble spread like ripples in a pond. Suddenly, people had less money with which to pay back their loans or to buy new goods. Because people could not repay their loans, many banks failed. People were not buying many products, so companies needed fewer workers. Many people lost their jobs and their savings. The Great Depression had begun. This was a ten-year period when many banks and businesses failed and large numbers of people could not find jobs.

THE GREAT DEPRESSION IN MICHIGAN

There were more factories and factory workers in Michigan than in most other states. Therefore, when people no longer could afford to buy cars or other products, states like Michigan suffered the most. By 1930 nearly one out of every five Michigan workers was without a job. Things were even worse in the cities, where one out of every two workers was jobless. Many people who did have jobs were only able to work part-time.

Businesses throughout Michigan slowed down production. Look at the graph below to see the change in Michigan's automobile production between 1929 and 1932. Other important Michigan businesses, such as mining in the Upper Peninsula and furniture manufacturing in Grand Rapids, also suffered during this time.

GRAPH SKILL: During the Great Depression, many people had to wait in line for food. As factories closed, fewer products were produced. How many fewer automobiles were made in 1932 than in 1929?

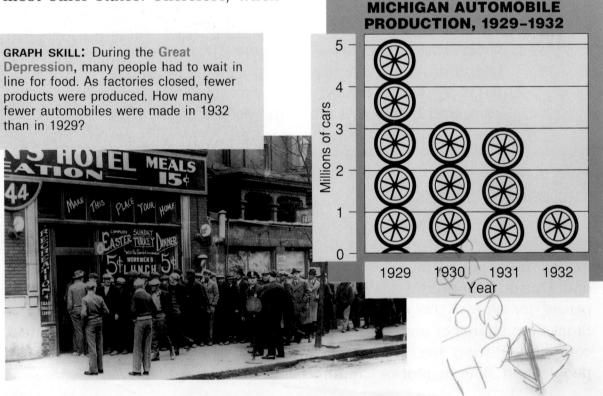

MICHIGAN AUTOMOBILE PRODUCTION, 1929–1932

Millions of cars / Year

212

As part of the New Deal, artists painted murals like this one in Clare and CCC Boys built shelters in state parks.

But the people who were already poor were hurt the most. Because of discrimination, African American factory workers were "the last hired and first fired." In Inkster, an African American community of factory workers near Detroit, almost everyone was without a job. People could not pay taxes and the town had to close its school. The power company even cut off the community's electricity.

THE GOVERNMENT STEPS IN

In the years that followed the "crash," the Great Depression worsened in Michigan and throughout the United States. Hoping for a change, voters elected Franklin D. Roosevelt as President in 1932.

President Roosevelt promised reforms known as the New Deal. These were government programs to help farmers and businesses to get going again. The New Deal spent government money for projects that put jobless people to work.

One of the most important New Deal programs was the Civilian Conservation Corps, also known as the CCC. It gave young men, called "CCC Boys," a chance to do useful work for their state. By the summer of 1935, nearly 17,000 CCC Boys lived in 103 camps around Michigan. They built bridges, parks, roads, and forest-fire lookouts.

Another New Deal program, the Works Progress Administration, or WPA, hired artists, musicians, writers, and teachers. Some of these artists were chosen to create murals, or wall paintings, for government buildings. Often the murals showed something about the local community. In Clare, Grayling, and Manistique the murals showed scenes of lumbering. In Marquette an artist painted a mural of Michigan's Native Americans.

MAKING DO IN MICHIGAN

The Great Depression continued throughout the 1930s. The New Deal programs put thousands of

Joe Louis was born in Detroit and went on to win the world heavyweight boxing championship 25 times.

On the weekends you'd have live music from the nightclubs. At New Year's you could get Times Square, and you could almost feel you were there.

Michigan athletes provided another source of excitement during these years. The Detroit Tigers defeated the Chicago Cubs in the 1935 World Series. In 1936, the Detroit Red Wings won the Stanley Cup and the longest game in National Hockey League history. Detroit's "Brown Bomber," Joe Louis, won the world's heavyweight boxing championship in 1937.

STRUGGLING IN MICHIGAN

The Great Depression started in 1929. Many Michiganians lost their jobs and faced poverty. The government tried to help people until the economy improved, but its efforts did not end the depression.

people to work. But people in Michigan and across the United States still had to struggle to pay for food, clothing, and heat for their homes. In 1935 Detroit newspapers reported that at least 1,000 children stayed home from school because they did not have enough warm clothes to wear.

People who lived through the Great Depression remember "making do" with what they had. They learned to make clothing out of burlap bags and furniture out of old crates. One man who grew up in Black Bottom during the Depression remembered that his mother was "a master at taking nothing and making something."

Movies and radio helped people to forget their worries for a while. As one woman remembered:

Check Your Reading

1. What are stocks?
2. What happened to factory workers in Michigan during the Great Depression?
3. Describe two examples of New Deal programs.
4. **THINKING SKILL:** What are three questions you could ask someone who lived during the Great Depression to learn more about life during that time?

2 The Rise of Unions

READ TO LEARN

Key Vocabulary
union
strike

Key People
Walter Reuther

Key Places
Flint

Read Aloud

I worked from 7 o'clock in the morning until 6 o'clock in the evening. . . . [It was] hot. . . . And you couldn't open up the windows because you'd dry up the [tobacco]. We were just cooped up. . . . And don't forget, we ate where we worked, on the same benches.

These are the words of a Detroit woman who worked in a cigar factory during the 1930s. In this lesson you will read about some of the ways in which people in our state struggled to improve their workplaces.

Read for Purpose

1. **WHAT YOU KNOW:** Why was life difficult for Michiganians during the Great Depression?
2. **WHAT YOU WILL LEARN:** How did unions change the lives of working people in our state?

EARLY UNIONS

During the years of the Great Depression, many unions were started in Michigan. A union is an organization formed by workers. These workers join together to ask for better pay and better working conditions.

Unions had existed long before the Great Depression. Printers had formed Michigan's first union in 1853. Craftworkers such as plumbers and shoemakers formed "craft unions" after the Civil War. In 1885 workers in the sawmills and lumber camps near Muskegon and Saginaw formed a union. They demanded the right to work for no more than ten hours every day.

Before the 1930s, however, few other Michiganians had joined unions. Jobs were plentiful and wages were higher in Michigan than they were elsewhere. Most factory workers were immigrants from many different countries. They often had formed neighborhood groups to help one another. For that reason they were less interested in joining together with workers who had come from countries other than their own.

UNIONS DURING THE DEPRESSION

As the Great Depression worsened, many workers looked to unions as a way to help themselves. When times grew hard, many employers treated workers poorly. Companies often cut workers' wages in order to stay in business.

Walter Reuther traveled throughout Michigan and the United States to speak to workers about joining unions.

In 1929 most Michigan auto workers earned about $1,600 a year. However, in 1932 they earned only half that amount.

Working conditions also grew worse. In some factories, the speed of the assembly line was increased. Supervisors would walk along the line and hit men on the back, telling them to work faster and harder. If workers complained, they were told to quit. There were plenty of other people who needed jobs.

In 1935, six years after the Depression had begun, Michigan auto workers decided to form a union. This union was named the United Auto Workers, or UAW. Walter Reuther (rü' thər), a 29-year-old toolmaker at General Motors, encouraged thousands to join the UAW. Reuther managed to get all of the different kinds of workers—including painters, welders, and janitors—together into one large union. One UAW member, Catherine Gelles, described the feeling of joining a union for the first time:

After we got together, we felt our strength. We felt that we were strong because we weren't individuals any longer. We were part of an organization.

STRIKES IN MICHIGAN

By the end of 1936, the UAW was ready to start the drive for higher wages and better working conditions. The UAW decided to test its

A "strike kitchen" provided food for striking workers during the **strike** at the General Motors factory in Flint.

strength against General Motors, the largest automaker in the world. In a factory in **Flint**, workers went on **strike** on December 30, 1936. A strike is when workers stop work in order to get higher pay or better working conditions.

The strike in Flint was one of the first "sit-down strikes" in the auto industry. In a sit-down strike the workers stay in the factory rather than walk out. This means that the company cannot bring in other workers to operate the machines.

For 44 days the General Motors leaders refused to meet with union leaders. The workers stayed in the Flint factory all that time. Their wives, mothers, and sisters organized a "strike kitchen" near the factory where they cooked food to take to the men. The women passed hot food, clean clothes, and magazines through the factory windows. Finally, General Motors agreed to meet with the union leaders. Each

side gave up some of its demands, and they reached a compromise. The workers won better pay and better working conditions, and the strike ended in February 1937.

Workers in other industries followed this example. At Woolworth's in downtown Detroit, salesclerks worked 52 hours each week and were paid only 28 cents an hour. One day in February 1937, a union organizer stepped to the center of the store, blew a whistle, and shouted "Strike!" For eight days Woolworth employees, most of them teenage girls, occupied the dime store. One teacher who joined the young workers in the strike said:

Some people say you're lawbreakers, but I'm here, a schoolteacher, proud to be among you.

On March 6 the salesclerks won a raise of 5 cents an hour.

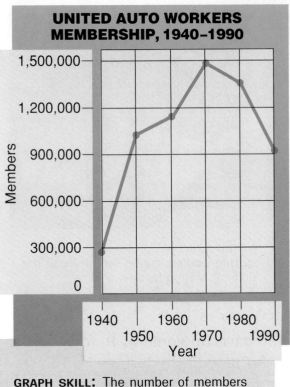

UNITED AUTO WORKERS MEMBERSHIP, 1940–1990

Members

1,500,000

1,200,000

900,000

600,000

300,000

0

1940　1950　1960　1970　1980　1990

Year

GRAPH SKILL: The number of members in the UAW continued to grow until 1970. In which year did the UAW have the most members?

From Detroit auto factories to Upper Peninsula copper mines, Michigan workers joined together during the Great Depression. The unions that they formed fought for better pay and safer workplaces.

UNIONS TODAY

By the end of the 1930s, unions had become an important part of our state. Men and women in many different jobs joined unions. Teachers, police officers, grocery clerks, and truck drivers all depended on their unions to get a better deal from employers. Many unions, especially the UAW, worked hard to gain more rights for African-American and women workers. They also set up programs to care for workers when they became sick or too old to work.

Look at the graph on this page to see the change in membership of the UAW. There are not as many union members in Michigan today. Factories are smaller and people do many new kinds of work. Critics say that big unions need to change some practices that are out-of-date. They also say that big wage increases for union workers cause the price of the union-made goods to rise.

A "UNION STATE"

During the Great Depression workers in Michigan formed unions. They found that by joining together they could make a better life. So many people joined unions that Michigan became known as the "union state."

Check Your Reading

1. What is a union?
2. How did the Great Depression change workers' opinions about unions?
3. Who was Walter Reuther and what did he accomplish?
4. **GEOGRAPHY SKILL:** Why did many unions form in cities?
5. **THINKING SKILL:** Predict what might have happened if unions had not formed in our state.

218

3 Michigan and World War II

READ TO LEARN

Key Vocabulary
World War II

Key Places
Willow Run

Read Aloud

Take my word that Minnie's in the money.
She hasn't got a guy who's got a diamond mine,
But she's a welder on the old assembly line
She's helping Uncle Sam to keep his people free.

These are words to a song that was popular during the 1940s. In this lesson you will read about some of the changes that took place in our state during this time.

Read for Purpose

1. **WHAT YOU KNOW:** Why were factories producing fewer cars and other products in the 1930s?
2. **WHAT YOU WILL LEARN:** How did World War II affect the lives of millions of Michiganians?

WAR BEGINS

In 1939, while Americans were struggling through the Great Depression, war broke out again in Europe and Asia. The Axis (ak' sis) powers of Germany, Italy, and Japan fought against the Allied powers of Great Britain, France, the Soviet Union, and China. This war became known as World War II.

Many Americans wanted little to do with this faraway war. But on December 7, 1941, Japan bombed the United States naval base at Pearl Harbor, Hawaii. The next day Congress voted to go to war against Japan. Germany and Italy then declared war on the United States.

Many thousands of Michiganians rushed to volunteer for the armed forces. Eventually, more than 600,000 men and women from Michigan served in Europe and in Asia. That's twice as many people as live in Michigan's Upper Peninsula today!

Thousands of Michiganians rushed to join the armed forces at the beginning of World War II.

THE ARSENAL OF DEMOCRACY

Soon, Michigan became known as the "arsenal of democracy." An arsenal is a place where military equipment is made. Factories throughout our state geared up to produce materials needed for the war. A steering wheel factory in Saginaw produced machine guns and rifles. An airplane factory at Iron Mountain made glider planes that could fly behind enemy lines. The Kalamazoo Sled Company built toboggans to carry cargo to the ski troops in the Arctic. Even Kellogg's cereal factory in Battle Creek helped the war effort. This factory packaged the "K rations" that were eaten by American soldiers everywhere.

Michigan's most famous war factory was the giant airplane plant built at Willow Run near Ypsilanti (ip sə lant' ē). The workers in this plant managed to build one B-24 bomber every hour! By June 1945 the Willow Run factory had built 8,645 aircraft, more than any other factory in the United States.

THE WAR AT HOME

All over the state, the people of Michigan helped the United States and its allies. Because so many of Michigan's workers were away fighting in the war, factories hired thousands of new workers. Some of them had come to Michigan from other states in search of high-paying factory jobs. Many of the new workers were women.

Some workers lived in tent cities that sprang up around factories. Others rented beds for only eight hours a day. Two other people would sleep in the same bed during different times of the day!

At Willow Run 15,000 women were on the job. They put on overalls and spent long hours operating welding torches, drills, and other machinery. This is how one 20-year-old woman described the difficult factory work.

> It was quite a difference going from a hospital to . . . popping rivets [bolts]. But it made me feel good, and that carried a lot of us over, I think.

Another group of men and women who were very important to the factory at Willow Run were "small people." These people, who were usually under 5 feet tall, helped to build B-24 bombers. They were the only workers who could fit inside the wings, tails, and other tight areas.

In the Upper Peninsula, iron ore and copper mines quickly increased production. Ships transported ore through the Soo Canal both day and night. In Sault Ste. Marie soldiers watched the sky, using searchlights and radar. They wanted to protect this important supply route from enemy airplanes.

Michigan farmers raised more and more crops. Women and children helped to plant and harvest, and they cared for animals. Boys and girls gathered milkweed pods so that the fibers could be used to fill life jackets for sailors. After ten years of the Great Depression, it now seemed that there was too much work to be done and not enough workers.

In 1945 both Germany and Japan surrendered to the United States and its allies. In small towns and big cities, people flooded into the streets, cheering, shouting, and waving flags. Whistles blew and bells rang. The troops would be coming home from war!

A TIME OF CHANGE

World War II changed the lives of the people of Michigan. Thousands of Michiganians went over-

During the war, many women went to work in Michigan factories that built airplanes and other war equipment.

seas to fight. Many women went to work in factories, and many new workers came to Michigan. The war brought an end to the Great Depression. But the war also created some new problems in our state. You will read about these in the next lesson.

Check Your Reading

1. What event brought the United States into World War II?
2. Why was Michigan called the "arsenal of democracy"?
3. How did life change for the people of Michigan during World War II?
4. **THINKING SKILL:** In what ways was World War II similar to World War I for the people of Michigan?

Understanding Cause and Effect

cause   effect

Lila forgot to set her alarm clock before going to bed. The next morning she overslept. Forgetting to set her alarm clock was the **cause** of her oversleeping. A cause is something that makes something else happen. Oversleeping was the **effect** of forgetting to set the alarm. An effect is what happens as a result of something else.

Read the two sentences below.

- Liz won the spelling bee.
- For weeks, Liz studied lists of words every evening.

The first sentence states an effect. The second sentence states the cause, or the reason that the event happened. Liz won the spelling bee because she studied lists of words every evening.

Identifying cause and effect will help you to understand how events are related. You will see how one event leads to another.

Trying the Skill

Read each sentence below. Then tell which sentence states a cause and which sentence states an effect.

- Many banks and factories were closed during the Depression.
- People all over Michigan lost their jobs.

How were you able to tell which sentence stated a cause and which sentence stated an effect?

HELPING YOURSELF

The steps on the left can help you to find causes and effects.
The example on the right shows one way to apply these steps to
the sentences on the previous page.

One Way to Identify Cause and Effect	Example
1 Look at the events being described.	Banks and factories were closed, and people were out of work.
2. In each sentence look for words that signal causes, such as *because*, *since*, and *as a result of*. If you do not find any word clues, ask yourself if one event is the reason that something else happened.	Did the closing of banks and factories cause something else to happen?
3. If the answer is yes, you have found a cause.	The closing of banks and factories was the reason that something else happened.
4. Look for words that signal effects, such as *so*, *therefore*, and *as a result*. If you do not find any word clues signaling effects, ask yourself what happened as a result of the cause. What happened is an effect.	Because of the closing of banks and factories, people were out of work.

Applying the Skill

Now apply what you have learned.
Read each pair of sentences below.
Tell which sentence states the cause
and which sentence states the effect.

- During the Great Depression many businesses closed.
- The 1929 stock market crash caused many problems in the economy.
- Many of Michigan's factory workers went to Europe and Asia to fight in World War II.
- Factories hired thousands of new workers.

Now check yourself by answering
the following questions.

1. What is the first thing you should do to identify cause and effect?
   a. Find the cause.
   b. Look at the events described.
   c. Ask what happened.
2. What was one effect of the New Deal?
3. What was one effect of Michigan workers fighting in World War II?

Reviewing the Skill

1. What is a cause? An effect?
2. What are four steps that you could follow to find the cause and effect?
3. Why is it important to be able to tell the difference between causes and effects?

4 The Struggle for Equal Rights

READ TO LEARN

Key Vocabulary

segregation
civil rights
integration

Key People

Martin Luther King, Jr.
Coleman Young
Richard Austin

Read Aloud

I will go out and carve a tunnel of hope through the mountain of despair [sadness]. *With this faith, I will go out with you and transform* [change] *dark yesterdays into bright tomorrows.*

Martin Luther King, Jr. spoke these words when he visited Michigan in 1963. In this lesson you will read how people throughout our state worked to build a "bright tomorrow" of equality and justice for all Michiganians.

Read for Purpose

1. **WHAT YOU KNOW:** What does the word *equality* mean to you?
2. **WHAT YOU WILL LEARN:** How did the civil rights movement change Michigan?

SEPARATE BUT NOT EQUAL

You have already read that blacks and whites had lived together in Michigan since the 1700s. But more than 200 years later, our state's African Americans were still suffering from discrimination.

In big cities like Grand Rapids and small towns like Monroe, African Americans were the victims of segregation (seg ri gā' shən). Segregation is the practice of keeping blacks and whites separate. Blacks were not allowed to join the same clubs, eat in the same restaurants, or go to the same schools as whites. The facilities that were used by African Americans were usually of poorer quality. Entire neighborhoods were often segregated.

224

Michigan's African Americans also faced anger and violence from the Ku Klux Klan. Klan members hated any people who they felt were different from themselves, especially African Americans, Catholics, and Jews. As more blacks came to Michigan after 1915, several thousand white Michiganians joined the Ku Klux Klan. They beat, bullied, and sometimes even killed African Americans.

ANGER IN DETROIT

As you have read, thousands of people came to Michigan during World War II to work in factories. In most cities these newcomers were jammed into neighborhoods that were already overcrowded. The war also meant that people worked very long hours. Many Michiganians were tired, and they were worried and anxious about what might happen in the war.

In this tense situation, disagreements could quickly become angry or even violent. On June 20, 1943, many black and white Detroiters were relaxing at Belle Isle, a city park. A fight broke out and it quickly spread. That night a riot filled the streets of Detroit. A riot is a violent disturbance by a crowd of people. Before this riot was over, 34 people had died.

THE STRUGGLE FOR RIGHTS

Blacks and whites throughout Michigan realized that changes were needed. Michiganians began to fight for civil rights. Civil rights are the rights of all people to be treated equally under the law. These rights include the right to vote, freedom of speech, and equal protection for all citizens.

During the 1950s and 1960s thousands of Michiganians joined the civil rights movement. Martin Luther King, Jr., an important leader of this movement, came to Detroit in June 1963. King led nearly

In the summer of 1963, Martin Luther King, Jr. led a march for civil rights through downtown Detroit.

125,000 people in a march down Woodward Avenue to the riverfront. In a speech, King described the goal of the civil rights movement:

Now is the time to make real the promises of democracy. . . . Now is the time to lift our nation from the quicksands of racial injustice to the solid rock of racial justice. Now is the time to get rid of segregation and discrimination.

In August 1963, Michigan became the first state to create a Civil Rights Commission. This group works to protect the rights of all Michigan citizens. Progress was made toward the integration of schools, restaurants, and transportation. Integration means the act of making something available to all groups of people.

Although the civil rights movement brought change to Michigan, many problems remained. Banks rarely gave loans to African Americans to start businesses in their own neighborhoods. Few African Americans were hired as teachers, police officers, or firefighters. African Americans still did not have the same opportunities to buy homes or to receive an education as whites did. Many African Americans felt that they had been denied their fair share in the United States.

RIOTS IN DETROIT

On July 23, 1967, these frustrations came to a head. Trouble broke out between police and young people in an African-American neighborhood of Detroit. It soon turned into a terrible riot. Federal troops

Riots in Detroit in 1967 caused terrible destruction and led Detroiters to look for new solutions to the city's problems.

came to Detroit to end the riot. By the end of the week, 43 people had died and hundreds of homes had been destroyed.

An African American newspaper, the *Michigan Chronicle,* wrote: "We are a city divided not only between its black and white citizenry, but within [these groups] as well." Few blacks or whites believed in violence as a solution. Brave women and men came forward in their schools, churches, and neighborhoods. Together they looked for solutions to the problem of inequality in Michigan.

MAYOR COLEMAN YOUNG

In 1973 Coleman Young was elected as Detroit's first African American mayor. As a union member and state senator, he had worked to bring integration and equality to Michigan. While he was mayor he increased the number of African American city workers. Young helped African American Detroiters to feel that they were a part of their city at last.

Throughout the state, African Americans took advantage of opportunities that had resulted from years of struggle. There were more laws now to protect their rights. More members of the African American community were able to go to college. In 7 of Michigan's 15 largest cities, African Americans were elected mayor. Michigan's

Richard Austin (*left*) and Coleman Young (*right*) both worked to bring equality to all Michiganians.

secretary of state, Richard Austin, was the longest- serving African American official in the United States.

A LONG STRUGGLE

African Americans in Michigan were denied equality for hundreds of years. In the 1960s, after years of struggle, they began to gain the civil rights that most Americans already had. Today, people throughout our state continue to work together to bring equality to all Michiganians.

Check Your Reading

1. What are civil rights?
2. Why was there trouble in Detroit during World War II?
3. What progress in civil rights was made in Detroit in the 1950s and 1960s?
4. **THINKING SKILL:** In what ways did the civil rights movement help to change the lives of Michigan's people?

227

A Children's MUSEUM

"The museum was built for children," said Dr. Charles Wright during a recent interview about the Museum of African American History in Detroit. In many ways the museum that Wright started is a result of his involvement in the civil rights movement.

When Dr. Wright was a member of the Medical Committee for Civil Rights in the 1960s, he met and marched with Dr. Martin Luther King, Jr. This experience helped Wright to decide that he "wanted to help my people find out who they are."

In 1965 Wright started the Museum of African American History in his home in Detroit. He began interviewing members of his community and recording their remarks on tape. He found that they were proud to show him artifacts of their family history. In time Wright was able to borrow, copy, or buy many of these artifacts for his museum. A favorite artifact of Wright's is the "Freedom Pass." This was a pass that African Americans before the Civil War had to carry at all times. Failure to carry the pass might have resulted in a person's being sold into slavery. When the collection became too large for his house, Wright needed to find a new place to put everything.

With the cooperation of the Detroit public schools, Wright began the "Buy a Brick" project. For each dollar that children collected, a brick was bought for the new museum, which opened on May 7, 1987. "The project raised $86,000," recalls Wright. "And now many of these kids are adults and they come to *their* museum."

Although Wright no longer runs the museum, he still serves as an adviser and speaker. "I've been pleased to see how the children have adopted the Museum," says Wright. "They have a sense of pride that they didn't have before."

REVIEWING VOCABULARY

Number a sheet of paper from 1 to 5. Beside each number write **C** if the underlined word is used correctly. If it is not, rewrite the sentence using the word correctly.

1. A <u>union</u> was a type of club for boys who needed jobs during the Great Depression.
2. A <u>strike</u> is a share of ownership in a company.
3. Under the practice of <u>segregation</u>, black children and white children attended school together.
4. <u>Civil rights</u> include the right to vote and the right to free speech.
5. Because of <u>integration</u>, black passengers and white passengers had to sit in separate cars on the same train.

REVIEWING FACTS

1. What was the purpose of the New Deal?
2. Why did Michiganians join unions in great numbers during the Great Depression?
3. How did Michigan's factories help the war effort during World War II?
4. What caused the Detroit riot in 1943?
5. How did the struggle for civil rights help African Americans? Which problems still remain?

WRITING ABOUT MAIN IDEAS

1. **Writing a Diary Entry:** Imagine that you are a fourth grader in Michigan during World War II. Write a diary entry telling about some of the ways in which your life was touched by the war.
2. **Writing an Interview:** Imagine that you are in the audience hearing Martin Luther King, Jr. speak in Detroit in June 1963. Write five questions that you would ask him about the civil rights movement.

BUILDING SKILLS: UNDERSTANDING CAUSE AND EFFECT

1. Which steps should you follow in order to find cause and effect?
2. Read the two sentences that follow and tell which states a cause and which states an effect.
   a. The Great Depression brought hardships for many people.
   b. President Roosevelt introduced the New Deal.
3. Why is it useful to know the difference between cause and effect?

REVIEWING VOCABULARY

civil rights	reform
discrimination	segregation
economy	strike
integration	suffrage
mass production	union

Number a sheet of paper from 1 to 10. Beside each number write the word or term from the list above that best completes the sentence.

1. _____ are the rights of all people to be treated equally under the law.

2. Under _____, blacks and whites were separated from each other.

3. Under _____, black children and white children could go to school together.

4. Ford's method of _____ helped to lower the price of the Model "T"

5. Workers went on _____ at the headquarters of General Motors in Flint on December 30, 1936.

6. Mexican Americans suffered _____ when they were unfairly treated differently from other people.

7. During the Great Depression, the _____ of the United States suffered.

8. Caroline B. Crane brought about _____, or changes for the better.

9. Anna Howard Shaw worked for women's _____, or the right to vote.

10. Many Michiganians joined an organization called a _____ to fight for better pay and working conditions.

WRITING ABOUT THE UNIT

1. **Listing Effects:** After Henry Ford introduced the assembly line at his automobile factory, many changes came to Michigan and the nation. List at least five changes that were brought about by the new cars.

2. **Writing a Comparing Paragraph:** Consider the way in which Native Americans were treated in Michigan in the 1800s and the way in which African Americans were treated in Michigan during World War II. Then write a paragraph telling how the methods of treatment were the same and how they were different.

ACTIVITIES

1. **Researching:** Find out more about one of the key people discussed in the unit. Learn about the person's life and accomplishments. Tell the rest of the class what you have learned by pretending to be the person and "introducing yourself" to the class.

2. **Making Illustrations:** In this unit, you read about two wars in which Michiganians fought—World War I and World War II. Choose one feature of these wars, such as uniforms, advances in technology, or strategies. Then find out how that feature had changed from the first to

the second world war. Prepare a set of illustrations showing the changes.

BUILDING SKILLS: UNDERSTANDING CAUSE AND EFFECT

Read the paragraph below and answer the questions that follow.

During the 1960s the civil rights movement brought change to Michigan. As a result, the Civil Rights Commission was formed to protect the rights of all Michigan citizens. Steps were taken toward the integration of schools, restaurants, and transportation.

1. What is the difference between a cause and an effect?
2. Identify a cause that appears in the paragraph. Identify an effect.
3. Which word or words might help you to recognize the difference between a cause and an effect?
4. Explain why it is important to be able to tell the difference between causes and effects.

 LINKING PAST, PRESENT, AND FUTURE

Since 1900 numerous advances in technology have changed life for people in Michigan. Changes have included new farm machinery, automobiles, airplanes, and household appliances. How does technology affect your daily life today? How do you think technology might change your life even further by the time you are an adult?

State tree:
White pine

State flag

UNIT

5

State bird:
Robin

MICHIGAN TODAY

LIFE IN OUR STATE

On these pages you see some of the symbols of Michigan. These are all things found in our state that make it different from any other. In the last three units you read the story of our state's past. Now let's find out what Michigan is like today.

State flower:
Apple blossom

233

CHAPTER 10

LIVING AND WORKING IN MICHIGAN

FOCUS

It was fun to go to work with my dad. He is a scientist who creates new car paints. We did experiments and tested new colors.

Krystal Gordon lives in Mount Clemens in Macomb County. Her father works in the automobile industry. In this chapter you will read about the many different jobs that people have in Michigan.

1 Rural Life

READ TO LEARN

Key Vocabulary

census   rural   tourism
urban   livestock

Key Places

Empire

Read Aloud

There are lots of things to do around where I live. In the summertime my family and I go fishing on Lake Superior. In the winter I can go downhill skiing on Marquette Mountain or cross-country skiing on the golf course that's right behind my house.

This is how nine-year-old Dwight Downs describes what it is like to live in the Upper Peninsula. Dwight and his classmates at Fisher Elementary School in Marquette feel lucky to live in the U.P. because they can do many different things outdoors. In this lesson you will read about other things that make life in the small towns and countryside of Michigan very special.

Read for Purpose

1. **WHAT YOU KNOW:** How has agriculture been important to our state's history?
2. **WHAT YOU WILL LEARN:** What are some of the ways in which rural life has changed in Michigan?

WHERE WE LIVE

Every ten years the United States government takes a census. A census is a count of the number of people living in a place. The census in 1990 found that you, your family, your friends, plus everyone else who lives in the state of Michigan added up to 9,328,784 people.

The 1990 census found that eight out of ten Michiganians live in urban areas—that is, in cities and large towns. It also found that two out of every ten Michiganians live in

235

MICHIGAN: URBAN AND RURAL POPULATION

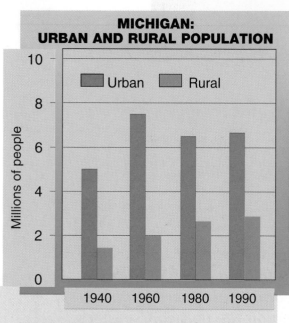

Millions of people

| | 1940 | 1960 | 1980 | 1990 |

Urban Rural

GRAPH SKILL: Gene and Darlene Rhodes live in rural Michigan. How many people lived in rural areas in 1990?

rural areas. The word *rural* means "having to do with the country or agriculture." Rural areas are small towns and farming communities. Look at the graph on this page. It shows the changes in Michigan's urban and rural populations over the last 50 years. How big was Michigan's rural population in 1940?

THE PUMPKIN PEOPLE

If you drive down Highway M-43 near Kalamazoo, you may see an orange tractor, orange barns, orange wagons, orange cars, and a yard filled with orange pumpkins! This is the farm of Gene and Darlene Rhodes. The Rhodeses are known as the "Pumpkin People."

When Myron Rhodes, Gene's grandfather, started the farm in 1885, he grew many different crops. He raised wheat, corn, hay, and a few pumpkins. He also raised livestock. We use this word to describe animals such as cows, pigs, and horses that are raised on a farm. Myron, like most Michigan farmers in the 1800s, was a subsistence farmer. The crops he grew and the livestock he raised were used mainly as food for his family.

In 1957 Gene and Darlene began raising only pumpkins and squash on the farm. Each year they grow 200 tons (181 metric t) of pumpkins and 70 tons (64 metric t) of squash. This adds up to a greater weight than that of 33 school buses! Like many Michigan farmers today, Gene and Darlene "specialize." This means that they produce one or two cash crops for the market. They use modern technology such as tractors and new types of fertilizers to grow

New machines, like this combine, have helped to make work easier for farmers. Scientists are also helping farmers to develop new and better crops.

larger and healthier pumpkins and squash. Gene and Darlene also sell some of their crops at a roadside stand.

In September and October Gene and Darlene are "walking advertisements" for their crops. During those months the "Pumpkin People" only wear orange clothing!

AGRICULTURE TODAY

There are fewer farmers in Michigan today than there were when Myron Rhodes started his farm in 1885. Because of new technology, a farmer today can produce much more food than a farmer could produce 100 years ago. Machines can plant, weed, fertilize, and harvest crops very quickly. Look at the graphs on page 312 of the Almanac to see some of the important crops that are grown in Michigan today.

Farmers and scientists in Michigan work together to find new ways to improve agriculture. For example, they have discovered new feeds that help cows to produce much more milk. Farmers and scientists also work to find new uses for crops. In the 1930s Henry Ford began to use soybeans to make plastic for the steering wheels of his Model Ts. Today, Michigan soybeans are used to make plastic, plywood, shampoo, and paint.

TIMBER AND MINING

You have already read about the many ways in which timber has been important to Michigan. Today about half of our state is covered with forests. In the northern part of Michigan, timber is still an important business. Towns such as Escanaba and Manistee are famous for their sawmills, just as they were in the 1800s. In factories throughout our state, workers turn trees into paper, furniture, boats, and other products. Michigan's trees provide many jobs for Michigan's people.

Our forests also provide opportunities for recreation. Michigan has 32 state forests and 5 national forests, more than any other state. These forests are areas that have been set aside by the government for use by all of Michigan's people. Some of the timber on this land is sold to logging companies. The government uses this money to build roads and to pay for schools. But much of this forested land is preserved for hiking, skiing, and hunting. Michigan's government also plants new trees in order to provide lumber and forests for recreation for many years to come.

Michigan is still one of our country's biggest producers of minerals. Our state is second only to Minnesota in the amount of iron ore mined. Most of this iron comes from mines in the Upper Peninsula. Today, the White Pine mine in

Ontonagon County is Michigan's only active copper mine. The White Pine mine also produces silver!

TOURISM

The 1990 census showed that some rural parts of Michigan are among the fastest-growing regions of our country. The area around Traverse City, for example, is attracting many new people. Why are these areas growing so quickly? Part of the answer is tourism. Tourism is the business of providing services to people who are on vacation.

Every year more and more tourists visit places of interest in our state. Some of these people come from Michigan, but many come from other states and other countries. These visitors stay at hotels, motels, and campgrounds. They eat Michigan food and buy souvenirs.

Michigan's wildlife, forests, and historical sites, such as the Empire Museum, help to make **tourism** a growing industry in our state.

They ski on Michigan slopes and swim at Michigan beaches. These tourists provide many jobs for the people of our state. In fact, more than 139,000 Michiganians work in our state's tourism industry.

Many rural communities offer tourists the chance to learn about our state's natural resources and history. In **Empire**, a tiny town in northwestern Michigan, local residents have built a museum that displays exhibits about early logging and farming. They have even rebuilt a one-room schoolhouse containing desks and books that are more than 100 years old!

CLOSE TO THE LAND

From the Rhodes' orange pumpkin farm to the museum in the little town of Empire, Michiganians are continuing a long tradition of living close to the land. The residents of rural areas work together to make Michigan a better state for all of us and for our visitors.

Check Your Reading

1. What does a census tell us about our state?
2. How are scientists and farmers working together to improve farming in Michigan?
3. What are some of the ways in which we use our state forests?
4. **GEOGRAPHY SKILL:** How has the geography of our state helped the timber, mining, and tourism industries?
5. **THINKING SKILL:** How has new technology changed life in rural Michigan today?

239

Recognizing Point of View

Key Vocabulary
point of view

Read what Ruth and Bill have to say about skiing.

Ruth: Skiing is fun for both skiers and spectators.
Bill: Skiing is a dangerous sport. Skiers can get hurt.

Ruth and Bill have different **points of view**. Point of view is the way a person looks at something. People often look at the same subject from different points of view. Being able to identify a person's point of view allows you to make up your own mind about the subject.

Trying the Skill
Gregory and Gail have two different points of view about places to visit in Michigan. Read them both carefully.

Gregory: I think that there is no better place to visit than Sleeping Bear Dunes National Lakeshore. I can enjoy swimming there.
Gail: I think that the most beautiful place in all of Michigan is Mackinac Island. There I can ride in a horse-drawn wagon.

How would you describe the two points of view?

HELPING YOURSELF

The steps on the left will help you to recognize a person's point of view. The example on the right shows one way to apply these steps to Gail's statement on page 240.

One Way to Recognize Point of View	Example
1. Identify the subject.	The subject is the place in Michigan that Gail likes to visit.
2. Identify the information included.	Gail likes visiting Mackinac Island.
3. Identify words that are expressions of opinion. They tell how a person feels about something.	Gail uses the words *I think that the most beautiful. . . .* These words tell you that she is giving her opinion.
4. Tell the point of view expressed.	Gail thinks that Mackinac Island is the most beautiful place to visit.

Applying the Skill

Now apply what you have learned. Identify the points of view expressed by Felicia and Spike.

Felicia: The Underground Railroad was a good system, but it really didn't make that much difference. Slavery still existed throughout the South.

Spike: The people who worked in the Underground Railroad made a huge difference in the lives of thousands. Over 2,000 enslaved people were led to freedom.

To check yourself, answer the following questions.

1. What topic are Felicia and Spike talking about?
   a. the risks of the Underground Railroad
   b. whether or not the Underground Railroad made a difference
   c. famous people who worked in the Underground Railroad

2. Which phrases helped you to determine Felicia's point of view?
   a. *really didn't make that much difference*
   b. *slavery still existed*
   c. *was a good system*

3. Spike's point of view is shown by
   a. the facts that Spike included.
   b. the words *made a huge difference.*

Reviewing the Skill

1. Define *point of view.*
2. What are some steps that you should take to identify point of view?
3. Why is it important to understand a person's point of view?

2 Urban Life

READL TO LEARN

🔲 Key Vocabulary

high-tech   service industry

Key Places

Chelsea

🔲 Read Aloud

There are maybe a million things I like about living in Detroit. All of my friends and all of my family live here. There's the park on Belle Isle and Tiger Stadium. I love sitting in the bleacher seats. It seems like I get to see about 100 games every season!

Joey Rashid is a fourth grader who lives in Detroit. Detroit is our state's biggest urban area. It is also the seventh-largest city in our country. In this lesson you will read about what it is like to live in urban Michigan.

🔲 Read for Purpose

1. **WHAT YOU KNOW:** How did people from different countries help Michigan's cities to grow?
2. **WHAT YOU WILL LEARN:** How have Michigan's urban areas changed in the last 100 years?

OUR CHANGING COMMUNITIES

The 1990 census showed that many of Michigan's communities have changed greatly in the last 100 years. Today, about eight out of ten Michiganians live in urban areas. In 1890 this number was only three out of ten.

In 1890 Chelsea was a rural farming town. Today, Chelsea is a small urban community. Some people in Chelsea are still farmers. However, most people work in stores, offices, or small factories such as the Chelsea Milling Company, producers of Jiffy Mix food products. Many people drive from their homes in Chelsea to jobs in larger cities such as Jackson, Detroit, or Ann Arbor.

Businesses in Chelsea have changed along with the town. *The*

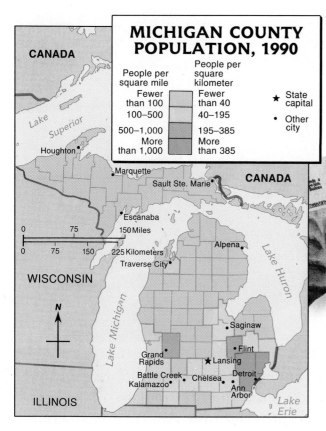

MICHIGAN COUNTY POPULATION, 1990

People per square mile | People per square kilometer
Fewer than 100 | Fewer than 40
100–500 | 40–195
500–1,000 | 195–385
More than 1,000 | More than 385

★ State capital
• Other city

CANADA

Lake Superior

Houghton

Marquette

Sault Ste. Marie

CANADA

Escanaba

0   75   150 Miles
0   75   150   225 Kilometers

Alpena

WISCONSIN

Traverse City

Lake Michigan

Lake Huron

N

Saginaw

Flint

Grand Rapids

★ Lansing

Battle Creek
Kalamazoo

Chelsea

Detroit

Ann Arbor

ILLINOIS

Lake Erie

MAP SKILL: *The Chelsea Standard* brings news to the people of Chelsea. How many people per square mile live in Chelsea?

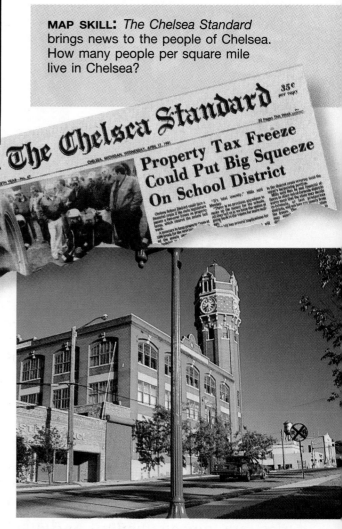

The Chelsea Standard

Property Tax Freeze Could Put Big Squeeze On School District

Chelsea Standard, the local newspaper, was started in 1871. In those days the employees ran the printing press and folded each paper by hand. Sometimes they had to travel 20 miles (32 km) by wagon to pick up paper and ink.

The *Standard* still brings the news to the people of Chelsea. In fact, some of today's readers are the great-grandchildren of the very first readers. Owned by the Heritage Newspaper chain, the *Standard* is managed and edited by Brian Hamilton. After working for the paper's previous owners for nine years, Hamilton left to start his own publication. Now he is back at the *Standard* working to keep the residents of Chelsea informed about their community.

MANUFACTURING

You have read how Michigan's cities have grown from tiny trading posts to bustling urban areas. Look at the map on this page. How many people per square mile live in the Grand Rapids area?

As manufacturing became more important, towns such as Detroit and Grand Rapids became centers for people to live and work. Today, new people, new jobs, and new technology are changing the face of our cities.

243

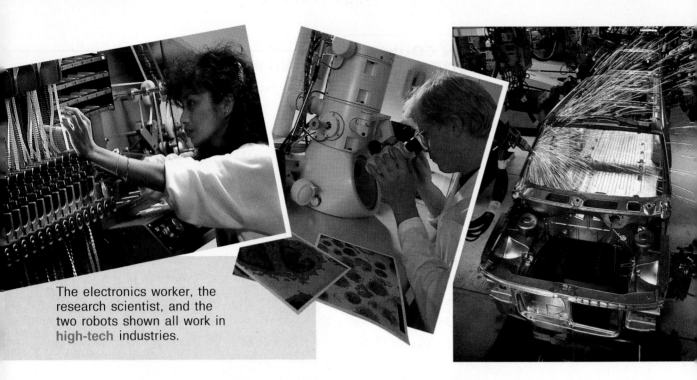

The electronics worker, the research scientist, and the two robots shown all work in high-tech industries.

In the 1920s as many as 15,000 people worked in a single, huge auto factory. Everything from hubcaps to steering wheels was made under one roof. Workers and their families lived in neighborhoods close to the factories.

Today most of Michigan's factories are much smaller. And like many of Michigan's farms, these factories have become specialized. Although cars are still assembled in one factory, the car parts are made in many different places. One small factory might make only brakes. As factories have moved out of cities, so have many workers.

Some industries have continued to change and grow right where they started. In Grand Rapids many companies still manufacture furniture, just as they did in the 1800s. But the furniture that they make has changed. For example, one Grand Rapids factory makes only computer furniture. Another makes only office chairs. Automobiles and highways make it possible for the people who work in these factories to live many miles from their jobs. Just like Detroit, Grand Rapids has "spread" into surrounding areas.

HIGH-TECH INDUSTRIES

Many new factories in Michigan are part of the high-technology, or high-tech, industry. This industry makes products that require much scientific knowledge.

Joey Mazzetti lives in Berkley, a Detroit suburb. Joey's dad works in a high-tech factory that has only 14 workers. These workers make only one product, control panels. These control panels are the "brains" that run the robots in auto factories.

Robots are among the most important high-tech products that are made in Michigan. In fact, our state has more than 15 robot companies. Robots are often used to do tiring or dangerous work. In an auto factory in Hamtramck, one robot can weld 87 places in just 47 seconds!

Because factories in Michigan have begun using robots and other types of technology, many workers have lost their jobs. This has prompted companies and unions to join together to train these workers for the new jobs that are appearing in our changing economy.

SERVICE INDUSTRIES

The fastest-growing areas of Michigan's economy are found in the service industries. These are industries that "serve" people. Doctors, cooks, lawyers, and teachers are all service workers. Tourism, about which you read in Lesson 1, is one of the most important service industries in our state. What are some examples of service workers in your community?

Many jobs in the service industries are also high-tech jobs. Doctors at the University of Michigan use computers to study the causes of cancer. They search through billions of pieces of information trying to find a cure. Like many new jobs in Michigan, cancer research requires years of study. This is one of the reasons that education is such an important part of Michigan's new economy.

Today, about one out of every four Michigan workers is a service worker. And by the time you finish high school, there will be more service jobs than manufacturing jobs in our state.

Cooks, doctors, and telephone repair people are some of the many service industry workers in our state.

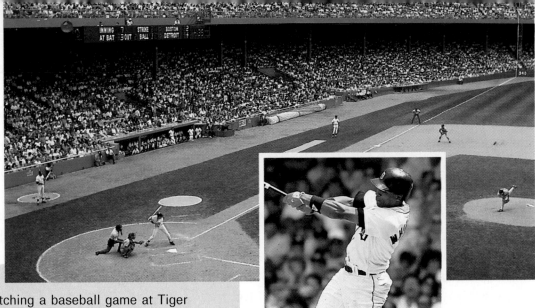

Watching a baseball game at Tiger Stadium is a special part of living in metropolitan Detroit.

ENJOYING URBAN LIFE

In the Read Aloud section you met Joey Rashid and learned some of the reasons that he likes living in metropolitan Detroit. What do you think are some of the special things about living in an urban area?

In an urban area there are many things to do nearby. You might find bowling lanes, an art museum, and a zoo all within a few miles. There are department stores and neighborhood shops. Some businesses stay open all night long!

In an urban area you can always find places to enjoy sports and hobbies. Joey Rashid loves baseball. Living near Tiger Stadium means that he can watch his favorite team play many times during the season. In the park at Belle Isle, he can play ball with his friends. Urban areas also offer tennis courts, ice rinks, orchestras, choirs, and art classes.

URBAN MICHIGAN

Many changes have come to Michigan's urban areas. Companies both large and small have found new ways to grow in a changing economy. High-tech industries and service industries have become more and more important. Urban Michigan continues to be an exciting place in which to live and work.

Check Your Reading

1. How have our state's automobile factories changed?
2. How are service jobs different from manufacturing jobs?
3. **GEOGRAPHY SKILL:** How have automobiles and highways had an effect on the way in which Michiganians live and work?
4. **THINKING SKILL:** Predict three new service jobs that might come to our state in the future.

3 Michigan and the World

READonly TO LEARN

Key Vocabulary

interdependent   environment   acid rain

export   pollute

import   recycle

Key Places

Ann Arbor

Read Aloud

Did you ever stop to think that you can't leave for your job [or school] *in the morning without being dependent on most of the world?*

Think about Martin Luther King, Jr.'s question for a moment. Where did the banana that you put on your morning cereal come from? Where were your clothes and shoes made? In this lesson you will read about the ways in which Michigan is linked with the rest of the world.

Read for Purpose

1. **WHAT YOU KNOW:** In what ways do you depend on other people to meet your daily needs?
2. **WHAT YOU WILL LEARN:** How is Michigan linked with other countries in the world today?

LINKS WITH THE WORLD

In Chapter 6 you have read that pioneers took almost one month to travel from New York to Michigan in the early 1800s. An airplane could make that trip in less than two hours today! Improvements in transportation have brought Michigan closer to the rest of the world.

If you look around your classroom, you will probably see many things that were made in other countries. Your pencils may have been made in Venezuela. Calculators in your classroom might have come from Japan. Your chairs might have been made in Canada.

AN INTERDEPENDENT WORLD

Today our state is part of an **interdependent** world—a world in which countries depend on each other to meet their needs and wants. One way in which countries are interdependent is through trade.

A large amount of Michigan's automobiles, iron, timber, and other products are exported, or sold to countries around the world. In turn, many goods that we need—such as petroleum and steel—are imported, or bought from other countries. The chart on this page lists some of the many products that Michigan exports and imports.

Our neighbor Canada is Michigan's most important trading partner. Michigan sells more of its goods to Canada than does any other state in the United States. If you were to visit Canada, you would probably see many American-made cars streaming along its highways. You probably would find your favorite breakfast cereal on the shelves of a Canadian supermarket, too!

Just as Canada imports products that it needs from Michigan, we import products that we need from our northern neighbor. For example, the natural gas and petroleum that we import from Canada helps to keep our homes warm in winter and our cars running all year round. Michiganians and Canadians like to say that they are "partners in prosperity [*wealth*]."

PROTECTING OUR ENVIRONMENT

As you have read, one reason that Michigan and Canada are interdependent is because of trade.

CHART SKILL: Michigan trades with many different countries. From which country does Michigan **import** bananas?

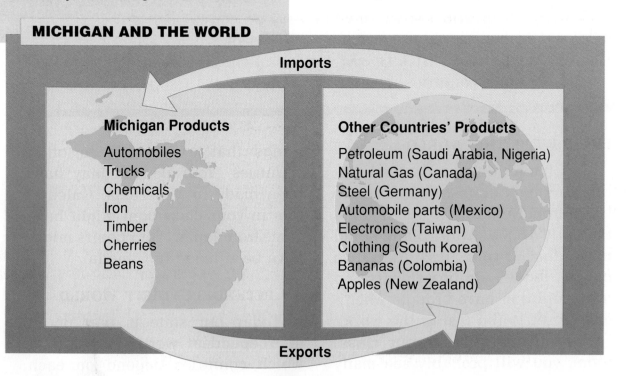

MICHIGAN AND THE WORLD

Imports

Michigan Products

Automobiles
Trucks
Chemicals
Iron
Timber
Cherries
Beans

Other Countries' Products

Petroleum (Saudi Arabia, Nigeria)
Natural Gas (Canada)
Steel (Germany)
Automobile parts (Mexico)
Electronics (Taiwan)
Clothing (South Korea)
Bananas (Colombia)
Apples (New Zealand)

Exports

Acid rain, which is formed by pollution from power plants and other factories, caused the deaths of these trees.

Another reason is because we share the same **environment**. The environment is made up of the surroundings in which people, animals, or plants live.

Both the United States and Canada border the largest group of freshwater lakes in the world—the Great Lakes. In the 1950s factories around the Great Lakes released tons of harmful waste materials into the lakes each day. As a result, they became badly **polluted**, or filled with harmful materials. This new problem alarmed Americans and Canadians alike.

Since then, Americans and Canadians have worked together to clean up the Great Lakes. The two countries have signed several agreements, stating that they will work together to improve the water quality in the lakes. Today the lakes are much cleaner than they were back in the 1950s, thanks to the efforts of Americans and Canadians. Some factories have begun to **recycle** materials used in manufacturing. To

recycle means "to use something again." Factories are also working to store their harmful waste materials in safe places.

Acid rain has become one of the most serious environmental problems facing the United States and Canada today. In the region around the Great Lakes, many power companies burn coal to produce energy. The burning of coal, however, causes an especially harmful kind of air pollution. Pollution is something that makes the air, soil, or water dirty. When the pollution from burning coal combines with moisture, the result is acid rain.

Acid rain badly damages trees, lakes, and streams. It can even kill all of the fish and other wildlife that live in a lake or stream. Canadians and Americans are working hard to end acid rain, but it remains a difficult problem today.

Students from Ann Arbor learn about a different culture when they visit their sister city of Hikone, Japan.

SISTER CITIES

Michiganians do more than work and trade with people who live in countries around the world. They also exchange thoughts and ideas. Several Michigan cities have "sister cities" in other countries. Sister cities help to build bridges of friendship between people of different cultures.

Ann Arbor has sister cities in Canada, Germany, Japan, and Nicaragua. Students in the Ann Arbor School District are involved in many programs with students in their sister cities. Every year they spend a weekend playing sports and computer games with students from Peterborough, Canada. Many students have become pen pals with students in Nicaragua. Others have had the opportunity to visit their sister cities in Japan and Germany.

BRIDGES WITH THE WORLD

There are many bridges that connect Michigan and its people with the rest of the world. Michiganians are linked together by trade, a concern for the environment, and other needs and wants. Sister-city programs are another way in which we are building bridges with people from around the world.

Check Your Reading

1. How do imports from other countries help Michiganians?
2. Name two ways in which Michigan and Canada have become interdependent.
3. **GEOGRAPHY SKILL:** Why does it seem as if Michigan is closer to the rest of the world today than ever before?
4. **THINKING SKILL:** Predict two ways in which Michigan may become more closely linked to the rest of the world.

REVIEWING VOCABULARY

export   service industry
import   urban
rural

Number a sheet of paper from 1 to 5. Beside each number write the word or term from the list above that best matches the definition.

1. Having to do with the country or with agriculture
2. Goods brought in from other countries
3. Workers, such as bus drivers and tour guides, who serve other people
4. Goods sold to other countries
5. Having to do with cities or large towns

REVIEWING FACTS

1. What are three ways in which Michigan agriculture has changed over the last 100 years?
2. List three jobs in the tourism industry that you would like to have.
3. Name two ways in which the high-tech industry is providing a service for the automobile industry.
4. What are two kinds of problems that Michiganians and Canadians have worked together to solve?
5. What causes acid rain? Why is it important to put an end to acid rain?

WRITING ABOUT MAIN IDEAS

1. **Writing a Paragraph:** Many Michiganians work in agriculture or in manufacturing. Write a paragraph explaining how these people are interdependent.
2. **Making a List:** Imagine that your community has a sister city in another part of the world. What activities or programs might children and adults share with their sister city? List at least five ideas.

BUILDING SKILLS: UNDERSTANDING POINT OF VIEW

Read the conversation below. Then answer the questions that follow.

Gerri: I think that there is no better place to live than in a city. There are always many things to do, like visiting a museum or going to a movie.

Sheila: I think that the best place to live is in the country. Only in the country can I go horseback riding.

1. Name some steps you could take to identify a person's point of view?
2. What is Gerri's point of view about living in a city? What is Sheila's point of view?
3. Why is it important to be able to recognize a person's point of view?

CHAPTER 11

MICHIGAN'S GOVERNMENT

FOCUS

I like all of the changes that have been made in the Capitol Building. They have fixed it up so that it looks pretty. I especially like the glass ceiling with the seals of all the states.

Alexandra Sophiea lives in East Lansing, just a few miles from our state capital. She visited one of the important rooms in our Capitol Building. In this chapter you will read about the people who meet in this room and make decisions about our state.

1 State Government

READ TO LEARN

Key Vocabulary

State Legislature   bill   veto
legislative branch   executive branch   judicial branch

Read Aloud

Of all our extraordinary resources, the most valuable are our people—all of our fellow citizens who pay the taxes, raise the children, farm the land, and build the future.

Governor John Engler spoke these words to the people of Michigan in January 1991. In this lesson you will read how the governor and other leaders of our state government work to improve our state. You will also read how you, too, can help to "build the future" of Michigan.

Read for Purpose

1. **WHAT YOU KNOW:** What are some rules that students at your school must follow?
2. **WHAT YOU WILL LEARN:** How does the government of Michigan work?

OUR STATE AND YOU

Have you ever visited our state's Capitol Building in Lansing? This beautiful building was recently restored so that it now looks the way it did more than 100 years ago. On the Chapter Opener page you can see one of the rooms in which our leaders meet.

Each day, decisions that affect life in Michigan are made in a room like this one. While you are busy at school, people in the Capitol Building are busy working to improve our state. They make sure that there is money for your school and that school buses are safe. And they work to see that the men and women who want to be your teachers have the opportunity to go to college.

Our state government also provides services such as fixing roads and taking care of parks. Of course, the government must pay for these services. Our state government is able to pay because it collects money from the people of Michigan. This money is called *taxes.*

The decisions that our state government makes about how much to spend on services determines the amount of taxes to be collected. The plan for spending the taxes is called a *budget.* Look at the circle graph on this page. It shows how Michigan spends each tax dollar. What is the biggest part of Michigan's budget?

Sometimes people in our state may disagree about how much money should be spent on one particular service. How are these decisions finally made? In order to answer this question, you need to know more about the way in which our government works.

THE LEGISLATIVE BRANCH

One of our state government's most important jobs is protecting our natural resources. Did you ever wonder why so many white pine trees grow in our state?

Part of the answer is our soil. Much of the Upper Peninsula and northern Lower Peninsula is covered with a fertile soil called Kalkaska soil. Kalkaska soil is perfect for growing white pine trees.

In 1990 Karl Hausler from Lansing became concerned about this valuable natural resource. Karl thought that if Kalkaska soil became our "state soil," Michiganians would work harder to protect this important part of our environment. But to make this official, the state would have to pass a law. How does this process work?

Karl brought his idea to the Michigan State Legislature. This is the legislative (lej' is lā tiv) branch of the Michigan government. A branch is a part of government. The members of the State Legislature meet and make laws. In Michigan the State Legislature is made up of two different parts: the House of Representatives and the Senate. The

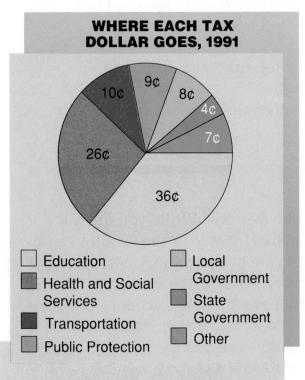

WHERE EACH TAX DOLLAR GOES, 1991

9¢
10¢
8¢
4¢
7¢
26¢
36¢

☐ Education
☐ Health and Social Services
☐ Transportation
☐ Public Protection
☐ Local Government
☐ State Government
☐ Other

GRAPH SKILL: How much of every tax dollar did Michigan spend on transportation in 1991?

Senator Connie Binsfeld *(right)* worked in the State Legislature to help Karl Hausler's state soil idea become a state law.

110 representatives and 38 senators are elected by the voters of our state. Representatives serve for two years, and senators serve for four years.

Karl discussed his idea with Connie Binsfeld, the senator from Kalkaska County. In 1991, Senator Binsfeld became our Lieutenant Governor. Senator Binsfeld agreed to write a bill to make Kalkaska soil our state soil. A bill is a plan for a law. The "soil bill," now called Senate Bill 236, was presented to the Senate. The senators liked the soil idea and voted to pass the bill.

Next, the bill was sent to the House of Representatives. Sometimes the representatives disagree with the senators and refuse to pass the bill. But in this case they agreed that the soil bill was a good idea,

and they also voted to pass the bill. Now, the governor of Michigan had to be convinced.

THE EXECUTIVE BRANCH

The governor is elected by the people of our state to head the executive (eg zek′ yə tiv) branch of our government. He or she makes sure that the laws are carried out. The governor also plays an important role in making laws.

After both houses of the State Legislature had passed Bill 236, it was sent to the governor for his

255

approval. The governor had two choices. He could sign the bill, which would make it a state law. Or else he could veto the bill, which means that he refuses to sign it. However, if two thirds of the members of the State Legislature still support the bill, they would be able to "override," or set aside, the governor's veto.

But the governor agreed that the Kalkaska soil was a good choice for our state soil. On December 14, 1990, he signed the bill into law. Look at the chart on this page to see how a bill becomes a law.

THE JUDICIAL BRANCH

The soil bill had become law. But one more branch of our state government may become involved with this law. This branch is called the judicial (jü dish' əl) branch. The word *judicial* means "relating to courts of law and to justice."

In Michigan the judicial branch has many judges and several kinds

CHART SKILL: This chart shows the steps a bill goes through to become a law. What happens if the governor vetoes the bill?

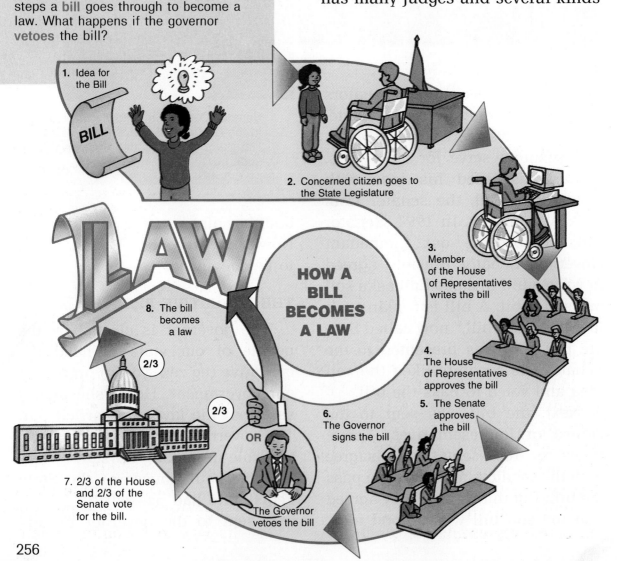

HOW A BILL BECOMES A LAW

1. Idea for the Bill

2. Concerned citizen goes to the State Legislature

3. Member of the House of Representatives writes the bill

4. The House of Representatives approves the bill

5. The Senate approves the bill

6. The Governor signs the bill

OR The Governor vetoes the bill

7. 2/3 of the House and 2/3 of the Senate vote for the bill.

8. The bill becomes a law

256

THE THREE BRANCHES OF GOVERNMENT

EXECUTIVE BRANCH
Governor
Carries out laws

LEGISLATIVE BRANCH
State Legislature
Passes laws

JUDICIAL BRANCH
Supreme Court
Makes judgments about laws

CHART SKILL: Michigan's constitution provides for three branches of government. What is the function of the **executive branch**?

of courts. The highest court is the Supreme Court. It is made up of seven justices who are elected by the voters of our state.

As you can see from the chart on this page, the judicial branch is responsible for making judgments about laws. If someone thought that the soil bill did not agree with the constitution, he or she could challenge the law in court. If the judges decided that the soil bill was unconstitutional, then the law would be thrown out.

RESPONSIBLE CITIZENS

Michigan's government is our government. By electing the members of our three branches of government, the people of Michigan decide who will serve us in our capital city, Lansing.

When you are older, you might become a representative, a senator,

a judge, or even governor of Michigan. When you are 18 you will be able to play a part in our state government by voting. You will be making choices that will affect the lives of the people of Michigan.

Check Your Reading

1. Name the three branches of government and explain the job that each branch performs.
2. What happens to a bill if the governor decides to veto it?
3. What are some ways in which you could become involved in our state government?
4. **THINKING SKILL:** List the steps that the "soil bill" went through on its way to becoming a law.

257

Reading Newspapers

Key Vocabulary

news article   headline
feature article   byline
editorial   dateline

In Lesson 1 you read about Karl Hausler, from Lansing, whose idea it was to make Kalkaska soil the state soil. How did people all over Michigan learn about this idea? One way was through newspapers. Every large American city and many small towns have their own newspaper. The newspaper covers stories of local, state, and national interest.

The Parts of a Newspaper

Newspapers are divided into several parts. The front part usually contains news articles. A news article reports about recent events. Most newspapers also have feature articles. A feature article reports in detail about a person, subject, or event. For example, a local newspaper might have a feature article on recycling or about a town's early history.

Other parts of the newspaper include sports articles, cartoons, and editorials. An editorial is an article in which the editor gives his or her opinion about an issue. An editor is the person who plans or runs the newspaper. Unlike a news article that includes only facts, an editorial gives an opinion. For example, an editorial might urge readers to support plans to build a new library. An editorial might also support a person who is running for government office such as the presidency.

Editorials often appear on a page with letters to the editor. These letters are written by the paper's readers. In them, readers give their opinions about an issue in the news. By printing letters from readers, newspapers can offer many different opinions about an issue.

The Parts of a News Article

A news article usually begins with a headline. The headline is printed in large type across the top of the article. It catches the reader's attention. Many news articles have a byline. The byline gives the name of the reporter who wrote the article. Some news articles also begin with a dateline. A dateline tells where and when the story was written.

A well-written news article begins by answering four questions: (1) *Who* was involved in the story? (2) *What* happened? (3) *When* did it happen? (4) *Where* did it happen? As you read the news article from *The Jewish News*, decide if the reporter answered the *Who*, *What*, *When*, and *Where* questions.

14-Year-Old Miracle Worker Holds Second MDA Carnival

by Michael Weiss

OAK PARK, August 25 — Most teenagers spend their summers going to camp, traveling with family or hanging out with friends.

Not Jeff Lazar. He's busy working to raise $6,000 at his second annual carnival for the Muscular Dystrophy Association to be held September 8 at the Crowne Pointe Office Center in Oak Park.

Fourteen-year-old Lazar has been collecting for MDA since the age of five. "He walked door-to-door and collected over $500 that first year," recalled his father. Since then, he's collected every summer, raising more money each time.

Last year, Lazar came up with the idea of holding a carnival for MDA. However, he was told he could not use money he had collected for MDA to pay for it.

Still determined, Lazar contacted local businesspeople and asked them to sponsor booths. Despite a rainstorm and a shortage of volunteers, Lazar collected more than $2,000.

"So naturally, this year he wanted to do something bigger and better," said his father. "He wanted rides. I said absolutely no. So we are having them."

After several months of contacting local businesses, Lazar has completed most of the planning. The owners of the Crowne Pointe Office Center at Lincoln and Greenfield have donated their parking lot for the carnival. Local businesses have donated $3,000. This is enough money for carnival rides, food and drinks.

Although this year's carnival is not even finished yet, Lazar is already planning the next one.

Reviewing the Skill

1. Name three parts of a newspaper.
2. What is one difference between a news article and an editorial?
3. Which four questions does a well-written news article answer?
4. Write another headline for the news article about Jeff Lazar.
5. Describe the events that were reported in the news article.
6. Why is it helpful to understand the different parts of a newspaper?

2 Local Government

READn TO LEARN

Key Vocabulary

board of commissioners   council
county manager   mayor
charter

Key People

Thomas Coogan

Read Aloud

In 1817 some Detroiters became angry because hogs were allowed to run loose through town. These hogs sometimes destroyed vegetable gardens. The leaders of Detroit passed a law to take care of this problem. This law said that a hog could roam freely only if the owner put a metal ring in its nose. The leaders knew that if a hog started to dig in a garden, the ring would hurt its nose.

When Detroit was only a small pioneer town, the citizens asked their leaders to pass laws to help their community. Today, Michigan's communities have new problems. In this lesson you will read about how local governments work to make decisions and pass laws.

Read for Purpose

1. **WHAT YOU KNOW:** In which city or town do you live?
2. **WHAT YOU WILL LEARN:** What are some services that local governments provide?

COMMUNITY GOVERNMENT

In the last lesson you read about the three branches that make up our state government. These three branches work together to make decisions that affect all the people of Michigan. But some issues are only important to the people who live in one place. People in a community might be concerned about buying a new traffic light or hiring more teachers for the school. These decisions about our communities are made by local governments.

COUNTY GOVERNMENT

As you have read, the United States is divided into 50 states. In the same way, Michigan is divided into smaller parts. Each of these parts is called a county. Michigan has 83 counties. You can learn more about them by looking at pages 307–309 of the Michigan Almanac. Each of these counties has its own government. And each part has a role in serving Michiganians like yourself.

The board of commissioners is the legislative branch of county government. The board might have as few as 5 or as many as 35 members. The number of members depends on the size of the county.

County governments also have an executive branch. In Michigan there is more than one type of executive. Counties with many residents, like Oakland, Bay, and Kent counties, elect a county executive. Some counties, however, have a county manager to run the executive branch. This person is hired by the board of commissioners.

Our county governments also collect taxes from their citizens. They use this money to build roads, run hospitals, and pay teachers. Look at the map on this page to find the county in which you live.

MAP SKILL: In which of Michigan's 83 counties is our state capital located?

MICHIGAN: Counties

— County boundary   ★ State capital

1. Alcona	27. Gogebic	40. Kalkaska	55. Menominee
2. Alger	28. Grand Traverse	41. Kent	56. Midland
3. Allegan	29. Gratiot	42. Keweenaw	57. Missaukee
4. Alpena	30. Hillsdale	43. Lake	58. Monroe
5. Antrim	31. Houghton	44. Lapeer	59. Montcalm
6. Arenac	32. Huron	45. Leelanau	60. Montmorency
7. Baraga	33. Ingham	46. Lenawee	61. Muskegon
8. Barry	34. Ionia	47. Livingston	62. Newaygo
9. Bay	35. Iosco	48. Luce	63. Oakland
10. Benzie	36. Iron	49. Mackinac	64. Oceana
11. Berrien	37. Isabella	50. Macomb	65. Ogemaw
12. Branch	38. Jackson	51. Manistee	66. Ontonagon
13. Calhoun	39. Kalamazoo	52. Marquette	67. Osceola
14. Cass		53. Mason	68. Oscoda
15. Charlevoix		54. Mecosta	69. Otsego
16. Cheboygan			70. Ottawa
17. Chippewa			71. Presque Isle
18. Clare			72. Roscommon
19. Clinton			73. Saginaw
20. Crawford			74. St. Clair
21. Delta			75. St. Joseph
22. Dickinson			76. Sanilac
23. Eaton			77. Schoolcraft
24. Emmet			78. Shiawassee
25. Genesee			79. Tuscola
26. Gladwin			80. Van Buren
			81. Washtenaw
			82. Wayne
			83. Wexford

Teachers, road workers, and firefighters all provide services for local governments.

CITIES AND TOWNS

Counties in Michigan are made up of townships. In rural areas, the township governments are very important. In urban areas, township governments are not as important. The reason is that city and town governments in urban townships take care of local government.

Most people in Michigan live in cities and towns. These communities can write charters, which are like local constitutions. When people in a community write a charter, they decide for themselves what kind of government they will have. For this reason, Michigan's cities and towns do not all have the same type of local government.

But most local governments have three branches. The council is the legislative branch of a town or city. A mayor is the head of the executive branch. Mayors in big cities usually work full-time at their jobs and receive a salary. In smaller towns and suburbs, mayors often volunteer to serve without pay, and they work as mayor only part-time.

A MAYOR'S JOB

James M. Kinard is the mayor of Melvindale in Wayne County. He is also president of his family business, located in Melvindale since 1962. Although Mayor Kinard keeps daily business hours at city hall, he also has one phone at his company's office that rings only when someone calls about city

262

business.

Kinard has been Melvindale's mayor since December, 1995. He works to provide better roads and schools for the city and to help its senior citizens. The mayor can also perform weddings and other ceremonies for the town's residents.

Recently the city faced a big challenge. Melvindale is located over one of the world's largest salt mines. Some people wanted to use this huge empty mine for storing dangerous waste materials. The previous mayor, Thomas Coogan, discussed this important issue with the people of the town. After Kinard was elected, he continued work with the people and city council for a solution that was best for Melvindale. They worked for a year against the idea. Finally, the owner of the mine gave up the proposal.

Mayor Kinard works hard to make his city a good place to live. He wants Melvindale to live up to its slogan, "The Little City with the Big Heart."

GOVERNMENTS WORK TOGETHER

As Michigan grows and changes, the role of government changes, too. In the 1800s people in our state were concerned about hogs running loose in the streets. Today, Michiganians are concerned about protecting our environment in different ways. People in our state also want

Mayor James Kinard handles city business and company business in Melvindale.

to improve our schools and care for our senior citizens.

Many of these problems cannot be solved entirely on the state, county, or local level. The people in all levels of government must work together to find solutions. In the next lesson you will read about the ways in which the United States government also helps to improve life in our state.

Check Your Reading

1. What is the role of local government in our state?
2. Why are township governments more important in rural areas?
3. What are some of the duties of a small-town mayor?
4. **THINKING SKILL:** What are three questions you could ask your mayor in order to learn more about his or her job?

263

Should Michiganians Put Their Garbage in a Landfill or Burn It?

Did you know that everyone in your class, including your teacher, produces about 5 pounds (2 kg) of garbage every day, or 35 pounds (16 kg) every week? Have you ever wondered what happened to that ice-cream wrapper or banana peel that you threw away? As you read in the last lesson, Michiganians are concerned about their environment. Many people have begun to recycle their garbage. But what about the garbage that is not recycled? Michiganians have different ideas about what to do with this garbage.

Right now most of the garbage you produce is buried in a landfill, which is an area of land that is filled in by garbage and then covered with soil. Some Michiganians believe that landfills are a safe and inexpensive way to take care of garbage. However, other Michiganians believe that landfills can be dangerous. They are concerned that garbage might leak out of the landfill and get into the water supply. Instead they would like to incinerate, or burn, the garbage. But those Michiganians who think that landfills are safer say that the burning of garbage causes air pollution. Should Michiganians put their garbage in a landfill or burn it?

Two DIFFERENT Viewpoints

Michiganians Should Put Their Garbage in Landfills

Many Michiganians think that landfills are not as harmful as the burning of garbage is. Landfills do not produce air pollution, but burning garbage does.

Patrick Johnson, chairperson of the Macomb County Solid Waste Planning Commission in St. Clair Shores, is in favor of landfills. He says:

> . . . with landfills, nothing is sent into the atmosphere like there would be with incineration. We are finding that materials do not rot in a landfill like we used to believe they did.

Greg Carpenter, vice president and general manager of the Pine Tree Acres Landfill in New Haven, says:

> Landfills are simply more economical. Landfills are much safer today . . . and have liners of clay and other materials to help control . . . possible leakage.

● Why do Patrick Johnson and Greg Carpenter think that landfills are safe?

Michiganians Should Burn Their Garbage

Some Michiganians are concerned that garbage might leak into the soil or water supply and produce effects that are harmful to people. They believe that it is safer to burn garbage than to use landfills.

Nancy Fagge, president of the Council for Rural Awareness in Warren, is in favor of burning garbage. She does not think that landfills are safe.

> All landfills eventually leak and create problems with wells, causing a loss of homes, sickness . . . and even death.

Ed Whedon, general manager of the Grosse Pointe/Clinton Refuse Disposal Authority in Mount Clemens, says:

> There used to be a fear of air pollution . . . but now we have better controls that have solved that problem. Incineration is a good system because it reduces the volume of trash into ash. . . .

● Why does Nancy Fagge want to burn garbage instead of using landfills?

BUILDING CITIZENSHIP

1. Why do some Michiganians want to use landfills?
2. Why do some Michiganians want to burn their garbage?
3. Which side do you think makes the stronger case? Why?

3 Michigan and Our Nation's Government

READ TO LEARN

 Key Vocabulary

House of
   Representatives
Senate

Key People

Carl Levin
Spencer Abraham
Gerald R. Ford, Jr.

Martha Griffiths
John Conyers, Jr.

 Read Aloud

*Every day the White House must have many bags of
trash. Do you recycle any of it? If you will help by recycling, it will let more trees live in Michigan.*

Ten-year-old Andy Vinyard wrote these words to President George Bush in 1991. In this lesson you will read
President Bush's reply to Andy. You will also read about
how you are connected with the nation's government.

 Read for Purpose

1. **WHAT YOU KNOW:** What are the three branches of
   Michigan's state government?
2. **WHAT YOU WILL LEARN:** How does our national government work, and why is it so important?

THE UNITED STATES GOVERNMENT

In this lesson you will read
about Michigan and the national
government. Like our state government, the national government has
three branches. The legislative
branch, called Congress, is made
up of the House of Representatives
and the Senate. The executive
branch is led by the President. The
judicial branch is made up of our
national, or federal, courts.

The number of people that a
state sends to the House of Representatives in Washington, D.C.,
depends on that state's population.
During the 1980s Michigan had 18
representatives. In 1990, however, a
national census found that some
states, such as California, are growing much faster than Michigan. For

this reason, California has added representatives and Michigan now has 16.

The number of Michigan's senators, however, never changes. Every state has two senators. Carl Levin was first elected to the Senate in 1978. Senator Spencer Abraham has served since 1995.

HOW THE NATIONAL GOVERNMENT WORKS

In many ways our national government is much like our state and local governments. For example, it depends on tax money to pay for the services it provides. But the national government is also different from state and local governments.

The national government handles matters that go beyond state borders. If you mail a letter to a friend in Arizona, the United States Postal Service carries your letter.

The national government works with other countries. For example, it might sign an agreement with Canada that works to prevent acid rain. The national government also maintains the armed forces to protect our country's interests.

SERVING THE NATION

In the Legacy lesson on pages 173–176, you read that public service has always been important in Michigan. The most famous Michiganian to serve in our national government was Gerald R. Ford, Jr., who was President from 1974 to 1977.

When Ford was a high school senior in Grand Rapids, he won a trip to Washington, D.C. Sixteen years later Ford became involved in national government himself. In 1948 he was elected to the United States House of Representatives for the first time. This was only the beginning of Ford's long career in government. He became Vice President in 1973. One year later, Gerald Ford became our nation's thirty-eighth President.

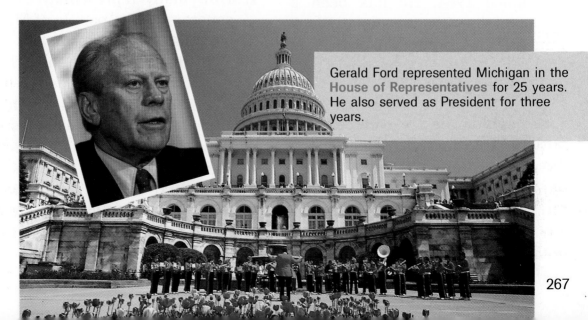

Gerald Ford represented Michigan in the House of Representatives for 25 years. He also served as President for three years.

John Conyers, Jr., and Martha Griffiths both served Michigan as members of the House of Representatives. Griffiths later became our lieutenant governor.

Many other Michiganians have served in our nation's government. Martha Griffiths was elected to the House of Representatives in 1954. She later served as lieutenant governor of our state. John Conyers, Jr., from Detroit, has been a representative since 1964. He has been a leader of the Congressional Black Caucus. This group works to gain equal rights for African Americans.

MAKING A DIFFERENCE

When you are 18 years old, you will be able to vote. But you can have a voice in government now!

Andy Vinyard is a fifth-grade student who lives in Pleasant Ridge. He helps to save the earth's resources by taking newspapers and bottles to a recycling center for elderly people in his neighborhood.

As you read in the Read Aloud, Andy wrote to President George Bush to find out what government leaders are doing about recycling. President Bush wrote back to say that the White House recycles cans and newspapers. He also wrote:

Your message tells me that you have a deep appreciation for our natural heritage. . . . Together, we will make the words of the song "America, the Beautiful" a reality.

YOUR GOVERNMENT

In this lesson you have read that the purpose of our nation's government is to serve all of its citizens. By voting for our leaders and by telling them our concerns, Michiganians help to make this a better country for all people.

Check Your Reading

1. How many representatives and senators do the people of Michigan elect to Congress?
2. Why does Michigan now have fewer seats in the House of Representatives than it did before?
3. What kinds of services does our national government provide?
4. **THINKING SKILL:** Compare the three branches of our national government with the three branches of Michigan's state government.

REVIEWING VOCABULARY

bill   mayor
charter   veto
House of
    Representatives

Number a sheet of paper from 1 to 5. Beside each number write the word or term from the list above that best completes the sentence.

1. The ____, or plan for a law, was introduced in Congress.
2. The ____ is the head of a city or town government.
3. A governor can ____ a bill to keep it from becoming a law.
4. The ____ of our small town says we can have a part-time mayor.
5. One of the lawmaking bodies of Congress is called the ____.

REVIEWING FACTS

Number a sheet of paper from 1 to 5. Beside each number write **T** if the statement is true. If the statement is false, rewrite it to make it true.

1. The job of the legislative branch is to carry out the laws.
2. The executive branch is a part of the judicial branch.
3. The lawmaking body of a county is called its township.
4. Cities and towns do not have a local government that makes laws.
5. Every state has the same number of representatives in the Senate.

WRITING ABOUT MAIN IDEAS

1. **Writing a Story:** Think of an idea that would make a good law for the people of Michigan. Following the steps of how a bill becomes a law, write a story telling how this idea might actually become a law.
2. **Writing a List of Elected Officials:** Find out who represents you in the different parts of government. Make a list of the names of your mayor, your board of commissioners, your governor, and your representatives in the United States Congress.

BUILDING SKILLS: READING A NEWSPAPER

1. A well-written news article begins by answering which four questions?
2. What is the difference between a news article and an editorial?
3. Reread the article on page 259. Then answer the following questions.
   a. What is the headline?
   b. What information is provided in the byline?
4. How can reading newspapers help you in school?

CHAPTER 12

ENJOYING MICHIGAN

FOCUS

I like living in this part of Michigan because it is peaceful. It was cold and windy on top of Mount Curwood. But being on top of the mountain is like being on top of Michigan!

Jessica Maki and Darrin Voskuhl live near L'Anse in the rugged country of Michigan's Upper Peninsula. They visited nearby Mount Curwood, which is one of the highest peaks in our state. What is special about the part of Michigan in which you live?

1 Who We Are

READ TO LEARN

Key Vocabulary

ancestor   reservation

Read Aloud

We have families [here] who are black, East Indian, French, German, Chaldean, Jewish, Taiwanese, Turkish, Korean, South American and Japanese. I see all the kids playing together.

These are the words of Diane McVety of West Bloomfield Township. She is proud to live in a community with so many different people. In this lesson you will read about some of the people who live in Michigan today.

Read for Purpose

1. **WHAT YOU KNOW:** From which countries did Michigan's immigrants come during the 1800s and 1900s?
2. **WHAT YOU WILL LEARN:** How is Michigan's population changing today?

MICHIGAN'S POPULATION

President Franklin Roosevelt once said, "Remember always that all of us . . . are descended from immigrants." He was pointing out something that you have already studied. That is, all Americans or their ancestors came from some other place. An ancestor is a person in your family, starting with your parents, who was born before you.

Today more than 9 million people live in Michigan. Only seven states in the United States have more people. People have come from all over the country and the world to live in our state.

WHO WE ARE TODAY

As you read in Chapter 3, the first people to live in Michigan were hunters who followed herds of animals to find food. These hunters were the ancestors of Michigan's Native Americans.

Today there are 56,000 Native Americans living in Michigan. Most belong to the groups of the Three Fires—the Chippewa, Ottawa, and Potawatomi. Thousands of Native Americans in Michigan live on reservations, or land set aside by the government. Many Chippewa live on the state's largest reservations near Sault Ste. Marie. Not all of Michigan's Native Americans live on reservations, however. Most live in the cities of Michigan.

In Michigan's cities, Native Americans live side by side with people whose ancestors escaped from slavery or migrated from New England. You read about the arrival of these pioneers in Chapter 6.

Other Michiganians have ancestors who came from countries in Europe. You have read that thousands of immigrants from western Europe came to Michigan in the 1800s to work as farmers, miners, and loggers. In the early years of the 1900s, thousands of people from southern and eastern Europe streamed into Michigan to work in the state's booming new factories.

RECENT ARRIVALS

In more recent years, immigrants have come to Michigan from still other places in the world. New families from countries in Asia, Latin America, and the Middle East have settled in our state. In fact, Michigan has the largest Arab-American community of any state. In all,

TIME LINE SKILL: In which year did the Great Migration begin?

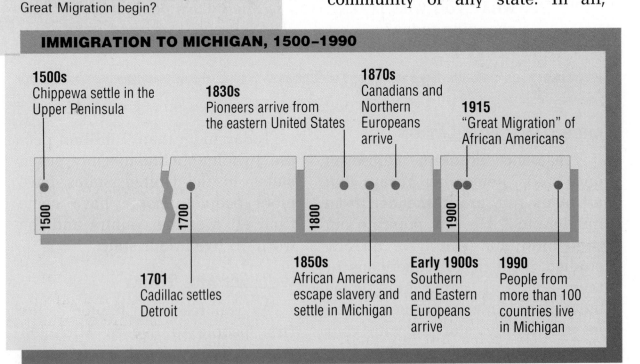

IMMIGRATION TO MICHIGAN, 1500–1990

1500s
Chippewa settle in the Upper Peninsula

1830s
Pioneers arrive from the eastern United States

1870s
Canadians and Northern Europeans arrive

1915
"Great Migration" of African Americans

1500

1700

1800

1900

1701
Cadillac settles Detroit

1850s
African Americans escape slavery and settle in Michigan

Early 1900s
Southern and Eastern Europeans arrive

1990
People from more than 100 countries live in Michigan

Michigan is home to people from more than 100 different countries!

Think about your own family for a minute. Where did your family's ancestors originally come from?

RELIGION IN MICHIGAN

Safriman Maamun is a student in Mrs. Frese's fourth-grade class at Spartan Village Elementary School in East Lansing. His parents moved to Michigan from Indonesia in 1988. In class, Safriman sits next to Lin Kou and Maria Siles. Together, they learn about Michigan's past and present.

On weekends, though, they are involved in different activities. Safriman is Muslim, so he worships with his family at a mosque on Friday. Lin is Protestant and Maria is Roman Catholic. They both go to church services on Sunday. However, they attend different churches.

Religion is an important part of life for Safriman and his friends, as it is for many Michiganians. Of course, not every Michiganian is a member of a religious group. And not all religious groups in our state have the same beliefs. Religious beliefs in Michigan are varied, just like its land and people.

MICHIGANIANS ALL

Our state's people are as different as Michigan's Porcupine Mountains are from the flatlands of the Lower Peninsula. But no matter

Today Michigan is home to people from more than 100 different countries.

where or how Michiganians live, we all help to make Michigan a special place. In the next lesson you will read about how art adds beauty to life in our state.

Check Your Reading

1. To which groups do most Native Americans in Michigan belong today?
2. From where have many of Michigan's immigrants come in recent years?
3. What are some of the religions practiced by Michiganians?
4. **THINKING SKILL:** What are three questions you could ask an immigrant to learn more about the place that he or she came from?

Reading Time Zone Maps

Key Vocabulary

time zone

Gene and Darlene Rhodes, about whom you read in Chapter 10, own a farm begun by Gene's ancestors. Like the Rhodeses, people in other states earn their living from farming. But when Gene and Darlene are just beginning their day, farmers in California are probably sound asleep. How is that possible?

Understanding Time Zones

The earth is divided into 24 time zones—1 for each hour of the day. The difference in time between most neighboring time zones is exactly one hour.

Because the earth rotates from west to east, in time zones east of yours it is always later than it is in your time zone. In time zones west of yours it is always earlier than it is in your time zone. For example, suppose that it is 6:00 A.M. where you live. In the time zone just east of yours it is 7:00 A.M. In the time zone just west of yours it is 5:00 A.M.

Reading a Time Zone Map

The map on page 275 shows the time zones of the United States. How many time zones are there in our country? What is the name of the easternmost time zone?

Look at the clock for the Central Time Zone. It shows 6:00 A.M. What time is it in the Pacific Time Zone when it is 6:00 A.M. in the Central Time Zone?

Remember that in most time zones it is one hour earlier or later than it is in the neighboring zone. If you know the time in one time zone, you can find the time anywhere by using these two rules.

1. Moving east, you must add an hour for each time zone you cross.
2. Moving west, you must subtract an hour for each time zone you cross.

Suppose that it is 3:00 P.M. in Chicago. Chicago is in the Central Time Zone. In Sault Ste. Marie (one time zone to the east) it is 4:00 P.M. (3:00 P.M. + 1 hour = 4:00 P.M.). In Los Angeles (two time zones to the west) it is 1:00 P.M. (3:00 P.M. − 2 hours = 1:00 P.M.).

Differences in time can be important. Suppose that you live in Denver. You want to talk with your aunt in Anchorage. She gets home from work at 5:00 P.M. To reach her by phone at home, you would have to call her after 7:00 P.M. Denver time.

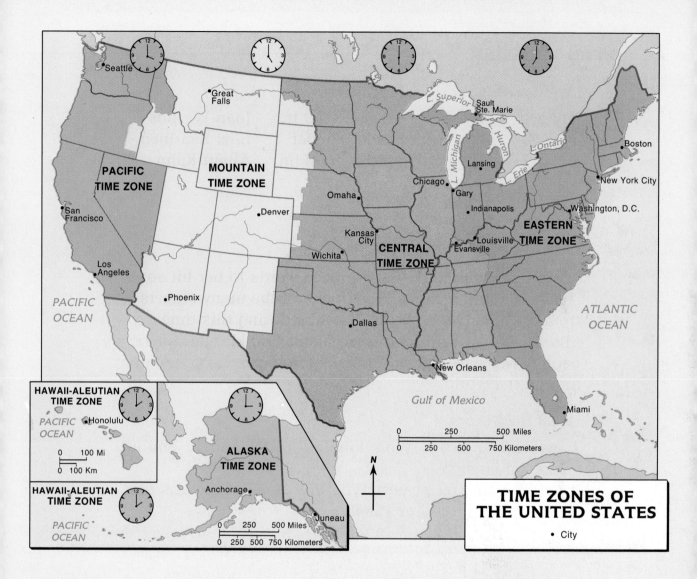

TIME ZONES OF
THE UNITED STATES

• City

Look at the map on this page. As you can see, most states in the United States are located within one time zone. However, some states are located within more than one time zone. Michigan is one of those states. Most of Michigan is located in the Eastern Time Zone. However, one small area in the western Upper Peninsula is located in the Central Time Zone.

Reviewing the Skill

1. What is a time zone?
2. When it is 5:00 A.M. in Phoenix, what time is it in Miami?
3. A friend in Seattle asked you to call at 7:00 P.M. Seattle time. You live in Lansing. At what time should you call?
4. Why is it important to be able to use a time zone map?

275

2 Culture and the Arts

READ TO LEARN

Key Vocabulary

folk art

jazz

Key People

Berry Gordy, Jr.

Stevie Wonder

Aretha Franklin

Joan W. Blos

Eliel Saarinen

Albert Kahn

Read Aloud

R-E-S-P-E-C-T,
Find out what it means to me . . .

Aretha Franklin first sang these words to her hit song, "Respect," in the 1960s. She is one of the many singers from Michigan who became famous during this time. In this lesson you will read more about Franklin and other people who have helped to make Michigan music popular around the world.

Read for Purpose

1. **WHAT YOU KNOW:** What kinds of books, music, and art do you enjoy?
2. **WHAT YOU WILL LEARN:** What are some of the arts that are important to our state?

CULTURE AND ART

In Chapter 3 you read that a culture is the way of life of a group of people. Culture includes a people's customs and beliefs. It also includes the art that people create— the books they write, the music they play, or the pictures they paint. It is an important part of life in Michigan today.

FOLK ART

Did you know that much of our art is created by everyday people? This kind of art is called **folk art**. Folk art can include a quilt that someone has sewn or a song that someone has written.

Different immigrant groups brought their own special types of folk art to Michigan. Lovely hand-painted eggs are an example of Ukrainian folk art. The skill of making these tiny treasures was brought by immigrants from the Ukraine and handed down from one generation to the next. What are some examples of folk art that are found in your community?

THE MUSIC OF MICHIGAN

The many groups of people that have come to live in Michigan have brought with them a rich tradition of music. Native Americans made music with drums and other hand-made instruments. French families held singing and dancing parties in their homes. Yankee pioneers played their "fiddles," or violins, at barn-raising parties.

African Americans who arrived from the South brought still other kinds of music to Michigan. One was the music that enslaved African Americans sang in the hot, dusty fields of the South, calling out to one another while they worked. Another kind of music spoke of people's longings for freedom and better lives. Both kinds of music had roots in African rhythms and styles.

By the early 1900s these African rhythms and styles began to be heard in a new kind of music—jazz. Detroit became a major center for jazz musicians. Jazz took a new turn in the 1950s when jazz artists began to recapture the "rhythm-and-blues" feel of the earlier forms of African-American music. One young man, Berry Gordy, Jr., set out to record this new style of music. In 1960 he started the Motown Record Corporation. *Motown* is short for Detroit's nickname, "Motor Town."

Gordy recorded many talented young singers from Detroit's African-American community. One of Motown's first hit songs was made by a 12-year-old singer and song-writer nicknamed Stevie Wonder. Other Motown hits followed, recorded by such groups as the Supremes and the Temptations. These performers created a special kind of music, known as the "Motown Sound."

Another singer from Detroit who first became popular in the 1960s was Aretha Franklin, whom you read about in the Read Aloud on

Berry Gordy, Jr. (*left*) and Stevie Wonder (*right*) helped make Michigan's "Motown Sound" famous throughout the world.

The Supremes (*above*) and Aretha Franklin (*above, right*) began their singing careers in Detroit. Ernest Hemingway (*below*) wrote many stories about northern Michigan.

page 276. Franklin began her singing career in the choir at Detroit's New Bethel Baptist Church. Today she performs in concert halls all over the world.

MICHIGAN WRITERS

The author Ernest Hemingway spent many of his childhood summers in northern Michigan. The days spent in Michigan's pine forests shaped the stories that Hemingway later wrote. When he was older Hemingway said, "Almost everything . . . I've written has been about that [part of the] country."

Novels, poems, and short stories by Michigan writers describe fur traders, lumberjacks, and ship captains of long ago. They tell about pioneers from Vermont, miners from Ireland, and Fourth of July celebrations in the Upper Peninsula.

Many Michigan writers have become famous throughout the country. For example, Michigan's Joan W. Blos has written award-winning books for young people. You can read two stories by Blos in the Legacy lessons on pages 144–149 and 200–204.

MICHIGAN ARCHITECTURE

You might not think of the buildings you see every day as works of

Eliel Saarinen designed the beautiful and simple architecture at Cranbrook Academy in Bloomfield Hills.

art. But architecture, or the style of a building, can show a person's feelings about a place.

Eliel Saarinen [el′ ē əl sär′ i nən] was one of Michigan's most famous architects. Saarinen was born in Finland in 1873. He was already a world-famous architect when he moved to Michigan in 1923 to design the Cranbrook Academy of Art.

Michigan's Albert Kahn was another famous architect. He came to Michigan from Germany in 1880. Kahn is best known for the automobile factories he designed for Henry Ford. Unlike many factories of the time, which were dark and dreary, Kahn's factories were airy and filled with windows.

ART FOR EVERYONE

You have just read about famous musicians, writers, and architects who have made art a rich part of life in our state. But you, too, can make art! Many schools have bands, orchestras, and choir programs. If you

like to write, perhaps your school has a newspaper.

If you love to draw, you might try to draw the things and people around you in your own neighborhood. In the Legacy lesson on pages 280–282, you will read about one man from Detroit who did just that—and went on to become a famous artist.

Check Your Reading

1. Why is folk art a special form of art?
2. Describe two kinds of music that developed in Michigan.
3. How did Albert Kahn change the design of Michigan's factories?
4. **THINKING SKILL:** In which ways is jazz similar to earlier forms of African-American music?

READ TO LEARN

📖 **Key Vocabulary**   **Key People**

portrait   Carl Owens

📖 **Read for Purpose**

1. **WHAT YOU KNOW:** What are some of the ways in which Michiganians express themselves through art?
2. **WHAT YOU WILL LEARN:** How is the pride that Carl Owens takes in his culture reflected in his artwork?

A MICHIGAN ARTIST
by Norman McRae

Carl Owens creates a painting in his Detroit studio.

In the last lesson you read about how Michiganians express themselves through the arts. In this lesson you will read about Carl Owens, who uses his artwork to show his pride in being an African American.

STORIES FROM THE PAST

When Carl Owens was growing up in Detroit in the 1930s, his mother used to tell him stories about great people in history—people like Elijah McCoy, Sojourner Truth, and other famous African Americans. Carl's favorite stories, though, were about his great-grandfather, Charles Henry Watt.

Watt was born into slavery in Maryland in 1821. Carl learned about what slavery was like for his great-grandfather and how his great-grandfather felt when he won his freedom in the 1840s. To Carl his great-grand-father was a hero and another great person in history.

These stories filled Carl's mind with many exciting images. He loved to draw these pictures on paper. Carl's mother encouraged him to draw pictures of family members and friends.

GROWING UP IN DETROIT

At Sampson Elementary School in Detroit, a teacher recognized Carl's talent as an artist. She taught him new skills and ways of improving his drawing. It was not long before Carl knew that he wanted to be an artist when he grew up.

After graduating from high school in 1947, Carl worked to put himself through college by selling his artwork. Every September he set up a booth at the Michigan State Fair in Detroit. There he drew pictures of fairgoers and their families. Carl graduated from Wayne State University in 1952 and returned to Detroit to work in the public schools as an art teacher.

Throughout his 15 years in the Detroit public schools, Carl never forgot the stories about African Americans. His mother's stories helped Carl to realize that people make history. When Carl became a full-time artist in 1968, he set out to make his images of history-makers come alive in his art.

STRONG WOMEN, STRONG MEN

On the next page you can see some of the portraits, or pictures of people, that Carl Owens has drawn. The portrait of Sojourner Truth is part of a drawing called *Strong Women*, which honors 34 African-American women who are famous for their courage and special talents. The hands in the drawing represent the strength that is found in members of the African-American community. Owens has also done a drawing called *Strong Men*, which highlights 35 African-American men who are heroes to people today.

Young Carl Owens, shown in a family photograph (*bottom, left*), drew the picture of a saxophone player when he was 11.

Carl Owens's portrait of Soujourner Truth is part of his drawing *Strong Women.*

SEEING THE WORLD

Today Carl Owens likes to travel to countries in Africa, the Caribbean, and Latin America. These trips help him to see how African culture is spread throughout the world. The sights, sounds, and colors help to shape Carl's drawings and paintings.

Carl Owens has come a long way since his first art lessons at Detroit's Sampson Elementary School. But Owens has never stopped being proud of his African-American roots. To Carl, his works of art "represent my personal tribute to [respect for] the courage and creativity of black people everywhere."

Check Your Reading

1. What did Carl Owens learn from the stories his mother told him as a child?
2. How did Carl Owens earn money to pay for college?
3. **THINKING SKILL:** In what ways did the stories about African Americans contribute to Carl Owens's artwork?

3 Sports and Recreation

READ TO LEARN

Key Vocabulary

professional

Key People

Ty Cobb   Earvin "Magic" Johnson
Gordie Howe   Sheila Young-Ochowicz

Read Aloud

We set out to win the National Championship and we reached our goal. The whole town of Marquette was behind us; the whole Upper Peninsula was behind us. It felt great!

Kevin Scott was a member of the Northern Michigan University ice hockey team that became the best in the country in 1991. In this lesson you will read about Michiganians like Kevin who enjoy sports and recreation in our state.

Read for Purpose

1. **WHAT YOU KNOW:** Which sporting events have you attended in our state?
2. **WHAT YOU WILL LEARN:** What kinds of recreational activities do people in Michigan enjoy?

ENJOYING OUR STATE

No matter where you live in Michigan there is always something fun to do. You might like to play hockey, go swimming, read a book, or take a walk. All of these activities are different kinds of recreation. Recreation is what people do to enjoy themselves. What are some kinds of recreation that you like?

THE GREAT OUTDOORS

Every time you step outside in the Great Lakes State, there are dozens of ways to enjoy yourself. Michiganians use the Great Lakes for swimming, fishing, canoeing, sailing, and ice skating. People even go scuba diving near shipwrecks in these lakes. Michigan also has hundreds of smaller lakes

Michigan's many lakes and rivers provide opportunities for people to enjoy different kinds of water recreation.

that are perfect for many kinds of water recreation.

Most of our state's 83 state parks are especially suited to outdoor activities. We also have three national parks where you might camp, hike, or just relax. Our state and national governments created these parks so that people of our state would be able to enjoy Michigan's great outdoors for many years to come.

SPORTS IN MICHIGAN

On a Saturday afternoon in October, Michiganians everywhere turn their attention to an old football rivalry. Some houses fly blue flags with a big yellow M. Other houses fly green flags that say STATE. Route 96, which runs between Ann Arbor and East Lansing, is jammed with traffic. People crowd into the football stadium or around televisions cheering and waving pennants. It is the day of the football game between the Wolverines of the University of Michigan and the Spartans of Michigan State University.

Watching the Wolverines play the Spartans is an exciting yearly event for many Michiganians. But it is not the only way in which people in our state enjoy sports. Most of the colleges and universities in our state offer athletic programs—from football and swimming to basketball and tennis.

Michigan is also the home to **professional** (prə fesh′ ə nəl) teams in every major sport—the Tigers in baseball, the Lions in football, the Red Wings in hockey, and the Pistons in basketball. A professional is a person who is paid to do a special job. For professional athletes, playing sports is their work.

Over the years Michigan has produced many gifted professional athletes. **Ty Cobb**, a Detroit Tiger from 1905 to 1926, was the first person to be named to the National Baseball Hall of Fame. Joe Louis, who was the world heavyweight boxing champion from 1937 to 1949, grew up in Detroit. Joe Louis Arena in Detroit is named for him. **Gordie Howe**, who played for the Detroit Red Wings from 1946 to 1971, is considered by many to be hockey's all time greatest player. **Earvin "Magic" Johnson** grew up in Lan-

sing and went to Michigan State University. He has led the Los Angeles Lakers to many national basketball championships.

Many Michiganians have also represented the United States in the Olympic Games. **Sheila Young-Ochowicz**, from Detroit, won three gold medals in speed skating in 1976. She went on to become a world-champion bicycle racer.

The Wolverines and the Spartans meet in a football game every October. Ty Cobb, "Magic" Johnson, and Sheila Young-Ochowicz all have made contributions to Michigan sports.

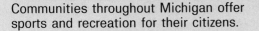

Communities throughout Michigan offer sports and recreation for their citizens.

YOUTH SPORTS IN MICHIGAN

If you drive into the town of Carney in Menominee County, you will see a sign announcing, "Home of the Michigan Girls' State Basketball Champions, 1991." The citizens of this Upper Peninsula town are proud that their high school team was the best in the state.

Most of Michigan's communities offer opportunities for many kinds of sports activities in their schools and in parks. People play for fun, for exercise, or with the hope of someday becoming a professional athlete. Have you participated in any sports at your school?

ENJOYING LIFE IN MICHIGAN

From the fresh blue waters of Lake Michigan to center field at Tiger Stadium, people find many ways to enjoy life in Michigan.

Whether you are bouncing a basketball in a city park or hiking on a quiet trail in the Upper Peninsula, there is always something fun to do in the Great Lakes State.

Check Your Reading

1. What are some of the ways in which you can enjoy Michigan's state and national parks?
2. Name two of the professional teams in Michigan.
3. **GEOGRAPHY SKILL:** Look at the map on page 305 and locate our state's three national parks.
4. **THINKING SKILL:** In what ways does the geography of Michigan shape the kinds of recreation that people enjoy in our state?

4 Michigan's Future

READ TO LEARN

Key Vocabulary

wetland

Read Aloud

I am Michigan, a world of constant wonders . . . I have many forests still. . . . I have islands near and far. . . . Come to know the miracles my waters hold for you.

These words were written to celebrate Michigan's 150th birthday. They help us remember our state's past, appreciate its present, and look forward to its future.

Read for Purpose

1. **WHAT YOU KNOW:** How is your life different from the lives of early Michiganians?
2. **WHAT YOU WILL LEARN:** What are some of the ways in which Michiganians can plan for the future?

PAST, PRESENT, AND FUTURE

By now you have read about many years of Michigan history. You have learned that our whole state was covered with water millions of years ago. You have studied the lives of Native Americans, of the first pioneers, of African Americans, and of the millions of eager immigrants. You have learned about Michigan in times of peace and in times of war.

The story you have read is a story of change. And this change contin- ues today. New problems such as pollution and acid rain threaten our environment. But many Michigan- ians continue to work together to find new solutions. The Kalkaska Soil law, which you read about in Chapter 11, is just one example of people coming together to help our state prepare for the future.

A PART OF THE WORLD

You have also read about the many ways in which Michigan's economy has changed. Today our

Students at East Jordan School build nesting boxes for birds that live in the **wetland** near their school.

state is part of an interdependent economy in which Michigan products are sent to countries around the world.

Leaders in Michigan industry, education, and government understand the importance of education for this interdependent economy. Governor John Engler is working with the University of Michigan to create an educational system based on the Internet called 'Auto U.' At home or in school, students can study the latest technology to ensure Michiganians a great future in the world economy.

YOU ARE THE FUTURE

You, too, are part of the story of our changing state. Students throughout Michigan are working in many ways to improve their communities and preserve their heritage. At the East Jordan School in Charlevoix County, many students have worked to save a **wetland** that is located next to their school. A wetland is a swampy area that is home to special plants and animals. The students study the birds, fish, and plants that live in this environment.

How this story continues depends on the choices that you will make. What will you make of tomorrow's Michigan—with its beauty, its resources, and its people? Perhaps when other students are studying Michigan's history 30 years from now, they will read your name among our state's "Key People"!

Check Your Reading

1. What are some of the problems facing Michigan today?
2. What are some ways in which Michiganians are working to prepare our state for the future?
3. How have schools in Michigan changed since pioneer times?
4. **THINKING SKILL:** Predict how you think Michigan might be different 100 years from now.

YOU Can Make a Difference

Throughout this book you have read about people who have worked hard to make a difference in Michigan. These people have helped their community and state with their effort, their determination—and their hope.

Al Martin has helped to save a dying waterway with the Clinton River Clean-Up Project. He continues to educate students and his community about the importance of keeping their environment clean. Katherine Afendoulis continues to teach children to have respect for themselves and for others. Dr. Charles Wright has made a difference by creating a museum to preserve the history of African Americans.

Al, Charles, and Katherine are only three of the many fine citizens who are helping their fellow Michiganians.

Chances are that there is someone who has worked hard to solve a problem in your own community. That person could be an adult. But he or she could also be a young person like you.

There are many ways in which you can help people in your community. Is there a park nearby with litter on the ground? A clean park is more pleasant for everybody. Is there a senior citizen in your neighborhood who might enjoy a visit from a young person? Do you have a neighbor who needs help carrying groceries?

You might be able to help out in instances like these, or you might think of other ways in which to help your community. The important thing is always to remember that *you*, too, can make a difference.

REVIEWING VOCABULARY

Number a sheet of paper from 1 to 5. Beside each number write **C** if the underlined word is used correctly. If it is not, rewrite the sentence using the word correctly.

1. Martha's granddaughter is one of her <u>ancestors</u>.
2. Some Native Americans live on land set aside for their use called <u>reservations</u>.
3. The members of the Little League were <u>professional</u> ballplayers.
4. The rain turned the playground into a muddy <u>wetland</u>.
5. <u>Jazz</u> is a form of folk painting that was developed during the 1920s.

REVIEWING FACTS

1. List five immigrant groups that make up Michigan's population.
2. What is folk art?
3. Name at least two famous musicians who came from Michigan.
4. For what is Joe Louis famous? For what is Gordie Howe famous? For what is Earvin "Magic" Johnson famous?
5. What are five ways in which Michiganians can enjoy themselves outdoors?

✏ WRITING ABOUT MAIN IDEAS

1. **Writing About Your Community:** What clues are there in your community that tell you its people come from different countries or religious backgrounds? Consider foods, celebrations, street names, names of public buildings, and so on. Write a paragraph about how you can tell that your community is made up of different groups of people.
2. **Writing a Paragraph:** Which sport do you most enjoy watching or participating in? Write a paragraph telling why you like this sport, and identify where someone could play or watch it.

BUILDING SKILLS: READING TIME ZONE MAPS

Use the time zone map on page 275 and your knowledge of time zones to answer these questions.

1. Why is the earth divided into 24 time zones?
2. Your favorite football team is playing in San Francisco at 6:00 P.M. You will be watching the game live on television. What time will it be for you when the game starts?
3. Why is it useful to understand time zones?

REVIEWING VOCABULARY

ancestor	rural
bill	service industry
export	urban
mayor	veto
reservation	wetland

Number a sheet of paper from 1 to 10. Beside each number write the word or term from the list above that best matches the definition.

1. Businesses that serve people
2. To refuse to sign a bill
3. A person in your family, starting with your parents, who was born before you.
4. The head of the executive branch of a city or town government
5. Having to do with farms and the country
6. Having to do with cities
7. A swampy area that is home to special plants and animals
8. A proposed law
9. To sell goods to other countries
10. Land set aside for Native Americans to live on

✐ WRITING ABOUT THE UNIT

1. **Interpreting Song Lyrics:** Read the words to the song "Michigan, My Michigan," which is found on page 4. Then write a paragraph that tells the main ideas of the song.

2. **Writing a Radio Advertisement:** Write a radio advertisement aimed at persuading people from other parts of the United States to vacation in Michigan. Tell why it would be fun, exciting, or interesting to visit our state.

ACTIVITIES

1. **Researching:** Choose one of the key people mentioned in this unit. Go to the library and research information about that person. Prepare a written report about him or her.

2. **Making a Scrapbook:** Choose a topic about Michigan that interests you. For two weeks read and clip out newspaper articles about that topic. Use the clippings to make a scrapbook. Write a short introduction for the scrapbook, giving a summary of what you learned from the articles you chose.

3. **Listening to Music:** Listen to examples of music of the early Motown sound. Then make a report comparing the music to your favorite type of music today.

4. **Working Together to Make a Mural:** With a small group of classmates, make a mural that shows Michigan in the year 2000. In addition to pictures, include a title and captions on the mural.

(continued on next page)

TULIP FESTIVAL IN FULL BLOOM

— by Nancy Gilbert —

HOLLAND, May 18—The annual Tulip Festival ended today, after a ten-day celebration. Holland, home of the only wooden-shoe factory in the United States, was founded by a group of immigrants from the nation of Holland in 1847. The residents planted thousands of tulips, and eventually started the tradition of holding a Tulip Festival every year.

The Tulip Festival, which features hundreds of flowers in bloom, takes place each year in May. One of the highlights of this year's festival was the Volksparade. As crowds watched, people in Dutch costumes scrubbed the streets of Holland. Many children enjoyed taking part in the Children's Costume Parade where they dressed in colorful costumes and wooden shoes. The closing ceremony was attended by hundreds of tourists. They came to watch the spectacular Parade of Bands which left everyone looking forward to next year's festival.

BUILDING SKILLS: READING A NEWSPAPER

Read the newspaper article above. Then answer the questions below.

1. What is the headline of the article?
2. What information does the dateline give?
3. What events are described in the newspaper article?
4. Write an editorial about the same topic.
5. Why is it helpful to know about the different parts of a newspaper?

LINKING PAST, PRESENT, AND FUTURE

Until the early 1900s Michigan was known for its beautiful forests and its many fur-bearing animals. In the early 1900s it became famous for its automobiles and its rhythm-and-blues music. What do you think or hope that Michigan will be known for in the future?

REFERENCE
SECTION

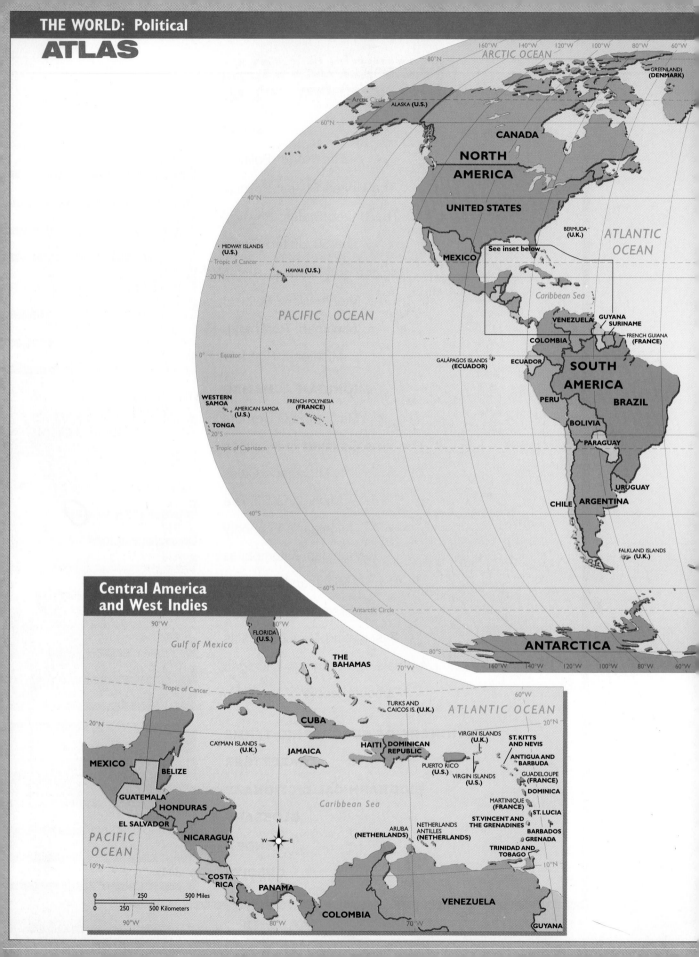

ARCTIC OCEAN

GREENLAND
(DENMARK)

Arctic Circle

ALASKA (U.S.)

CANADA

NORTH
AMERICA

UNITED STATES

BERMUDA
(U.K.)

ATLANTIC
OCEAN

MIDWAY ISLANDS
(U.S.)

Tropic of Cancer

MEXICO

See inset below

HAWAII (U.S.)

Caribbean Sea

PACIFIC OCEAN

VENEZUELA

GUYANA
SURINAME

COLOMBIA

FRENCH GUIANA
(FRANCE)

Equator

GALÁPAGOS ISLANDS
(ECUADOR)

ECUADOR

SOUTH
AMERICA

WESTERN
SAMOA

AMERICAN SAMOA
(U.S.)

FRENCH POLYNESIA
(FRANCE)

PERU

BRAZIL

TONGA

BOLIVIA

Tropic of Capricorn

PARAGUAY

URUGUAY

CHILE

ARGENTINA

FALKLAND ISLANDS
(U.K.)

Antarctic Circle

ANTARCTICA

Central America
and West Indies

Gulf of Mexico

FLORIDA
(U.S.)

THE
BAHAMAS

Tropic of Cancer

TURKS AND
CAICOS IS. (U.K.)

ATLANTIC OCEAN

CUBA

CAYMAN ISLANDS
(U.K.)

JAMAICA

HAITI

DOMINICAN
REPUBLIC

VIRGIN ISLANDS
(U.K.)

ST. KITTS
AND NEVIS

ANTIGUA AND
BARBUDA

MEXICO

BELIZE

PUERTO RICO
(U.S.)

VIRGIN ISLANDS
(U.S.)

GUADELOUPE
(FRANCE)

DOMINICA

GUATEMALA

MARTINIQUE
(FRANCE)

ST. LUCIA

HONDURAS

Caribbean Sea

EL SALVADOR

ST. VINCENT AND
THE GRENADINES

BARBADOS

PACIFIC
OCEAN

NICARAGUA

ARUBA
(NETHERLANDS)

NETHERLANDS
ANTILLES
(NETHERLANDS)

GRENADA

TRINIDAD AND
TOBAGO

COSTA
RICA

PANAMA

COLOMBIA

VENEZUELA

GUYANA

0   250   500 Miles

0   250   500 Kilometers

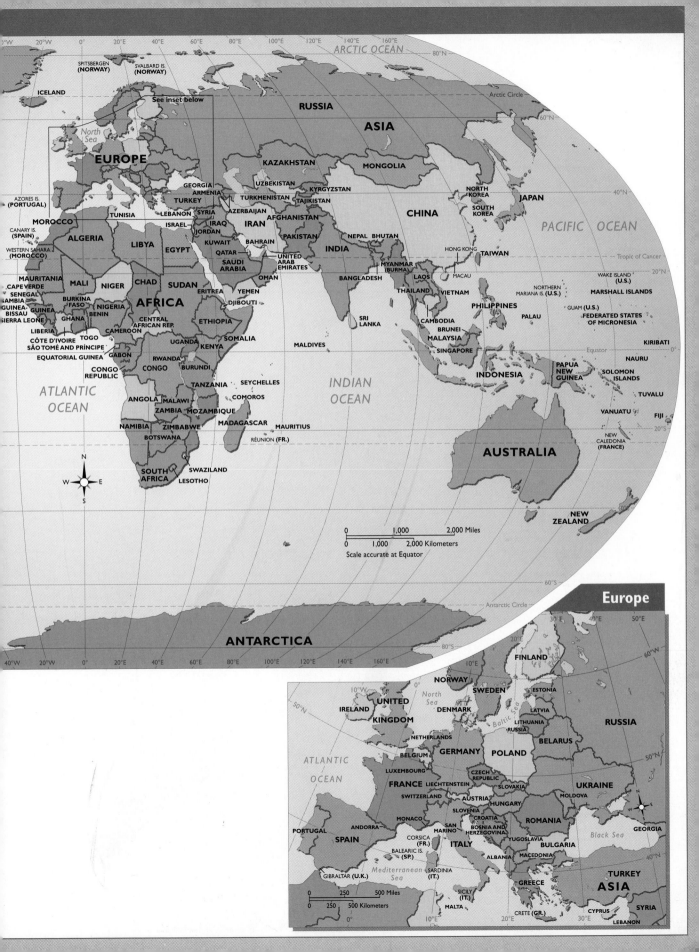

RUSSIA

ARCTIC OCEAN

70°N

ALASKA

Arctic Circle

60°N

180°

Nome

• Fairbanks

Yukon River

CANADA

170°W

160°W

150°W

140°W

• Anchorage

Juneau ★

PACIFIC OCEAN

0   250   500 Miles
0   250   500 Kilometers

40°N

CANADA

Seattle •
★ Olympia
WASHINGTON
Spokane •

River

Great Falls •

Missouri River

Helena ★

MONTANA

Billings •

Columbia

Portland •

★ Salem

• Eugene

OREGON

IDAHO

★ Boise

Snake River

Pocatello •

WYOMING

Casper •

Cheyenne ★

Reno •
★ Carson City

NEVADA

Great Salt Lake

Ogden •
★ Salt Lake City

• Provo

COLORADO

San Francisco •
Oakland •
San Jose •

★ Sacramento

UTAH

Denver ★

Colorado Springs •

Pueblo •

PACIFIC OCEAN

30°N

CALIFORNIA

Las Vegas •

Colorado River

Los Angeles •
Long Beach •

San Diego •

ARIZONA

Albuquerque •

Santa Fe ★

NEW MEXICO

★ Phoenix

Tucson •

El Paso •

Rio Grande

130°W

N
W ★ E
S

MEXICO

160°W   PACIFIC OCEAN   155°W

Kauai

Niihau

Oahu

Honolulu ★

Molokai

Lanai   Maui

Kahoolawe

HAWAII

Hawaii   Hilo •

20°N

0   100   200 Miles
0   100   200 Kilometers

120°W   110°W

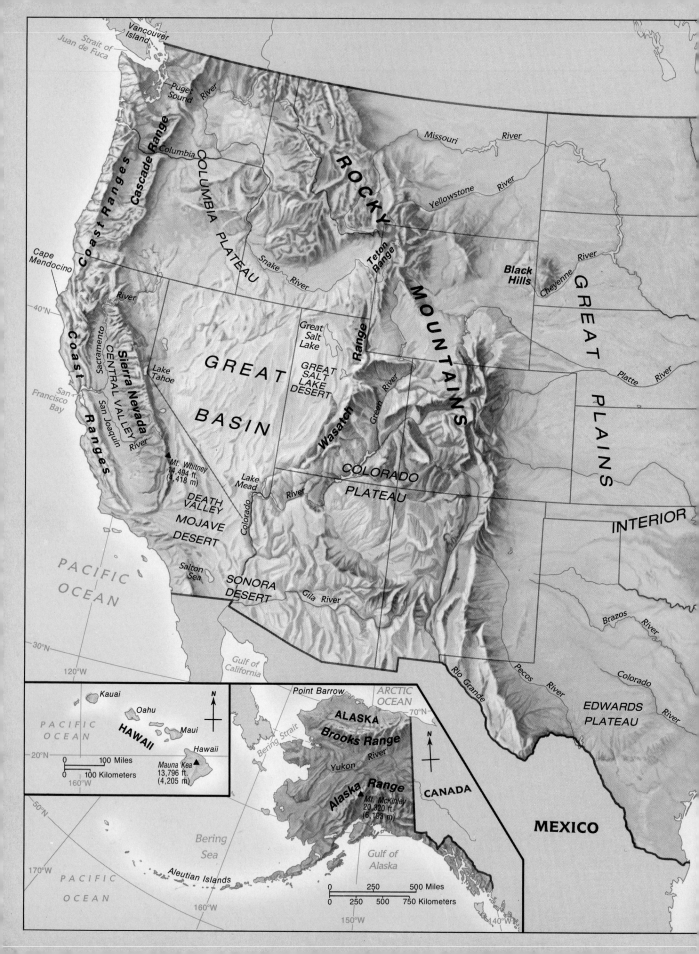

CANADA

Lake of
the Woods

Mesabi Range

Lake Superior

GREAT

LAKES

Mississippi

CENTRAL   PLAINS

River

Lake Michigan

Lake Huron

St. Lawrence River

White Mts.

Green Mts.

Adirondack
Mts.

Lake Ontario

Hudson River

Bay of
Fundy

Cape
Cod

Lake Erie

ALLEGHENY
PLATEAU

River

Susquehanna

Delaware R.

Long Island

40°N

Wabash   River

Ohio   River

Missouri

River

PLAINS

OZARK
PLATEAU

Arkansas

River

**Ouachita
Mountains**

Mississippi

River

Kentucky
Lake

Tennessee

River

River

Allegheny Mountains

APPALACHIAN   MOUNTAINS

PIEDMONT

Potomac R.

Delaware Bay

Chesapeake Bay

70°W

ATLANTIC   COASTAL   PLAIN

Cape Hatteras

ATLANTIC

OCEAN

Savannah River

Alabama

River

Chattahoochee

River

GULF COASTAL PLAIN

Red

River

30°N

Galveston Bay

Mobile Bay

Mississippi Delta

Gulf of Mexico

Lake
Okeechobee

90°W

N

THE UNITED STATES
Physical

0   100   200   300 Miles

0   100   200   300   400 Kilometers

Florida Keys

Straits of Florida

80°W

WEST INDIES

299

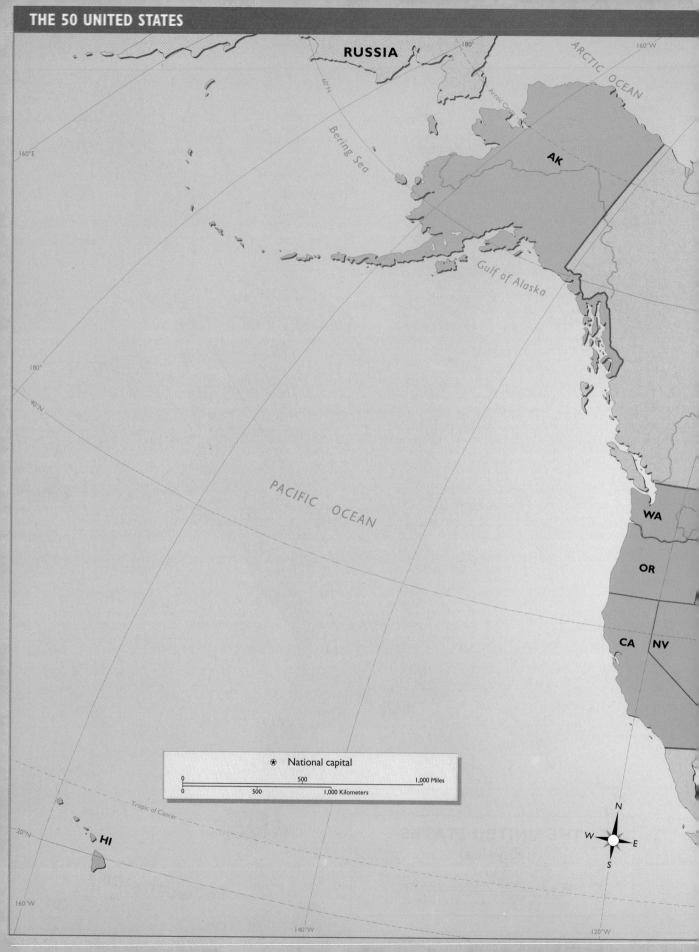

RUSSIA

ARCTIC OCEAN

Bering Sea

AK

Arctic Circle

Gulf of Alaska

PACIFIC OCEAN

WA

OR

CA NV

National capital

| 0 | 500 | 1,000 Miles |
| 0 | 500 | 1,000 Kilometers |

Tropic of Cancer

HI

N
W E
S

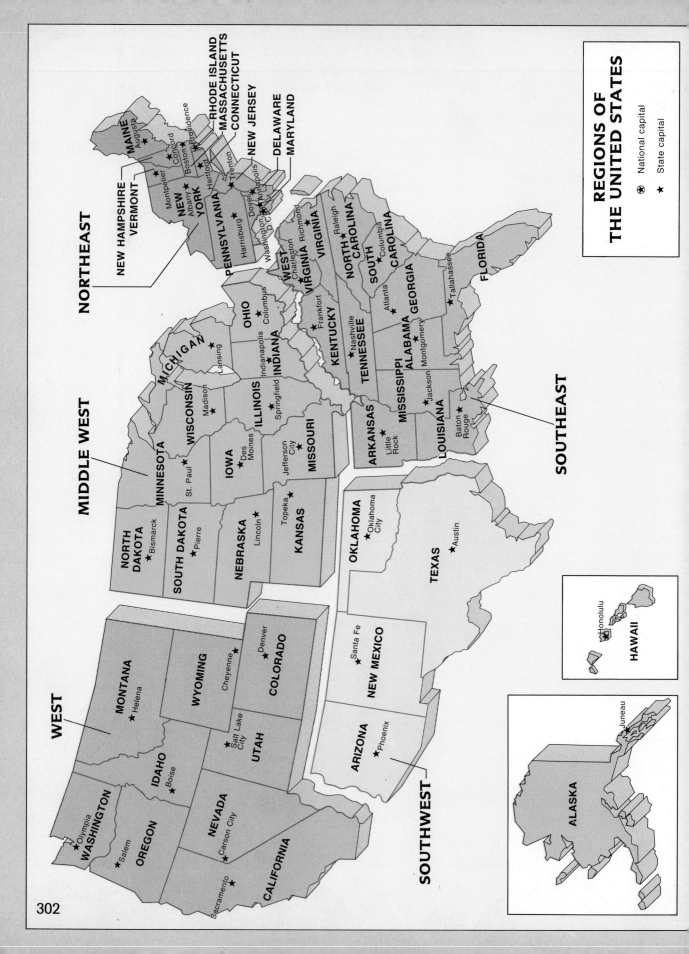

REGIONS OF
THE UNITED STATES

⊛ National capital
★ State capital

NORTHEAST

MIDDLE WEST

WEST

SOUTHWEST

SOUTHEAST

MAINE ★ Augusta
NEW HAMPSHIRE
VERMONT
★ Montpelier
★ Concord
NEW YORK ★ Albany
Boston ★
★ Providence
RHODE ISLAND
MASSACHUSETTS
CONNECTICUT
Hartford ★
NEW JERSEY
Trenton ★
DELAWARE
Dover ★
MARYLAND
★ Annapolis
Washington D.C. ⊛
PENNSYLVANIA
★ Harrisburg

WEST VIRGINIA
★ Charleston
VIRGINIA ★ Richmond
NORTH CAROLINA ★ Raleigh
SOUTH CAROLINA
★ Columbia
GEORGIA
★ Atlanta
FLORIDA
★ Tallahassee

OHIO ★ Columbus
MICHIGAN ★ Lansing
INDIANA ★ Indianapolis
ILLINOIS ★ Springfield
KENTUCKY ★ Frankfort
TENNESSEE ★ Nashville
ALABAMA ★ Montgomery
MISSISSIPPI ★ Jackson

WISCONSIN ★ Madison
MINNESOTA ★ St. Paul
IOWA ★ Des Moines
MISSOURI ★ Jefferson City
ARKANSAS ★ Little Rock
LOUISIANA ★ Baton Rouge

NORTH DAKOTA ★ Bismarck
SOUTH DAKOTA ★ Pierre
NEBRASKA ★ Lincoln
KANSAS ★ Topeka
OKLAHOMA ★ Oklahoma City
TEXAS ★ Austin

MONTANA ★ Helena
WYOMING ★ Cheyenne
COLORADO ★ Denver
NEW MEXICO ★ Santa Fe
IDAHO ★ Boise
UTAH ★ Salt Lake City
ARIZONA ★ Phoenix
WASHINGTON ★ Olympia
OREGON ★ Salem
NEVADA ★ Carson City
CALIFORNIA ★ Sacramento

HAWAII ★ Honolulu

ALASKA ★ Juneau

302

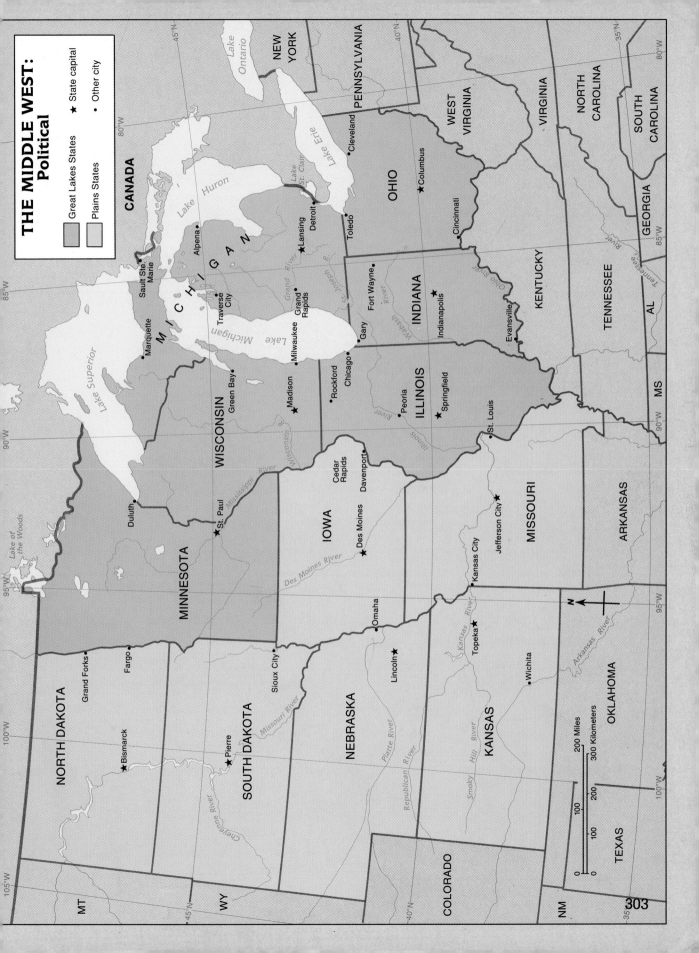

THE MIDDLE WEST: Political

★ State capital
• Other city

Great Lakes States
Plains States

303

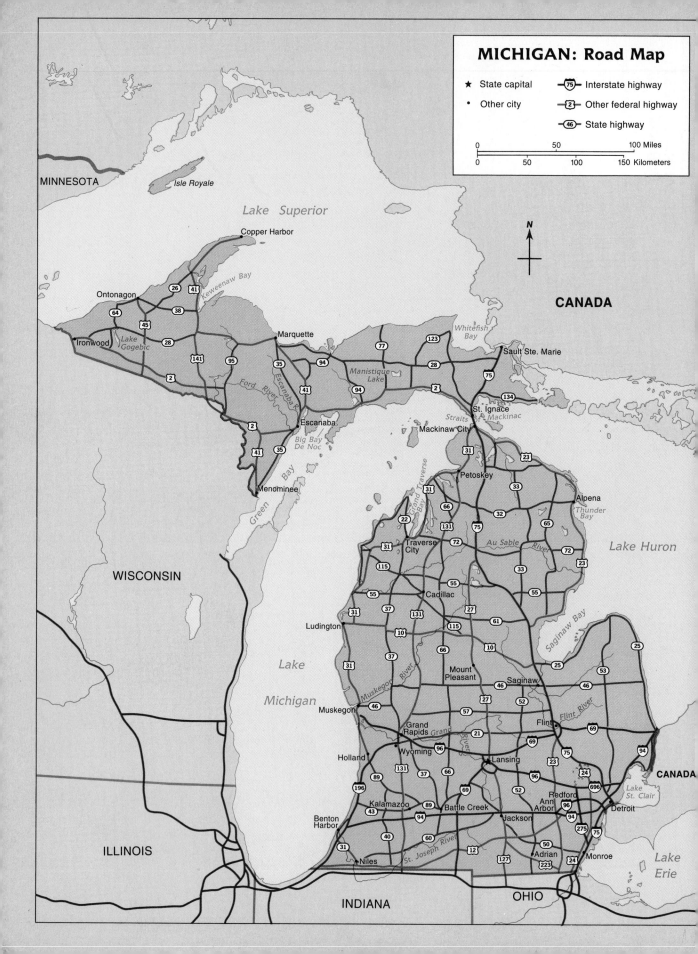

MICHIGAN: Road Map

★ State capital   75 Interstate highway
• Other city   2 Other federal highway
   46 State highway

0   50   100 Miles
0   50   100   150 Kilometers

N

MINNESOTA

Isle Royale

Lake Superior

Copper Harbor

CANADA

Ontonagon   26   41   *Keweenaw Bay*

64   38

45   Marquette

Ironwood   *Lake Gogebic*   28

141   95   35   94   77   123   *Whitefish Bay*

2   *Ford River*   *Escanaba R.*   41   94   *Manistique Lake*   28   Sault Ste. Marie

2   2   75

Escanaba   134

Big Bay De Noc   *Straits of Mackinac*   St. Ignace

41   35   Mackinaw City

Menominee   *Green Bay*   31   23

Petoskey   33

22   66   32   65   Alpena

31   *Grand Traverse Bay*   131   75   *Thunder Bay*

WISCONSIN   Traverse City   72   *Au Sable River*   72   *Lake Huron*

31   115   33   23

55   Cadillac   55   55

55   37   131   27   61

Lake Michigan   Ludington   31   10   115   10   25

31   37   66   Mount Pleasant   25   53

Muskegon River   46   Saginaw   46

Muskegon   46   27   52   *Flint River*

57   *Saginaw Bay*

Grand Rapids   *Grand River*   21   Flint   69

Holland   Wyoming   96   69   75   94   CANADA

131   37   66   Lansing   23   96   24   696   *Lake St. Clair*

196   89   69   52   Redford   Ann Arbor   96   Detroit

Kalamazoo   89   Battle Creek   94   Jackson   94   275   75

43   40   60   *St. Joseph River*   50   Monroe   *Lake Erie*

Benton Harbor   12   223

31   Niles   127   Adrian   24

ILLINOIS

INDIANA   OHIO

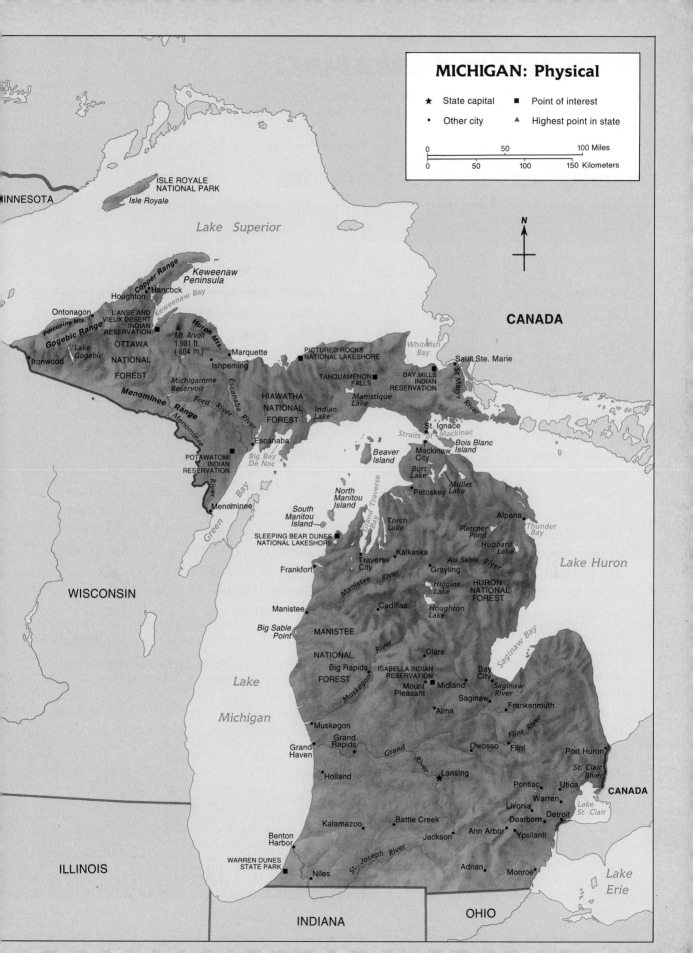

MICHIGAN: Physical

★ State capital   ■ Point of interest

• Other city   ▲ Highest point in state

| 0 | 50 | 100 Miles |

| 0 | 50 | 100 | 150 Kilometers |

MINNESOTA

ISLE ROYALE
NATIONAL PARK
Isle Royale

Lake Superior

N

CANADA

Copper Range

*Keweenaw
Peninsula*

Houghton • Hancock

Keweenaw Bay

Ontonagon

Porcupine Mts.

L'ANSE AND
VIEUX DESERT
INDIAN
RESERVATION

Gogebic Range

Huron Mts.

OTTAWA

Mt. Arvon
1,981 ft.
(604 m)

Whitefish
Bay

Sault Ste. Marie

Ironwood

*Lake
Gogebic*

NATIONAL

FOREST

• Marquette

PICTURED ROCKS
NATIONAL LAKESHORE

BAY MILLS
INDIAN
RESERVATION

St. Mary's River

• Ishpeming

Menominee Range

*Michigamme
Reservoir*

TAHQUAMENON
FALLS

Ford River

Escanaba River

HIAWATHA

NATIONAL

FOREST

*Manistique
Lake*

*Indian
Lake*

St. Ignace

Straits of Mackinac

POTAWATOMI
INDIAN
RESERVATION

Menominee River

• Escanaba

*Big Bay
De Noc*

Beaver
Island

Mackinaw
City

Bois Blanc
Island

WISCONSIN

• Menominee

Green Bay

*North
Manitou
Island*

*South
Manitou
Island*

SLEEPING BEAR DUNES
NATIONAL LAKESHORE

Grand Traverse Bay

Burt
Lake

• Petoskey

*Mullet
Lake*

Alpena

*Thunder
Bay*

*Torch
Lake*

Fletcher
Pond

Hubbard
Lake

Frankfort

Traverse
City

Kalkaska

Au Sable River

Manistee River

• Grayling

Higgins
Lake

HURON
NATIONAL
FOREST

Lake Huron

• Manistee

Cadillac

Houghton
Lake

*Big Sable
Point*

MANISTEE

NATIONAL

FOREST

Manistee River

• Clare

Saginaw Bay

Big Rapids

ISABELLA INDIAN
RESERVATION

Muskegon River

Mount
Pleasant

Midland

Bay
City

Saginaw
River

*Lake

Michigan*

Saginaw

Frankenmuth

• Alma

• Muskegon

Grand
Rapids

Grand River

Flint River

Grand
Haven

Owosso

Flint

Port Huron

*St. Clair
River*

Lansing ★

• Holland

Pontiac

Utica

CANADA

Warren

*Lake
St. Clair*

Livonia

Detroit

Kalamazoo

Battle Creek

Dearborn

Benton
Harbor

Jackson

Ann Arbor

Ypsilanti

WARREN DUNES
STATE PARK

• Niles

St. Joseph River

Adrian

Monroe

*Lake

Erie*

ILLINOIS

INDIANA

OHIO

MICHIGAN ALMANAC

An almanac is a collection of important and interesting information. The Michigan Almanac will help you to learn more about your state.

MICHIGAN'S GOVERNORS

Governor	Political Party	Term
Stevens T. Mason	D	1835-1840
William Woodbridge	W	1840-1841
James W. Gordon	W	1841
John S. Barry	D	1842-1845
Alpheus Felch	D	1846-1847
William L. Greenly	D	1847
Epaphroditus Ransom	D	1848-1849
John S. Barry	D	1850-1851
Robert McClelland	D	1852-1853
Andrew Parsons	D	1853-1854
Kinsley S. Bingham	R	1855-1858
Moses Wisner	R	1859-1860
Austin Blair	R	1861-1864
Henry H. Crapo	R	1865-1868
Henry P. Baldwin	R	1869-1872
John T. Bagley	R	1873-1876
Charles M. Croswell	R	1877-1880
David H. Jerome	R	1881-1882
Josiah W. Begole	D, G	1883-1884
Russell A. Alger	R	1885-1886
Cyrus G. Luce	R	1887-1890
Edwin B. Winans	D	1891-1892
John T. Rich	R	1893-1896
Hazen S. Pingree	R	1897-1900
Aaron T. Bliss	R	1901-1904
Fred M. Warner	R	1905-1910
Chase S. Osborne	R	1911-1912

Governor	Political Party	Term
Woodbridge N. Ferris	D	1913-1916
Albert E. Sleeper	R	1917-1920
Alexander J. Groesbeck	R	1921-1926
Fred W. Green	R	1927-1930
Wilbur M. Brucker	R	1931-1932
William A. Comstock	D	1933-1934
Frank D. Fitzgerald	R	1935-1936
Frank Murphy	D	1937-1938
Frank D. Fitzgerald	R	1939
Luren D. Dickinson	R	1939-1940
Murray D. Van Wagoner	D	1941-1942
Harry F. Kelly	R	1943-1946
Kim Sigler	R	1947-1948
G. Mennen Williams	D	1949-1960
John B. Swainson	D	1961-1962
George W. Romney	R	1963-1969
William G. Milliken	R	1969-1982
James T. Blanchard	D	1983-1990
John Engler	R	1991-

D = Democratic Party   R = Republican Party
G = Greenback Party   W = Whig Party

The Governor's Residence, home to Michigan's governors since 1969, is located on Oxford Road in Lansing.

THE COUNTIES OF MICHIGAN

County Name	County Seat	County Population (1995)	Area In Sq. Miles	Named for	Year Formed
Alcona	Harrisville	10,145	670	an Indian word meaning "beautiful plain"	1869
Alger	Munising	9,850	905	Governor Russell A. Alger	1885
Allegan	Allegan	97,513	826	the Allegan Indians	1835
Alpena	Alpena	30,797	565	an Indian word that means "partridge"	1857
Antrim	Bellaire	19,836	476	County Antrim, Northern Ireland	1863
Arenac	Standish	16,146	367	a compund of Latin words that means "a sandy place"	1883
Baraga	L'Anse	8,140	901	missionary Rev. Frederic Baraga	1875
Barry	Hastings	52,737	554	William T. Barry, postmaster general under President Andrew Jackson	1839
Bay	Bay City	111,587	447	Saginaw Bay	1857
Benzie	Beulah	13,576	316	a mispronounciation of the French word *bec-scie,* or "saw-bill," a local type of duck	1869
Berrien	St. Joseph	161,733	580	John M. Berrien, U.S. attorney general under President Andrew Jackson	1831
Branch	Coldwater	42,100	506	John Branch, secretary of the navy under President Andrew Jackson	1833
Calhoun	Marshall	140,871	709	John C. Calhoun, Vice President under President Andrew Jackson	1833
Cass	Cassopolis	48,846	491	Territorial Governor Lewis Cass	1829
Charlevoix	Charlevoix	23,151	414	Jesuit missionary Pierre F. X. Charlevoix	1869
Cheboygan	Cheboygan	22,811	721	a Native American name for a local site that means "Chippewa water"	1853
Chippewa	Sault Ste. Marie	37,080	1,590	the Chippewa Indians	1843
Clare	Harrison	28,192	571	County Clare, Ireland	1871
Clinton	Saint Johns	61,597	572	DeWitt Clinton, governor of New York	1839
Crawford	Grayling	13,625	561	Colonel William Crawford, an early surveyor of Michigan and the Ohio Valley	1879
Delta	Escanaba	38,747	1,177	its original shape, like the Greek letter delta	1861
Dickenson	Iron Mountain	27,095	757	Donald M. Dickenson, postmaster general under President Grover Cleveland	1891
Eaton	Charlotte	97,658	577	John H. Eaton, secretary of war under President Andrew Jackson	1837
Emmet	Petoskey	27,520	461	Irish patriot Robert Emmet	1853
Genesse	Flint	434,003	642	Genesse County, NY, from the Seneca word *Jenishiyeh* meaning "beautiful valley"	1836
Gladwin	Gladwin	24,416	503	British Major Henry Gladwin	1875
Gogebic	Bessemer	27,971	1,107	an Indian word of uncertain meaning	1887

County Name	County Seat	County Population (1995)	Area In Sq. Miles	Named for	Year Formed
Grand Traverse	Traverse City	70,776	462	the French words for "the great crossing"	1865
Gratiot	Ithaca	39,887	566	Captain Charles Gratiot	1855
Hillsdale	Hillsdale	45,146	600	local hills and dales	1835
Houghton	Houghton	36,576	1,017	Douglas Houghton, state geologist	1846
Huron	Bad Axe	35,274	819	the Huron Indians	1859
Ingham	Mason	277,360	559	Samuel D. Ingham, secretary of the treasury under President Andrew Jackson	1838
Ionia	Ionia	59,685	575	a region of ancient Greece	1837
Iosco	Tawas City	23,425	544	a word of uncertain origin which may mean "waters of light"	1857
Iron	Crystal Falls	13,095	1,171	local deposits of iron ore	1885
Isabella	Mount Pleasant	57,445	572	Queen Isabella of Spain	1859
Jackson	Jackson	154,100	698	President Andrew Jackson	1832
Kalamazoo	Kalamazoo	230,097	562	an Indian word that means "reflecting river"	1830
Kalkaska	Kalkaska	14,780	566	a Chippewa word of unknown meaning	1871
Kent	Grand Rapids	524,506	857	James Kent, New York lawyer	1836
Keweenaw	Eagle River	1,930	528	an Indian word that means "portage"	1861
Lake	Baldwin	9,893	571	the 46 lakes in the county	1871
Lapeer	Lapeer	82,701	658	the French words la pierre, which mean "the stone," referring to a rocky riverbed	1835
Leelanau	Leland	18,486	345	an Indian word that means "delight of life"	1863
Lenawee	Adrian	96,491	753	a word of uncertain origin, either Shawnee for "Indian" or French for "sluggish"	1826
Livingston	Howell	132,485	572	Edward Livingston, U.S. secretary of state under President Andrew Jackson	1836
Luce	Newberry	5,542	906	Cyrus G. Luce, governor of Michigan	1887
Mackinac	Saint Ignace	10,981	1,014	a Native American word for Mackinac Island, Michilimackinac	1849
Macomb	Mount Clemens	730,220	480	General Alexander Macomb	1822
Manistee	Manistee	22,875	552	a Native American name that may mean "spirit of the woods"	1855
Marquette	Marquette	70,199	1,829	Jacques Marquette, a Jesuit missionary	1846
Mason	Ludington	27,584	490	Stevens T. Mason, governor of Michigan	1855
Mecosta	Big Rapids	39,033	560	a Potawatomi chief whose name means "Big Bear"	1859
Menominee	Menominee	24,441	1,038	the Menominee Indians	1863

County Name	County Seat	County Population (1995)	Area In Sq. Miles	Named for	Year Formed
Midland	Midland	80,651	520	its location near the middle of Michigan	1850
Missaukee	Lake City	13,663	565	an Ottawa chief also known as Nesaukee	1871
Monroe	Monroe	138,889	557	President James Monroe	1822
Montcalm	Stanton	57,696	712	French General Louis de Montcalm	1835
Montmorency	Atlanta	9,624	555	either the dukes of Montmorency, France, or Bishop Montmorency-Laval, of Canada	1881
Muskegon	Muskegon	164,253	501	an Indian word meaning "marshy river"	1859
Newaygo	White Cloud	43,729	849	a Chippewa leader named Naw-wa-goo	1851
Oakland	Pontiac	1,155,160	867	the large oak forests formerly in the county	1821
Oceana	Hart	23,769	536	its long shoreline on Lake Michigan	1851
Ogemaw	West Branch	20,597	571	a Chippewa word that means "chief"	1873
Ontonagon	Ontonagon	8,622	1,316	a Chippewa word that means "bowl"	1848
Osceola ·	Reed City	21,699	581	a Seminole chief	1869
Oscoda	Mio	8,652	563	a word created by Henry Rowe Schoolcraft	1881
Otsego	Gaylord	20,573	527	a New York county whose name is the Mohawk word for "clear water"	1875
Ottawa	Grand Haven	209,518	563	the Ottawa Indians	1839
Presque Isle	Rogers City	14,088	648	French words that mean "almost an island"	1871
Roscommon	Roscommon	22,421	521	County Roscommon, Ireland	1875
Saginaw	Saginaw	210,742	814	a Native American word that means "place of the Sauk Indians"	1835
Saint Clair	Port Huron	153,733	723	Saint Clara d'Assisi	1821
Saint Joseph	Centreville	60,271	506	Saint Joseph	1829
Sanilac	Sandusky	41,945	961	a Wyandotte Indian chief	1848
Schoolcraft	Manistique	8,656	1,181	explorer Henry Rowe Schoolcraft	1846
Shiawassee	Corunna	72,011	540	a Native Indian word that means "the river that twists about"	1837
Tuscola	Caro	57,961	815	a word of uncertain meaning which was invented by Henry Rowe Schoolcraft	1850
Van Buren	Paw Paw	74,635	603	President Martin Van Buren, also secretary of state under President Andrew Jackson	1837
Washtenaw	Ann Arbor	292,320	711	an Indian word that means "land near water"	1829
Wayne	Detroit	2,052,248	605	General Anthony Wayne	1815
Wexford	Cadillac	28,572	559	County Wexford, Ireland	1869

MICHIGAN ALMANAC

MICHIGAN'S CITIES

City Name	City Population	City Name	City Population
Adrian	22,097	Lincoln Park	41,832
Albion	10,066	Livonia	100,850
Allen Park	31,092	Madison Heights	32,196
Alpena	11,354	Marquette	21,977
Ann Arbor	109,592	Melvindale	11,216
Auburn Hills	17,076	Midland	38,053
Battle Creek	53,540	Monroe	22,902
Bay City	38,936	Mount Clemens	18,405
Benton Harbor	12,818	Mount Pleasant	23,285
Berkley	16,960	Muskegon	40,283
Big Rapids	12,603	Muskegon Heights	13,176
Birmingham	19,997	Niles	12,456
Burton	27,617	Norton Shores	21,755
Cadillac	10,104	Novi	32,998
Clawson	13,874	Oak Park	30,462
Dearborn	89,286	Owosso	16,322
Dearborn Heights	60,836	Pontiac	71,166
Detroit	1,027,974	Portage	41,042
East Detroit	35,283	Port Huron	33,694
East Grand Rapids	10,807	River Rouge	11,314
East Lansing	50,677	Riverview	13,894
Ecorse	12,180	Rochester Hills	61,766
Escanaba	13,659	Romulus	22,897
Farmington	10,132	Roseville	51,412
Farmington Hills	74,652	Royal Oak	65,410
Ferndale	25,084	Saginaw	69,512
Flint	140,761	St. Clair Shores	68,107
Fraser	13,899	Sault Ste. Marie	14,689
Garden City	31,849	Southfield	75,728
Grand Haven	11,951	Southgate	30,771
Grand Rapids	189,126	Sterling Heights	117,810
Grandville	15,624	Sturgis	10,130
Grosse Point Farms	10,092	Taylor	70,811
Grosse Pointe Park	12,857	Traverse City	15,155
Grosse Pointe Woods	17,715	Trenton	20,586
Hamtramck	18,372	Troy	72,884
Harper Woods	14,903	Walker	17,279
Hazel Park	20,051	Warren	144,864
Highland Park	20,121	Wayne	19,899
Holland	30,745	Westland	84,724
Inkster	30,772	Woodhaven	11,631
Jackson	37,446	Wyandotte	30,938
Kalamazoo	80,277	Wyoming	63,891
Kentwood	37,826	Ypsilanti	24,846
Lansing	127,321		

All cities with a population greater than 10,000 based on the 1990 Census have been listed.

MICHIGAN'S CLIMATE

112°F.
44° Celsius
The highest temperature ever recorded in Michigan was on July 13, 1936, at Mio in Oscoda County.

-49°F.
−44° Celsius
The lowest temperature ever recorded in Michigan was on February 9, 1934, at Vanderbilt in Otsego County.

33
inches
The largest snowfall ever recorded in Michigan in a 24 hour period was on March 30, 1960 at Baldwin in Mecosta County.

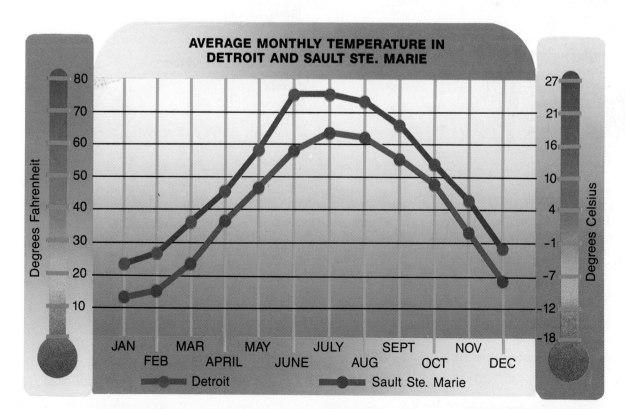

AVERAGE MONTHLY TEMPERATURE IN DETROIT AND SAULT STE. MARIE

Degrees Fahrenheit

Degrees Celsius

JAN FEB MAR APRIL MAY JUNE JULY AUG SEPT OCT NOV DEC

●— Detroit   ●— Sault Ste. Marie

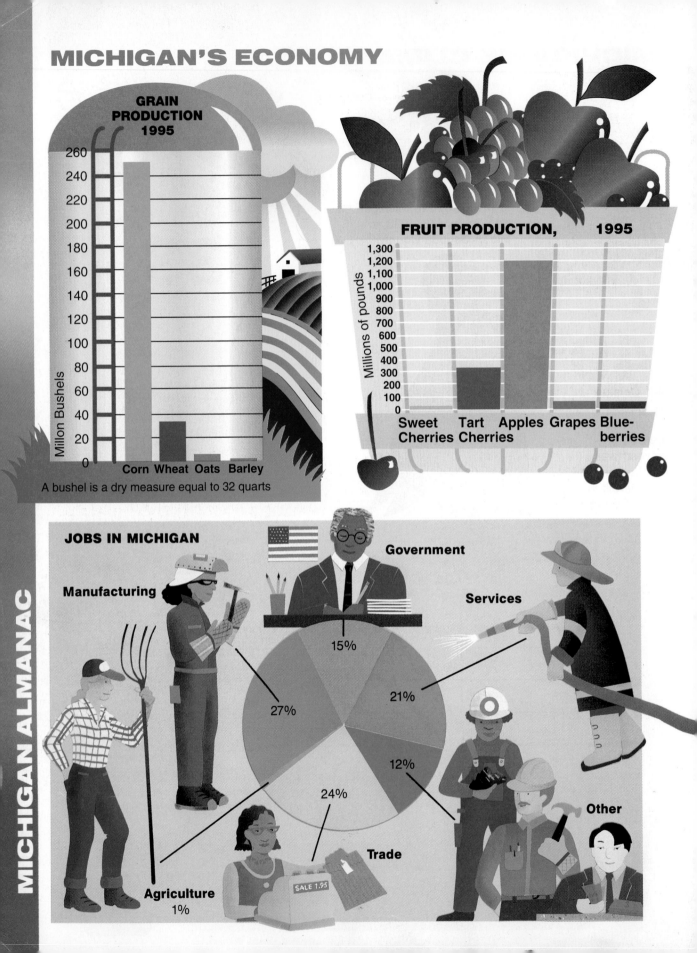

MICHIGAN'S ECONOMY

GRAIN PRODUCTION 1995

Millon Bushels

260
240
220
200
180
160
140
120
100
80
60
40
20
0

Corn Wheat Oats Barley

A bushel is a dry measure equal to 32 quarts

FRUIT PRODUCTION, 1995

Millions of pounds

1,300
1,200
1,100
1,000
900
800
700
600
500
400
300
200
100

Sweet Cherries Tart Cherries Apples Grapes Blue-berries

JOBS IN MICHIGAN

Manufacturing
Government
Services

27%
15%
21%
24%
12%

Agriculture 1%
Trade
Other

MICHIGAN ALMANAC

MICHIGAN AUTOMOBILES

1901-1903 **Oldsmobile Runabout**
The Runabout was the first mass-produced automobile ever made in Michigan. About 10,000 were sold. Like most early cars, the Runabout looked like a horse-drawn buggy.

1908-1927 **Model T Ford**   The Model T, also called the "Tin Lizzie," was one of the most successful cars in history. Over 15 million were sold. The Model T was tough, easy to repair, and was very inexpensive.

1934 **Chrysler Airflow**
The Airflow was the first car to have a fully streamlined shape. Streamlined things, like birds and airplanes, move easily through the air.

1941-1945 **Jeep**   In 1940 the U.S. Army asked auto makers for a vehicle that could carry nearly anything and go almost anywhere. The Jeep, short for "general purpose," was the answer.

1959 **Cadillac Coupe de Ville**   During the 1950s car companies competed to build the cars with the largest rear fins. In 1959 the Coupe de Ville had taller fins than any other car.

1964 **Ford Mustang**   In 1964 Ford designed the first "pony car," the Mustang, named for a wild horse. Pony cars were low-priced, stylish sports cars.

1991 **Dodge Neon**   The Neon was designed to use up fewer scarce resources. It is made partly of recycled materials. Other parts can be recycled after the Neon wears out.

313

MICHIGAN TIME LINE

40,000-10,000 years ago Asian nomads cross the Beringia land bridge into North America

1754-1760 France and Great Britain, with Native Americans fighting on both sides, clash in the French and Indian War

1763 Pontiac leads Native Americans in a rebellion against the British

About 1,000 years ago Chippewa, Ottawa, and Potawatomi migrate to Michigan

1679 Robert La Salle and his men build Fort Miami on the shore of Lake Michigan

1805 William Hull becomes the first governor of the Michigan Territory

1812-1814 The United States and Great Britain fight the War of 1812

1600s | 1700s | 1800s

1620 Etienne Brulé is the first European to set foot in Michigan

1701 Antoine de Cadillac founds Fort Pontchartrain du Détroit

1837 Michigan becomes the twenty-sixth state

About 3,000 years ago Mound builders make permanent communities in Michigan

1775-1781 The American Revolution brings independence to the Thirteen Colonies

1841 The copper boom begins in the Upper Peninsula

1795 Native American leaders sign the Treaty of Greenville, giving up large areas of land in Michigan and Ohio

1668 Jacques Marquette founds Sault Ste. Marie, the first European settlement in Michigan

1850s Sojourner Truth gives speeches about the abolition of slavery

1897 Hazen Pingree becomes governor of Michigan

1936-1937 The United Auto Workers (UAW) union holds a large sit-down strike in Flint

1963 Martin Luther King, Jr. leads nearly 125,000 Michiganians through Detroit on a march for civil rights

1861-1865 Michigan contributes 90,000 soliders and many tons of wood, iron, and copper to help the Union win the Civil War

1917-1918 175,000 Michigans serve with the allied forces in World War I

1957 The Mackinac Bridge connects the Upper Peninsula and the Lower Peninsula

1991 More than 5,000 Michiganians who served in the war in the Persian Gulf begin to come home

1900s

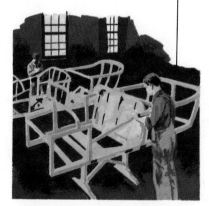

1903 Henry Ford founds the Ford Motor Company

1929 The stock market crashes in October and begins the Great Depression

1973 Coleman Young is elected Detroit's first African-American mayor

1918 Women win the right to vote in Michigan

1915 The "Great Migration" of African Americans to northern states is at its height in Michigan

1941-1945 600,000 Michiganians serve in the armed forces in World War II, thousands of Michigan women go to work in factories at home

1860 A wave of immigration from foreign countries begins which will bring about 700,000 people to Michigan before 1900

MICHIGAN ALMANAC

315

ANNUAL EVENTS IN MICHIGAN

SUMMER

JUNE
Buzzard Festival, Hell
Lake Front Days, Cadillac
Arabian Horse Show, Mason
Lilac Festival, Mackinac Island
Trout Tournament, Charlevoix
Battle Creek International Balloon
    Championship, Battle Creek
Day-of-the-Eagle Powwow, East Jordan
Experimental Aircraft Show, Ludington
International Freedom Festival, Detroit/Windsor

JULY
Bay City Fireworks Festival, Bay City
International Cherry Pit-Spitting Championship,
    Eau Claire
Van Buren County Youth Fair, Hartford
Jazz Festival, Buchanan
Bluegrass Festival, Ypsilanti
Black Fine Arts Competition, Kalamazoo
Woodland Indian Cultural Arts Festival,
    Traverse City

AUGUST
Nautical Festival, Rogers City
Michigan Festival, East Lansing
Upper Peninsula State Fair, Escanaba
Danish Festival, Greenville
Michigan State Fair, Detroit

FALL

SEPTEMBER
Carry Nation Festival, Holly
Mexican Festival, Grand Rapids
Michigan Peach Festival, Romeo
Mackinac Bridge Walk, Mackinaw City and
    St. Ignace
Salmon Derby and Festival, Sault Ste.
    Marie
Michigan Wine and Harvest Festival,
    Kalamazoo and Paw Paw
Michigan Fireman's Memorial Festival,
    Roscommon

OCTOBER
Harvest Home Festival, Troy
Fall Harvest Day and Art Fair, Jackson
Norwegian Pumpkin Rolling Festival,
    Williamsburg
Wildlife Art Exhibit, St. Johns

NOVEMBER
Festival of Trees, Saginaw
Fruitbelt Woodcarving Show, Bridgeman
Antique Toy Circus Maximus, Kalamazoo
Christmas Arts and Crafts Festival,
    Wakefield

WINTER

DECEMBER
Victorian Christmas, Benton Harbor
Holiday Crafts and Flowers Show,
    Madison Heights
Dog Show, Lansing

JANUARY
Ice Sculpture Spectacular, Plymouth
World of Cars, Saginaw
Perch Festival, Whitehall
Winter Carnival, Marine City

FEBRUARY
VASA Cross-Country Ski Race, Acme
Broomball Tournament, Lexington
Ice-Fishing Contest, Pentwater
Orchid Show, Okemos

SPRING

MARCH
Figure Skating Show, Traverse City
Irish Festival, Clare
Sugaring and Shearing, Marquette

APRIL
Fiddler's Jamboree and Dance, Battle Creek
Picnic in the Snow, Copper Harbor
Blossomtime Festival,
    Benton Harbor/St. Joseph
Italian Festival, Wyandotte

MAY
The Great Chili Cook-off, Saline
Tulip Time Festival, Holland
Dawn Patrol, Charlotte
Corvette Celebration, Hastings
Alma Highland Festival and Games, Alma
Fort Michilimackinac Pageant,
    Mackinaw City

FASCINATING MICHIGAN FACTS

The Upper Peninsula might have become a separate state. After Michigan became a state in 1837, the Upper Peninsula began to grow in wealth and population. Some Upper Peninsula residents did not want to be part of Michigan. Throughout the late 1800s and early 1900s, they spoke of forming a new state, the State of Superior.

Some of Michigan's most important historical sites are underwater. Michigan's underwater archaeologists study history by diving to sunken ships. For example, by examining the wreck of the *Regina*, which sank in Lake Huron in 1913, archaeologists discovered that the engines had been turned to "stop" when the ship sank. Clues like this help to tell the story of the crew's struggle to save their ship.

Cold breakfast cereals were invented in Michigan as food for hospital patients. In 1877 Dr. Harvey Kellogg took charge of a Battle Creek hospital that was run by the Seventh Day Adventist Church. Patients at the hospital had to eat a vegetarian diet as part of their treatment. Dr. Kellogg experimented with cold breakfast foods to make his patients' meals more tasty. After Charles W. Post, a former patient, began selling a similar breakfast food called "Grape Nuts," Kellogg decided to go into business, too. His first product, corn flakes, is still popular today.

The only wooden-shoe factories in the United States are in Holland, Michigan. Holland was settled by Dutch immigrants in 1847. All of the wooden shoes, or *klompen,* in Holland were originally made by hand for dancers in the annual Tulip Time Festival. Today, machines make thousands of klompen every year.

The world's largest dog, Joshua, lives in Grand Rapids, Michigan. Joshua, a Saint Bernard, weighs a whopping 310 pounds (141 kg). The average weight for a Saint Bernard is about 165 pounds (75 kg). Joshua belongs to Thomas and Anne Irwin, who have been breeding Saint Bernards for over 50 years.

MICHIGAN ALMANAC

ANIMALS AND PLANTS OF MICHIGAN

1. Peregrine falcon*
2. Apple tree
3. Sandhill crane
4. Wild turkey
5. Moose
6. Trout
7. Smelt
8. Pike
9. Catfish
10. Osprey
11. Painted turtle
12. Otter
13. Trillium
14. Beaver
15. Water snake
16. Red fox
17. Elk
18. American chestnut*
19. Kirtland's warbler*
20. Black spruce
21. Red oak
22. Black bear
23. White pine
24. Lynx*
25. Birds-eye maple
26. Timber wolf*
27. Raccoon
28. Snowshoe hare
29. White birch
30. Robin

* = endangered species in Michigan

FAMOUS PEOPLE OF MICHIGAN

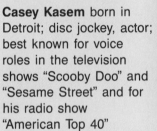

Carolyn Forché born in Detroit in 1950; poet, translator, has written several volumes of poetry including *Gathering the Tribes,* and *The Country Between Us,* and translated poetry by Spanish-speaking poets into English

Helen Thomas born in Winchester, Kentucky, in 1920, moved to Detroit in 1924; journalist; wire service reporter for United Press International (UPI) from 1943 to 1974, and UPI Washington Bureau Chief since 1974

Casey Kasem born in Detroit; disc jockey, actor; best known for voice roles in the television shows "Scooby Doo" and "Sesame Street" and for his radio show "American Top 40"

Lily Tomlin born in Detroit in 1939; actor; winner of six Emmy Awards; best known for roles in television show "Rowan and Martin's Laugh-In" and films *Nine to Five* and *All of Me*

Alvin Loving born in Detroit in 1935; artist; his work is held in major museums in New York and Detroit, best known for public commissions for Millender Station in Detroit, and Kennedy Airport, New York City

John Lee Hooker born in Clarkdale, Mississippi, in 1917, moved to Detroit in 1943; singer, guitarist; his first blues hit "Boogie Chillen," recorded in 1948, is a song about music and life in Detroit; winner of a Grammy Award in 1990 for his album *The Healer*

Tom Selleck born in Detroit in 1945; actor; best known for roles in the film *Three Men and a Baby* and the television show "Magnum P.I."

Madonna Louise Ciccone better known as Madonna, born in Bay City in 1958; singer, dancer, actor; best known for her many hit albums including *Madonna* and *True Blue,* and roles in the films *Desperately Seeking Susan* and *Dick Tracy*

George Peppard born in Detroit in 1928 and died in 1994; actor; starred in television shows "Banacek" and "The A Team"

Diana Ross born in Detroit in 1944; singer, actor, fashion designer; lead singer for The Supremes 1960-1969, solo artist since 1969; film roles include *Lady Sings the Blues* and *The Wiz*

DICTIONARY OF
GEOGRAPHIC TERMS

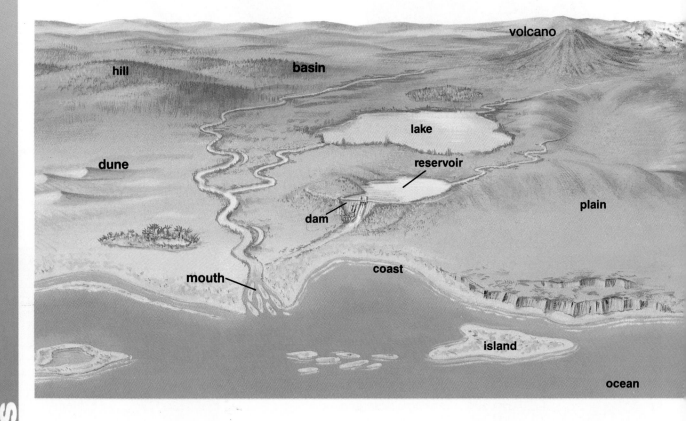

basin (bā′ sin) A low, bowl-shaped landform surrounded by higher lands. *See also* river basin.

bay (bā) A part of an ocean, sea, or lake that extends into the land.

canal (kə nal′) A waterway built to carry water for navigation or irrigation. Navigation canals usually connect two other bodies of water.

coast (kōst) The land along an ocean or sea.

dam (dam) A wall built across a river to hold back flowing water.

dune (dün) A mound or ridge of sand that has been piled up by the wind.

glacier (glā′ shər) A large sheet of ice that moves slowly over the land.

harbor (här′ bər) A protected place along a shore where ships safely anchor.

hill (hil) A rounded, raised landform that is not as high as a mountain.

island (ī′ lənd) A body of land completely surrounded by water.

lake (lāk) A body of water completely or almost completely surrounded by land.

mountain (moun′ tən) A high, rounded, or pointed landform with steep sides. A mountain is higher than a hill.

mountain range (moun′ tən rānj) A row or chain of mountains.

mouth (mouth) The part of a river where it empties into another body of water.

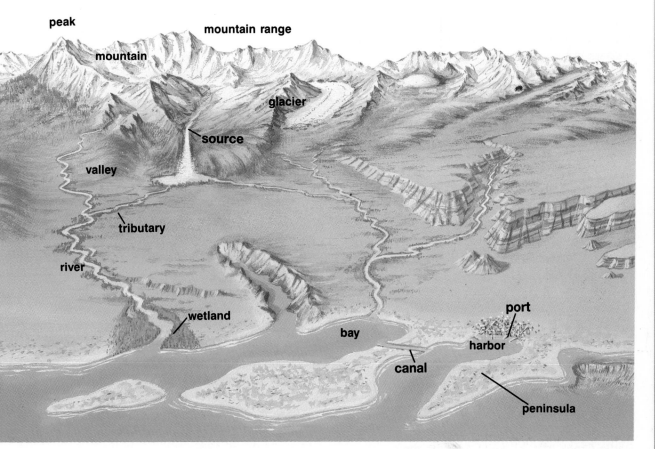

peak

mountain range

mountain

glacier

source

valley

tributary

river

wetland

bay

port

harbor

canal

peninsula

ocean (ō′ shən) One of the earth's four largest bodies of water. The four oceans are really a single connected body of salt water that covers about three fourths of the earth's surface.

peak (pēk) The pointed top of a mountain or hill.

peninsula (pə nin′ sə lə) A body of land nearly surrounded by water.

plain (plān) A large area of flat or nearly flat land.

port (pôrt) A place where ships load and unload goods.

reservoir (rez′ ər vwär) A natural or artificial lake used to store water.

river (riv′ ər) A large stream of water that flows in a natural channel across the land.

river basin (riv′ ər bā′ sin) All the land drained by a river and its tributaries.

source (sôrs) A spring, lake, or other body of water where a river or stream begins.

tributary (trib′ yə târ ē) A river or stream that flows into a larger river or stream.

valley (val′ ē) An area of low land between hills or mountains.

volcano (vol kā′ nō) An opening in the earth through which lava, rock, and gases are forced out.

wetland (wet′ land) A swampy area that is home to special plants and animals.

GEOGRAPHIC TERMS

GAZETTEER

This Gazetteer is a geographical dictionary that will help you to pronounce and locate the places discussed in this book. Latitude and longitude are given for cities and some other places. The page number tells you where each place appears in the text for the first time.

PRONUNCIATION KEY

a	cap	hw	**wh**ere	oi	**coi**n	ü	m**oo**n
ā	c**a**ke	i	b**i**b	ôr	**f**ork	ū	c**u**te
ä	f**a**ther	ī	k**i**te	ou	c**ow**	ûr	t**er**m
är	c**ar**	îr	p**ie**rce	sh	**sh**ow	ə	**a**bout, tak**e**n,
âr	d**are**	ng	so**ng**	th	**th**in		penc**i**l, apr**o**n,
ch	**ch**ain	o	t**o**p	th	**th**ose		helpf**u**l
e	h**e**n	ō	r**o**pe	u	s**u**n	ər	lett**er**, doll**ar**,
ē	m**e**	ô	s**aw**	u̇	b**oo**k		doct**or**

A

Ann Arbor (an är′ bər) A city in the southeastern part of the Lower Peninsula; site of the University of Michigan; 42°N, 84°W. (p. 130)

B

Battle Creek (bat′ əl krēk) A city in the south-central part of the Lower Peninsula; 42°N, 85°W. (p. 44)

Beringia (bär′ ən gē ə) An area of dry land that once formed a "land bridge" between Asia and North America, which now are separated by the Bering Strait. (p. 62)

Bering Strait (bîr′ ing strāt) The narrow body of water that separates North America from Asia. (p. 62)

Black Bottom (blak bot′ əm) An African-American neighborhood in Detroit. (p. 191)

C

Cassopolis (kə sop′ ə ləs) A community in the southwestern part of the Lower Peninsula. It was an important stop on one route in the Underground Railroad; 42°N, 86°W. (p. 160)

Chelsea (chel′ sē) An urban community in the southeastern part of the Lower Peninsula; 42°N, 84°W. (p. 242)

Copper Harbor (kop′ ər här′ bər) A community at the northwestern tip of the Upper Peninsula; 47°N, 88°W. (p. 33)

D

Dearborn (dîr′ bôrn) An industrial city in the southeastern part of the Lower Peninsula; 42°N, 83°W. (p. 186)

Detroit (di troit′) The largest city in Michigan, located in the southeastern part of the state; 42°N, 83°W. (p. 12)

E

Empire (em′ pīr) A community in the northwestern part of the Lower Peninsula; 45°N, 86°W. (p. 239)

Erie Canal (îr′ ē kə nal′) A canal in New York State that opened in 1825 and provided a water route between the Great Lakes and the Atlantic Ocean. (p. 135)

Escanaba (es kə näb′ ə) A city in the southwestern part of the Upper Peninsula; 46°N, 87°W. (p. 238)

F

Flint (flint) A city in the southeastern part of the Lower Peninsula; important site of automobile manufacturing; 43°N, 84°W. (p. 44)

Fort Mackinac (fôrt mak′ ə nak) A fort, on Mackinac Island in the Straits of Mackinac, attacked by the British and Native Americans during the War of 1812; 45°N, 84°W. (p. 121)

Fort Michilimackinac (fôrt mish ə le mak′ ə nak) A fort on the northern tip of the Lower Peninsula, on the Straits of Mackinac. It was captured by Native Americans during Pontiac's Rebellion; 45°N, 84°W. (p. 101)

Fort Pontchartrain (fôrt pon′ chər trān) A French settlement established in 1701 in what is now Michigan. It is the site of the present city of Detroit; 42°N, 83°W. (p. 92)

Fort St. Joseph (fôrt sānt jō′ zəf) A fort located near the present city of Niles in the southwestern Lower Peninsula. It is the only site in Michigan to have been ruled by four nations: France, Britain, Spain, and the United States; 41°N, 86°W. (p. 112)

G

Grand Rapids (grand rap′ idz) A city on the Grand River in the Lower Peninsula; 43°N, 85°W. (p. 43)

Grand River (grand riv′ ər) A river that flows through Lansing and Grand Rapids on its way to Lake Michigan. (p. 43)

Great Lakes (grāt lāks) The world's largest freshwater lakes, located between the northern United States and Canada. The Great Lakes include: Lake Superior, Lake Michigan, Lake Huron, Lake Erie, and Lake Ontario. (p. 20)

H

Hamtramck (ham tram′ ik) A suburb of Detroit where many Polish Americans live; 42°N, 83°W. (p. 190)

I

Inkster (ingk′ stər) A community west of Detroit where many African Americans live; 42°N, 83°W. (p. 213)

Isle Royale (īəl rôi′ əl) An island in Lake Superior off the north coast of Michigan's Upper Peninsula; now a national park; 48°N, 89°W. (p. 64)

J

Jackson (jak′ sən) A city in the south-central part of the Lower Peninsula, where Jackson automobiles were manufactured in the early 1900s; 42°N, 84°W. (p. 200)

K

Kalamazoo (kal ə mə zü′) A city in the southwestern part of the Lower Peninsula; 42°N, 86°W. (p. 64)

Keweenaw Peninsula (kē′ wi nô pə nin′ sə lə) A peninsula on the northern tip of the Upper Peninsula; the site of many rich copper mines. (p. 53)

L

Lake Erie (lāk ir′ ē) The southernmost of the Great Lakes. It borders the southeastern part of Michigan's Lower Peninsula. (p. 20)

Lake Huron (lāk hyùr′ ən) The second-largest of the Great Lakes. It forms part of Michigan's eastern border. (p. 20)

Lake Michigan (lāk mish′ i gən) The third-largest of the Great Lakes. It forms the western border of Michigan's Lower Peninsula. (p. 20)

Lake Ontario (lāk on târ′ ē ō) The smallest of the Great Lakes. It is the only one that does not border Michigan. (p. 20)

Lake St. Clair (lāk sānt clâr) A lake northeast of Detroit located on the border between the United States and Canada. (p. 18)

Lake Superior (lāk sə pir′ ē ər) The largest of the Great Lakes. It borders most of the northern part of Michigan. (p. 20)

Lansing (lan′ sing) The capital of Michigan. It is located in the south-central part of the Lower Peninsula; 43°N, 85°W. (p. 44)

M

Mackinaw City (mak′ ə nô sit′ ē) A city at the north-central tip of the Lower Peninsula; 46°N, 85°W. (p. 36)

Manistee (man ə stē′) A city in the northwestern part of the Lower Peninsula; 44°N, 86°W. (p. 238)

Manistee River (man ə stē riv′ ər) A river that flows through the northwestern Lower Peninsula and empties into Lake Michigan. (p. 24)

GAZETTEER

Manistique (man ə stēk′) A city in the south-central part of the Upper Peninsula; 46°N, 86°W. (p. 213)

Marquette (mär ket′) A city on the northern shore of the Upper Peninsula, important for iron mining; 47°N, 87°W. (p. 53)

Marshall (mär′ shəl) A community in southeastern Michigan; 42°N, 84°W. (p. 136)

Monroe (man rō′) A city in the southeastern corner of the Lower Peninsula. It was the site of a battle during the War of 1812; 42°N, 83°W. (p. 121)

Morenci (mə ren′ sē) A community in the southeastern part of the Lower Peninsula. It was a stop on an Underground Railroad route; 41°N, 84°W. (p. 160)

Mount Arvon (mount är′ von) Michigan's highest peak, located in the western part of the Upper Peninsula; 47°N, 88°W. (p. 52)

Mount Curwood (mount kûr′ wǔd) One of Michigan's highest peaks, located on the Upper Peninsula; 46°N, 88°W. (p. 270)

Muskegon (mə skē′ gən) An industrial city, on Lake Michigan, in the western part of the Lower Peninsula; 43°N, 86°W. (p. 153)

Muskegon River (mə skē′ gən riv′ ər) A river of the Lower Peninsula. It begins in Houghton Lake and flows southwest into Lake Michigan at Muskegon. (p. 43)

N

New France (nü frans) A French colony in North America from 1609 to 1763. (p. 85)

Niles (nīlz) A city near the site of Fort St. Joseph in the southwestern part of the Lower Peninsula; 42°N, 86°W. (p. 109)

Northwest Territory (nôrth west′ ter′ i tôr ē) A former United States frontier area that included the present states of Illinois, Indiana, Michigan, Ohio, Wisconsin, and part of Minnesota. (p. 114)

P

Pontiac (pon′ tē ak) A city in the southeastern part of the Lower Peninsula, named for the Ottawa chief who led Pontiac's Rebellion in 1763; 43°N, 83°W. (p. 207)

Porcupine Mountains (pôr′ kyə pīn moun′ tənz) The mountains, popular for skiing, that are located in the northwestern part of the Upper Peninsula. (p. 52)

Port Huron (pôrt hyür′ ən) A community of the eastern part of the Lower Peninsula. It was a point on an Underground Railroad route; 43°N, 83°W. (p. 112)

R

River Raisin (riv′ ər rā′ zin) A river in the southeastern corner of the Lower Peninsula that was the site of a battle during the War of 1812; 41°N, 83°W. (p. 121)

S

Saginaw (sag′ ə nô) An industrial city in the eastern part of the Lower Peninsula, on the Saginaw River; 43°N, 84°W. (p. 124)

Saginaw Bay (sag′ ə nô bā) An inlet of Lake Huron located on the eastern shore of the Lower Peninsula. (p. 123)

Saginaw River (sag′ ə nô riv′ ər) A river of the Lower Peninsula. It flows into Saginaw Bay, an inlet of Lake Huron. (p. 43)

Sault Ste. Marie (sü sānt mə rē′) A city on the St. Marys River in the eastern part of the Upper Peninsula; site of the Soo Canal; 46°N, 84°W. (p. 53)

Schoolcraft (skül′ kraft) A community of the southwestern part of the Lower Peninsula. It was a stop on an Underground Railroad route; 42°N, 85°W. (p. 156)

Sleeping Bear Dunes (slē′ ping bâr dünz) A national park located on the shore of Lake Michigan in the northwestern part of the Lower Peninsula. (p. 13)

St. Ignace (sānt ig′ nəs) A city on the southeastern shore of the Upper Peninsula. Today this city is a popular summer resort; 46°N, 85°W. (p. 37)

St. Marys River (sānt mâr′ ēz riv′ ər) A body of water that connects the Soo Locks to Lake Huron; it is located along the eastern edge of the Upper Peninsula. (p. 53)

Straits of Mackinac (strāts əv mak′ ə nak) The narrow body of water between the Upper and Lower peninsulas that connects Lake Michigan with Lake Huron. (p. 51)

GAZETTEER

T

Toledo Strip (tə lē′ dō strip) A piece of land in northern Ohio on which the port of Toledo is located. In the 1830s it was claimed by both Michigan and Ohio. (p. 129)

Traverse City (trav′ ərs sit′ ē) A city in the northwestern part of the Lower Peninsula; 45°N, 86°W. (p. 12)

V

Vermontville (vər mont′ vil) A community established in the southern part of the Lower Peninsula by settlers from Vermont; 43°N, 85°W. (p. 136)

W

Willow Run (wil′ ō run) The site of a huge airplane plant that operated during World War II, located near Ypsilanti; 42°N, 84°W. (p. 220)

Y

Ypsilanti (ip sə lant′ ē) An industrial city in the southeastern part of the Lower Peninsula; 42°N, 84°W. (p. 220)

a cap; ā cake; ä father; är car; âr dare; ch chain; e hen; ē me; hw where; i bib; ī kite; îr pierce; ng song; o top; ō rope; ô saw; oi coin; ôr fork; ou cow; sh show; th thin; th those; u sun; u̇ book; ü moon; ū cute; ûr term; ə about, taken, pencil, apron, helpful; ər letter, dollar, doctor

GAZETTEER

BIOGRAPHICAL DICTIONARY

The Biographical Dictionary will help you to pronounce the names of and to identify the Key People in this book. The page number tells you where each name first appears in the text.

PRONUNCIATION KEY

a	cap	hw	**wh**ere	oi	c**oi**n	ü	m**oo**n
ā	c**a**ke	i	b**i**b	ôr	f**or**k	ū	c**u**te
ä	f**a**ther	ī	k**i**te	ou	c**ow**	ûr	t**er**m
är	c**ar**	îr	p**ier**ce	sh	**sh**ow	ə	**a**bout, tak**e**n,
âr	d**are**	ng	so**ng**	th	**th**in		penc**i**l, apr**o**n,
ch	**ch**ain	o	t**o**p	th	**th**ose		helpf**u**l
e	h**e**n	ō	r**o**pe	u	s**u**n	ər	lett**er**, doll**ar**,
ē	m**e**	ô	s**aw**	ù	b**oo**k		doct**or**

A

Abraham, Spencer (ā′ brä ham), United States Senator from Michigan. (p. 267)

Artis, Kinchen (är′ tis, kin′ chən), 1830–1905 Soldier from Battle Creek who volunteered to serve in the First Michigan Colored Regiment during the Civil War. (p. 173)

Austin, Richard (ôs′ tin), 1913– Secretary of state of Michigan since 1971. (p. 227)

B

Blos, Joan W. (blōs), 1928– Author of *Brothers of the Heart*, a story of pioneer Michigan. She is also the author of *Old Henry, The Heroine of the Titanic,* and *A Gathering of Days,* for which she won the Newbery Medal and the American Book Award in children's fiction. (p. 144)

Brulé, Etienne (brü lā′, ā tyen), 1592–1632 French explorer who sailed up Lake Huron, St. Marys River, and Lake Superior in 1620; the first European to explore present-day Michigan. (p. 85)

C

Cadillac, Antoine de la (kȧ′ dē yȧk, an′ twän), 1658–1730 French colonial commander and the founder of Detroit in 1701. (p. 92)

Cass, Lewis (kas), 1782–1866 Michigan governor from 1813 to 1831 who persuaded Native Americans to sell large amounts of their land to the Michigan government. In 1831 he moved to Washington, D.C., to become an adviser to President Andrew Jackson, and in this position he encouraged settlers to move west to Michigan. (p. 123)

Champlain, Samuel de (sham plān′), 1567–1635 French explorer and mapmaker who founded Quebec City and sent out explorers to the area around present-day Michigan in search of the Northwest Passage. (p. 85)

Chandler, Elizabeth (chan′ dlər), 1807–1834 Quaker woman who was a leader in the abolitionist movement in Michigan. (p. 158)

Cobb, Ty (kob), 1886–1961 Baseball player for the Detroit Tigers from 1905 to 1926 and the first player named to the Baseball Hall of Fame. (p. 285)

Columbus, Christopher (kə lum′ bəs), 1451?–1506 European explorer who reached North America while sailing west in search of Asia in 1492. (p. 83)

Conyers, John, Jr. (kän′ yûrz), 1929– Member of the U.S. House of Representatives from Michigan since 1964; leader of the Congressional Black Caucus. (p. 268)

Crane, Caroline Bartlett (krān), 1858–1935
Progressive reformer from Kalamazoo who
worked to bring an end to unclean
conditions in meatpacking houses during
the late 1800s. (p. 195)

Custer, George (kus' tər), 1839–1876
Leader, from Monroe, of the Michigan
Cavalry Brigade during the Civil War.
(p. 170)

D

De Baptiste, George (də bap tēst'), African-
American conductor on Michigan's
Underground Railroad who helped enslaved
African Americans to escape to freedom.
(p. 160)

De Sable, Jean (də säb' lə, zhän), 1745–
1818   Haitian-born American from the
Great Lakes region who was captured by
the British as a suspected spy during the
American Revolution. (p. 112)

E

Edison, Thomas Alva (ed' ə sən), 1847–1931
Inventor of hundreds of items, including the
light bulb and the record player; he grew up
in Port Huron. (p. 179)

Edmonds, Sara Emma (ed' məndz), 1841–
1898   Woman from Flint who disguised
herself as a man and fought in several
battles during the Civil War. (p. 170)

F

Ford, Gerald R., Jr. (fôrd), 1913–   Native of
Grand Rapids who was first elected to
represent Michigan in the United States
House of Representatives in 1948. In 1973
he became Vice President, and from 1974 to
1977 he served as the thirty-eighth
President of the United States.
(p. 267)

Ford, Henry (fôrd), 1863–1947   Founder of
the Ford Motor Company in 1903. He also
introduced assembly-line techniques that
made automobiles affordable for the average
American. (p. 197)

Franklin, Aretha (frang' klin), 1942–   World-
famous singer who grew up in Detroit and
started her singing career in the choir of
Detroit's New Bethel Baptist Church.
(p. 276)

G

Gordy, Berry, Jr. (gôr' dē), 1929–   Promoter
of the "Motown Sound" through his record
company, Motown, which has recorded
such stars as Stevie Wonder, the Supremes,
and the Temptations. (p. 277)

Griffiths, Martha (grif' iths), 1912–   Member
of the House of Representatives from
Michigan since 1954, and a former
lieutenant governor of Michigan. (p. 268)

H

Hamilton, Henry (ham' əl tən), 1740?–1796
British commander in Detroit during the
American Revolution. (p. 111)

Harrison, William Henry (har' ə sən), 1773–1841
American general who led the recapture of
Detroit for the United States during the War
of 1812. (p. 121)

Haviland, Laura (hav' ə lənd), 1808–1898
Conductor on Michigan's Underground
Railroad who helped enslaved African
Americans to escape to freedom. (p. 161)

Houghton, Douglass (hōt' ən), 1809–1845
Scientist whose report that there were large
copper deposits in the Keweenaw Peninsula
led to the development of the copper
industry in Michigan during the 1800s.
(p. 153)

Howe, Gordie (hou), 1928–   One of hockey's
most famous players; played for the Detroit
Redwings from 1946 to 1971. (p. 285)

Hull, William (hul), 1753–1825   First
governor of the Michigan Territory from 1805
to 1812. (p. 116)

J

Johnson, Earvin "Magic" (jon' sən), 1959–
Professional basketball player who grew up
in Lansing and attended Michigan State
University. He has led the Los Angeles
Lakers to many national championships.
(p. 285)

BIOGRAPHICAL DICTIONARY

K

Kahn, Albert (kän), 1869–1942   Architect from Germany who is best remembered for his factory designs that provided workers with more air and light. (p. 279)

King, Martin Luther, Jr. (king), 1929–1968   Important civil rights leader during the 1950s and 1960s. In 1963 he visited Detroit and made a stirring speech in front of almost 125,000 people. (p. 225)

L

La Salle, Robert (lə sal′), 1643–1687   French explorer who founded Fort Miami, the first European fort in Michigan's Lower Peninsula. (p. 90)

Levin, Carl (le′ vən), 1934–   United States senator from Michigan. (p. 267)

Lincoln, Abraham (ling′ kən), 1809–1865   Sixteenth President of the United States; led the country during the Civil War. (p. 167)

Lindbergh, Charles (lind′ bûrg), 1902–1974   Pilot from Detroit who became the first person to fly alone across the Atlantic Ocean; in 1927 he flew the *Spirit of St. Louis* from New York to Paris. (p. 208)

Louis, Joe (lü′ is), 1914–1981   World heavyweight boxing champion from 1937 to 1949 who grew up in Detroit and was nicknamed the "Brown Bomber." (p. 214)

M

Marquette, Jacques (mär ket′, zhäk), 1637–1675   French missionary and explorer who founded Sault Ste. Marie and St. Ignace in the 1660s. (p. 87)

Mason, Stevens T. (mā′ sən), 1811–1843   The "boy governor" who began serving as secretary of the Michigan Territory when he was only 20 years old. He became acting governor of the Michigan Territory in 1834 when he was 23 years old. (p. 128)

McCoy, Elijah (mə koi′), 1843–1929   Detroit inventor of a number of inventions, including the "oil cup," which helped trains to run more smoothly. (p. 179)

N

Nicolet, Jean (nik ə lā′), 1598–1642   French explorer of the shoreline of Michigan's Upper Peninsula in 1634. (p. 86)

O

Olds, Ransom E. (ōldz), 1864–1950   Founder of the world's first automobile factory, which began operating in 1899 in Lansing. (p. 198)

Owens, Carl (ō enz), 1929–   Artist from Detroit whose work has become known throughout the world. (p. 280)

P

Perry, Oliver Hazard (per′ ē), 1785–1819   American naval officer who defeated the British in the Battle of Put-in-Bay during the War of 1812; he said, "We have met the enemy and they are ours." (p. 122)

Pingree, Hazen (ping′ grē), 1840–1901   Mayor of Detroit and governor of Michigan in the late 1800s who tried to make life better for working people. (p. 195)

Pontiac (pōn′ tē ak), 1720–1769   Ottawa chief who united Native Americans against the British in 1763. Leader of what became known as Pontiac's Rebellion, Pontiac later worked to bring about peace between Native Americans and the British. (p. 100)

R

Reuther, Walter (rü′ thər), 1907–1970   President of the United Auto Workers Union from 1946 to 1970. (p. 216)

Roosevelt, Franklin D. (rōz′ velt), 1882–1945   President of the United States during the Great Depression and World War II. (p. 213)

S

Saarinen, Eliel (sär′ i nen), 1873–1950   Award-winning architect from Finland who moved to Michigan in 1923 and designed the Cranbrook Academy of Art. (p. 279)

Shaw, Anna Howard (shô), 1847–1919   Leader of the women's rights movement in Michigan who grew up in Big Rapids. As a result of Shaw's and other people's work, the Michigan Constitution was changed in 1918 to allow women to vote. (p. 196)

BIOGRAPHICAL DICTIONARY

T

Tecumseh (tə kum′ sə), 1768–1813
Shawnee chief who tried to organize Native Americans in order to slow down the advance of American settlement on their lands; ally of the British during the War of 1812. (p. 120)

Truth, Sojourner (trüth), 1797?–1883
Former slave, whose real name was Isabella Baumfree; settled in Battle Creek and became a famous speaker in support of the abolition of slavery. She also spoke powerfully in support of women's rights. (p. 159)

W

Wayne, Anthony (wān), 1745–1796
American general who, in 1794, defeated Native Americans at the battle of Fallen Timbers in Ohio. This defeat led to the signing of the Treaty of Greenville, in which Native Americans agreed to give up large areas of land in southeastern Michigan. (p. 115)

Wilson, Woodrow (wil′ sən), 1856–1924
President of the United States during World War I. (p. 205)

Wonder, Stevie (wun′ dər), 1950– Musician and singer from Detroit who first became famous when the "Motown Sound" became popular throughout the world in the 1960s. (p. 277)

Woodward, Augustus (wůd′ wərd), 1774–1827 Territorial judge who designed the new city of Detroit after its terrible fire in 1805. (p. 117)

Y

Young, Coleman (yung), 1918– Detroit's first African–American mayor; he was elected to office in 1973. He was a union member and a state senator before becoming mayor. (p. 227)

a cap; ā cake; ä father; är car; âr dare; ch chain; e hen; ē me; hw where; i bib; ī kite; îr pierce; ng song; o top; ō rope; ô saw; oi coin; ôr fork; ou cow; sh show; th thin; <u>th</u> those; u sun; ů book; ü moon; ū cute; ûr term; ə about, taken, pencil, apron, helpful; ər letter, dollar, doctor

BIOGRAPHICAL DICTIONARY

GLOSSARY

This Glossary will help you to pronounce and understand the meanings of the Key Vocabulary in this book. The page number at the end of the definition tells where the word first appears.

PRONUNCIATION KEY

a	cap	hw	**wh**ere	oi	c**oi**n	ü	m**oo**n
ā	c**a**ke	i	b**i**b	ôr	f**or**k	ū	c**u**te
ä	f**a**ther	ī	k**i**te	ou	c**ow**	ûr	t**er**m
är	c**ar**	îr	p**ier**ce	sh	**sh**ow	ə	**a**bout, tak**e**n,
âr	d**are**	ng	so**ng**	th	**th**in		penc**i**l, apr**o**n,
ch	**ch**ain	o	t**o**p	th	**th**ose		helpful
e	h**e**n	ō	r**o**pe	u	s**u**n	ər	lett**er**, doll**ar**,
ē	m**e**	ô	s**aw**	ů	b**oo**k		doct**or**

A

abolitionist (ab ə lish′ ə nist) A person who wanted to abolish or end slavery. (p. 158)

acid rain (as′ id rān) A form of pollution created when rain mixes with chemicals from the burning of fuels. (p. 249)

agriculture (ag′ ri kul chər) The business of raising crops and farm animals. (p. 44)

ancestor A person in your family, starting with your parents, who was born before you. (p. 271)

archaeologist (är kē ol′ ə jist) A scientist who studies the way people lived a long time ago. (p. 62)

artifact (är′ tə fakt) Something made by people, such as tools or pottery, used in earlier times. (p. 62)

assembly line (ə sem′ blē līn) A way of working in which workers and machines are arranged so each worker does one job in turn. (p. 198)

B

barter (bär′ tər) To trade goods for other goods without using money. (p. 91)

basin (bā′ sin) A low, bowl-shaped landform surrounded by higher land. (p. 22)

bill (bil) A plan for a law. (p. 255)

board of commissioners (bôrd əv kə mish′ ə nərz) The legislative branch of Michigan's county governments. (p. 261)

byline (bī′ līn) The line in a newspaper story that tells who wrote the article. (p. 258)

C

canal (kə nal′) A waterway dug across land for ships to travel on. (p. 129)

cardinal directions (kär′ də nəl di rek′ shənz) The four main directions of the compass; north, east, south, and west. (p. 10)

cash crops (kash krops) Crops that are grown to sell for money. (p. 178)

cause (kôz) Something that makes something else happen. (p. 222)

census (sen′ səs) An official count of the people living in a place. (p. 235)

ceremony (ser′ ə mō nē) An act that people perform on a special occasion. (p. 64)

332

charter (chär′ tər) A written statement that gives a person or a group certain rights. (p. 265)

circle graph (sûr′ kəl graf) A graph that shows how something can be divided into parts. (p. 139)

civil rights (siv′ əl rīts) The rights of all people to be treated equally under the law. (p. 225)

clan (klan) A large group of related families. (p. 70)

climate (klī′ mit) The type of weather an area has over a long period of time. (p. 24)

colony (kol′ ə nē) A place or settlement that is ruled by another country. (p. 84)

compass rose (kum′ pəs rōz) A small drawing showing directions. (p. 10)

compromise (kom′ prə mīz) An agreement by which each side gives up part of what it wants. (p. 129)

Confederacy (kən fed′ ər ə sē) The Southern United States that formed their own country during the Civil War. (p. 167)

constitution (kon sti tü′ shən) A plan of government. (p. 128)

continent (kon′ tə nənt) One of the seven large bodies of land on earth. (p. 8)

council (koun′ səl) The legislative branch of a town or city. (p. 262)

culture (kul′ chər) The way of life of a group of people. (p. 69)

D

dateline (dāt′ līn) The line in a news article that tells where and when the story was written. (p. 258)

decision (di sizh′ ən) A choice. (p. 66)

degree (di grē′) A measure of distance between lines of latitude or longitude. (p. 28)

discrimination (di skrim ə nā′ shən) An unfair difference in the treatment of people. (p. 189)

E

economy (i kon′ ə mē) The system of using money, goods, and natural resources to meet a group's needs and wants. (p. 189)

editorial (ed i tôr′ ē əl) A newspaper article in which the editors give their opinions about an issue. (p. 258)

effect (i fekt′) What happens as a result of something else. (p. 222)

elevation (el ə vā′ shən) The height of land above sea level. (p. 40)

Emancipation Proclamation (i man sə pā′ shen prok lə mā′ shən) The announcement issued by President Lincoln in 1863 that said that all slaves in the Confederate states were free. (p. 171)

environment (en vī′ rən mənt) The surroundings in which people, animals, or plants live. (p. 249)

equator (i kwā′ tər) The imaginary line that lies halfway between the North Pole and the South Pole. (p. 9)

executive branch (eg zek′ yə tiv branch) The part of a government that makes sure the laws are carried out. (p. 255)

expedition (ek spi dish′ ən) A journey made for a special purpose. (p. 84)

export (ek spôrt′) To send goods to another country for sale or trade. (p. 248)

F

fact (fakt) A statement that can be proved true. (p. 162)

feature article (fē′ chər är′ ti kəl) A newspaper story that reports in detail about a person, subject, or event. (p. 258)

fertile (fûr′ təl) Good for growing crops. (p. 32)

folk art (fōk ärt) Art made by everyday people. (p. 276)

frontier (frun tîr′) The land that is at the edge of a settled area. (p. 109)

G

geography (jē og′ rə fē) The study of the earth and the way people live on it and use it. (p. 21)

glacier (glā′ shər) A huge sheet of ice that moves slowly over the land. (p. 21)

global grid (glō′ bəl grid) The lines of latitude and longitude on a world map that make it possible to locate places. (p. 30)

graph (graf) A diagram that allows you to compare different facts and figures. (p. 138)

grid map (grid map) A map with two sets of lines that cross each other to form squares; the grid is used to locate places on the map. (p. 13)

H

headline (hed′ līn) The title of a newspaper article, printed at the top of the story (p. 258)

hemisphere (hem′ i sfîr) A half of a sphere. (p. 8)

high-tech (hī tek) An industry that makes products that require much scientific knowledge. (p. 244)

history (his′ tə rē) Events of the past that have been preserved in written records. (p. 61)

House of Representatives (hous əv rep ri zen′ tə tivz) One of the two houses of Congress that make up the legislative branch of the United States government. (p. 266)

I

immigrant (im′ i grənt) A person who comes to another country to live. (p. 136)

import (im pôrt′) To bring in goods from another country for sale or use. (p. 248)

industry (in′ də strē) A group of companies that makes a certain product or provides a certain service. (p. 152)

integration (in ti grā′ shən) The act of making something available to all groups of people. (p. 226)

interdependent (in tər di pen′ dənt) Depending upon one another to meet needs and wants. (p. 247)

intermediate directions (in tər mē′ dē it di rek′ shənz) The directions that lie halfway between the cardinal directions. (p. 10)

J

jazz (jaz) A musical style with African rhythms that first appeared in the early 1900s. (p. 277)

judicial branch (jü dish′ əl branch) The part of a government made up of courts. (p. 256)

L

landform (land′ form) A feature of the earth's surface, such as a valley or a mountain. (p. 21)

latitude (lat′ i tüd) Imaginary lines on a map or globe that measure distance in degrees north or south of the equator. (p. 28)

legislative branch (lej′ is lā tiv branch) The part of a government that makes laws. (p. 254)

legislature (lej′ is lā chər) A group of people who have the power to make laws. (p. 130)

line graph (līn graf) A drawing that shows changes over a period of time. (p. 138)

livestock (līv′ stok) Animals that are raised on a farm. (p. 236)

lock (lok) Narrow, concrete passages in canals, in which the water level can be raised or lowered. (p. 54)

longitude (lon′ ji tüd) Imaginary lines on a map or globe that measure distance in degrees east or west of the prime meridian. (p. 29)

M

manufacturing (man yə fak′ chər ing) The making of products with the use of machinery. (p. 44)

map key (map kē) A guide that explains the meaning of each symbol used on a map. (p. 11)

mass production (mas prə duk′ shən) Making, quickly and cheaply, large numbers of one particular product. (p. 198)

mayor (mā′ ər) The person who is the official head of a city or town government. (p. 262)

meridian (mə rid′ ē ən) A line of longitude. (p. 29)

migrate (mī′ grāt) To move from one area to another. (p. 78)

mineral (min′ ər əl) A natural substance located below the earth's surface. (p. 33)

missionary (mish′ ə ner ē) A person who teaches his or her religion to other people who have different beliefs. (p. 86)

N

natural resource (nach′ ər əl rē′ sôrs) Something found in nature that is useful to people. (p. 32)

New Deal (nü dēl) President Franklin Roosevelt's plan for helping people who were hurt by the Great Depression. (p. 213)

news article (nüz är′ ti kəl) A newspaper story that reports about recent events. (p. 258)

Northwest Passage (nôrth west′ pas′ ij) A supposed water route through the North American continent connecting the Atlantic Ocean to the Pacific Ocean. (p. 85)

O

ocean (ō′ shən) A very large body of salt water. (p. 8)

opinion (ə pin′ yən) A belief or feeling that a person has about something. (p. 162)

outline (out′ līn) A plan that lets a person organize ideas about a subject. (p. 192)

P

parallel (par′ ə lel) A line of latitude. (p. 28)

peninsula (pə nin′ sə lə) A body of land surrounded almost entirely by water. (p. 19)

pioneer (pī ə nîr′) One of the first people to move into a frontier area. (p. 115)

point of view (point əv vū) The way a person looks at something. (p. 240)

pollute (pə lüt′) To make dirty with harmful materials. (p. 249)

population (pop yə lā′ shən) The number of people who live in a place. (p. 43)

precipitation (pri sip i tā′ shən) The moisture that falls to the earth as rain, snow, sleet, or hail. (p. 25)

prehistory (prē his′ tə rē) A period in the past before writing was invented. (p. 61)

prime meridian (prīm mə rid′ ē ən) The first line used for measuring lines of longitude. (p. 29)

product map (prod′ əkt map) A map that shows the kinds of things that are made or grown in a specific area. (p. 15)

professional (prə fesh′ ən əl) A person who is paid to do a job. (p. 284)

profile (prō′ fīl) A side view of part of the earth. (p. 41)

Progressive (prə gres′ iv) A person who tries to improve the quality of life for people in a state or country. (p. 195)

Prohibition (prō ə bish′ ən) The period (in Michigan from 1918 to 1933) when alcoholic beverages were illegal to manufacture, sell, or drink in the United States. (p. 208)

R

recreation (rek rē ā′ shən) The activities that people do to enjoy themselves. (p. 45)

reform (ri fôrm′) A change or improvement. (p. 195)

region (rē′ jən) An area with common features that set it apart from other areas. (p. 38)

religion (ri lij′ ən) The way people worship the God or gods they believe in. (p. 71)

reservation (rez ər vā′ shən) Land set aside by the government for a specific purpose. (p. 272)

rural (rür′ əl) Having to do with the country or agriculture. (p. 236)

S

scale (skāl) The relationship between distances shown on a map and the actual distances between places on the earth. (p. 12)

secede (si sēd′) To withdraw from a group, organization, or country. (p. 167)

segregation (seg ri gā′ shən) The practice of keeping one group of people separate from other groups. (p. 224)

Senate (sen′ it) One of the two houses of Congress that make up the legislative branch of the United States government. (p. 266)

service industry (sûr′ vis in′ də strē) An industry that serves people. (p. 245)

slavery (slā′ və rē) The practice of making one person the property of another. (p. 97)

---

a cap; ā cake; ä father; är car; âr dare; ch chain; e hen; ē me; hw where; i bib; ī kite; îr pierce; ng song; o top; ō rope; ô saw; oi coin; ôr fork; ou cow; sh show; th thin; <u>th</u> those; u sun; ù book; ü moon; ū cute; ûr term; ə about, taken, pencil, apron, helpful; ər letter, dollar, doctor

GLOSSARY

State Legislature (stat lej′ is lā chər) The branch of state government that makes laws. (p. 254)

stock (stok) A share of ownership in a company. (p. 211)

stockade (sto kād′) A tall fence of upright posts used to protect an area. (p. 92)

strait (strāt) A narrow waterway that connects two larger bodies of water. (p. 51)

strike (strīk) An action by which workers refuse to do their jobs until the employer agrees to their demands. (p. 217)

subsistence farmer (səb sis′ təns fär′ mər) A farmer who is able to provide for most of his or her own needs. (p. 143)

suburb (sub′ ûrb) A community close to a city. (p. 44)

suffrage (suf′ rij) The right to vote. (p. 196)

surveyor (sər vā′ ər) A person who uses special tools to measure land. (p. 133)

symbol (sim′ bəl) Something that stands for, or represents, something else. (p. 11)

T

tax (taks) Money that people pay to support the government. (p. 110)

technology (tek nol′ ə jē) The use of new ideas and tools to meet people's needs. (p. 177)

temperature (tem′ pər ə chər) A measure of how hot or cold the air is. (p. 25)

territory (ter′ i tôr ē) Land that belongs to a country but is not a state of that country. (p. 114)

timber (tim′ bər) Trees that can be used for building or to make wood products. (p. 34)

time line (tīm līn) A diagram that shows when events took place. (p. 88)

time zone (tīm zōn) One of the 24 divisions of the earth used to measure time. (p. 274)

tourism (tür′ iz əm) The business of providing services to people on vacation. (p. 238)

tourist (tür′ ist) A person who travels for enjoyment. (p. 42)

transportation map (trans pər tā′ shən map) A map that shows the different ways to travel from one place to another. (p. 13)

treaty (trē′ tē) An agreement between two countries. (p. 98)

U

Underground Railroad (un′ dər ground′ rāl′ rōd) A system of secret routes that escaping slaves followed to freedom. (p. 159)

union (ūn′ yən) An organization of workers formed to improve pay and working conditions. (p. 215)

Union (ūn′ yən) The Northern states that remained part of the United States during the Civil War. (p. 167)

urban (ûr′ bən) Relating to cities and large towns. (p. 235)

V

veto (vē′ tō) To refuse to sign a bill. (p. 256)

voyageur (voi ə zhər′) French-speaking fur trappers who transported furs from the trading posts to Quebec. (p. 91)

W

weather (weth′ ər) How hot or cold and how wet or dry a place is. (p. 24)

wetland (wet′ land) A swampy area that is home to special plants and animals. (p. 288)

a cap; ā cake; ä father; är car; âr dare; ch chain; e hen; ē me; hw where; i bib; ī kite; îr pierce; ng song; o top; ō rope; ô saw; oi coin; ôr fork; ou cow; sh show; th thin; th those; u sun; ù book; ü moon; ū cute; ûr term; ə about, taken, pencil, apron, helpful; ər letter, dollar, doctor

GLOSSARY

INDEX

Page references in italic type that follow an *m* indicate maps. Those following a *p* indicate photographs, artwork, or charts.

INDEX

CREDITS

MAPS
R. R. Donnelly and Sons Company Cartographic Services

CHARTS AND GRAPHS
Tom Cardamone Associates, Inc.

ILLUSTRATION CREDITS
Anthony Accardo: p. 66; **Jo Lynn Alcorn:** p. 317; **Gill Ashby:** pp. 173-176; **Joe Boddy:** pp. 46-50; **Mike Eagle:** pp. 201-204; **Len Ebert:** pp. 184-185; **Alan Eitzen:** p. 105; **Ann Feiza:** pp. 4-5; **Joe Forte:** pp. 112, 314-315; **Howard Friedman:** pp. 26, 322; **Hank Iken:** p. 199; **Ron Jones:** pp. 144-149, 141; **Allan Kikuchi:** p. 54; **Ann Neumann:** pp. 318-319; **Hima Pamodejo:** pp. 2-3; **Tom Pohrt:** pp.73-75; **Joel Snyder:** pp. 77-80; **Gary Torrisi:** pp. 16-17; **Elizabeth Wolf:** pp. 6-7 background

PHOTOGRAPHY CREDITS
All photographs are by the Macmillan/McGraw-Hill School Division (MMSD) except as noted below.

Front Matter: 2: t. Andy Sacks for MMSD; m.l. Andy Sacks for MMSD; m. Gordon Alexander for MMSD; b. Andy Sacks for MMSD; 4-5: t. Andy Sacks, Tony Stone Images; b.m. Mitch Kezar; 4: b.l. D. E. Cox, Tony Stone Images; 5: t. David Wisse, Uniphoto; b.r. Al Messerschmidt, Folio, Inc.; 4-5: background: Terry Donnelly, Tony Stone Images; 6: b. W. Cody, West Light; 6-7: t. Environmental Research Institute of Michigan, Ann Arbor, Michigan; 7: t. Morris Best, Uniphoto; b.r. Bruce Forster, Tony Stone Images; b.l. Terry Donnelly, Tony Stone Images; **Chapter 1:** 18: Andy Sacks for MMSD. 21: l. Jack Kausch/Exhibit Museum, University of Michigan; r. James L. Amos/Photo Researchers. 22: Lee Foster/Bruce Coleman Inc. 23: Andy Sacks for MMSD. 27: l. Terry Vitaco/Nawrocki Stock Photo; m. Gabe Palmer/Stock Market; r. D. E. Cox. 34: l. Richard Gross/Stock Market; b.l. Roy Morsch/Stock Market; b.r. Paul Steel/Stock Market. **Chapter 2:** 36: Gordon Alexander for MMSD. 38: l. Dick Pietrzyk/TSW-Click Chicago; m. Mark E. Gibson/Stock Market; r. D. E. Cox. 39: l. D. E. Cox/TSW-Click Chicago; r. Messana Photos. 44: Peter Vadnai/Stock Market. 45: l. Victoria Beller-Smith; r. Kindel Furniture Co. 52: D. E. Cox. **Chapter 3:** 60: Andy Sacks for MMSD. 62: Mark E. Gibson/Stock Market. 63: Field Museum of Natural History, Chicago neg. #110160. 64: l. State Archives of Michigan; r. Field Museum of Natural History, Chicago neg. #110026. 65: Grand Valley State University. 70-71: Field Museum of Natural History, Chicago neg. #14492. 70: t. State Archives of Michigan; l. Minnesota Historical Society. 72: l. Bettmann Archive; m., r. Cranbrook Institute of Science. 80: Cranbrook Institute of Science. **Chapter 4:** 82: Andy Sacks for MMSD. 84: The Granger Collection. 85: Buffalo Bill Historical Center. 86: The State Historical Society of Wisconsin. 87: l. Collection, Haggerty Museum of Art Marquette Univ., Milwaukee, WI., © 1991 Marquette University; r. Chicago Historical Society neg. #1963.7621. 93: The Granger Collection. 94: State Archives of Michigan. 98, 101, 102: The Granger Collection. **Chapter 5:** 108: Gordon Alexander for MMSD. 110: The Granger Collection. 111: l. By Permission of the Houghton Library, Harvard University; r. Smithsonian Institution. 117: l. National Portrait Gallery, Smithsonian npg 84-177; r. Courtesy of the Burton Historical Collection of the Detroit Public Library. 122: U.S. Naval Academy, Beverley R. Robinson Collection. 124: Western Reserve Historical Society, Cleveland, OH. 125, 126: State Archives of Michigan. 127: Gary Boynton. 130: l. State Archives of Michigan; r. Bentley Historical Collection, University of Michigan. **Chapter 6:** 132: Andy Sacks for MMSD. 135: Albany Institute of History and Art. 136: Dr. Benjamin C. Wilson/Western Michigan University. 137: Courtesy of the Burton Historical Collection of the Detroit Public Library. 142: l. The Granger Collection; r. State Archives of Michigan. 143: William L. Bailey/Children's Museum, Detroit. 150: Andy Sacks for MMSD. 151: State Archives of Michigan. 152: l. From the Collection of the Mercer Museum of the Bucks County Historical Society; m. From the Collection of the Mercer Museum of the Bucks County Historical Society. 152-153: Grand Rapids Public Library. 153: State Archives of Michigan. 154: Phil Schermeister. **Chapter 7:** 156: Andy Sacks. 158: l. Sophia Smith Collection, Smith College; m. State Archives of Michigan; r. Art Work of the State of Arkansas 1905. Published by the Harney Photogravure. 159: Cincinnati Art Museum. 161: State Archives of Michigan. 162: Andy Sacks for MMSD/Courtesy of Niles Public Library. 167: The Granger Collection; r. Courtesy of the Burton Historical Collection of the Detroit Public Library. 170: l. State Archives of Michigan; m. Library of Congress; r. National Archives. 171: r. The Granger Collection; l. Bentley Historical Collection, University of Michigan. 172: t. Courtesy of the Burton Collection of the Detroit Public Library; b. Michigan Capitol Committee/Peter Glendinning. 173: Courtesy of Mrs. Florence Connerly/MMSD. 178: Michigan State University Archives & Historical Collection. 179: l. Brown Brothers; r. Courtesy of the Burton Historical Collection of the Detroit Public Library. 180, 183: The Granger Collection. **Chapter 8:** 186: Andy Sacks for MMSD. 188: l. From the Collections of Henry Ford Museum & Greenfield Village; m. Courtesy of First Publishing Corporation; r. Andy Sacks for MMSD. 191: Bentley Historical Collection, University of Michigan. 195: Courtesy of the Burton Historical Collection of the Detroit Public Library. 196: l. Grand Rapids Public Library; r. Bentley Historical Collection, University of Michigan. 198-206t.: From the Collections of Henry Ford Museum & Greenfield Village. 206: b. State Archives of Michigan. 207: l. Bettmann Archive; m.l., m.r., r. Courtesy of the Strong Museum, Rochester, NY. 208: t. Bettmann Archive; b. Pete Saloutos/Stock Market. **Chapter 9:** 210: Andy Sacks for MMSD. 212: l. Archives of Labor and Urban Affairs, Wayne State University. 213: l. Dirk Bakker; r. State Archives of Michigan. 216: Archives of Labor & Urban Affairs, Wayne State University. 217: UPI/Bettmann Newsphotos. 218: Courtesy of UAW/MMSD. 220: State Archives of Michigan. 221: Chrysler Corporation. 225: l. UPI/Bettmann Newsphotos; r. Flip Schulke/Black Star. 226: UPI/Bettmann Newsphotos. 227: r. Mayor's Office, City of Detroit; l. Michigan Dept. of State. 228: Andy Sacks for MMSD. **Chapter 10:** 231: t. Flip Schulke; b. Archives of Labor & Urban Affairs, Wayne State University. 232: t.l. Noble Proctor/Photo Researchers. 232: Robert P. Carr/Bruce Coleman. 233: Rod Planck/TSW. 234: Andy Sacks for MMSD. 236: Gordon Alexander for MMSD. 237: t. Ziggy Kaluzny/TSW; b. Courtesy of Upjohn. 238-239: Balthazar Korab. 238: l. Joseph R. Pearce/DRK Photo. 239: Andy Sacks for MMSD. 243: Courtesy of the Chelsea Standard. 244: l. Gabe Palmer/Stock Market; m. Ted Horowitz/Stock Market; r. Andy Sacks/TSW. 245: l. David R. Frazier/TSW; r. Gabe Palmer/Stock Market. 246: m. Bill Smith/Sports Illustrated; t. John Biever/Sports Illustrated. 249: l. Brad Inverson/TSW; r. TSW. 250: Susan Finch/Mr. Kiyokazu Ogura. **Chapter 11:** 252: Andy Sacks for MMSD. 255: t. Michigan Travel Bureau; b. Andy Sacks for MMSD. 257: Gary Boynton. 259: The Jewish News. 262: t. Gordon Alexander for MMSD; m. Andy Sacks for MMSD; b. Gordon Alexander for MMSD. 263: Andy Sacks for MMSD. 264: l., m. D. E. Cox; r. W. Eastep/Stock Market. 267: t. Bob Daemmrich/Uniphoto; b. Everett C. Johnson/Folio, Inc. 268: l. Duane Belanger/The Detroit News; r. Stan Barouh/Uniphoto. **Chapter 12:** 270: Gordon Alexander for MMSD. 273: Gordon Alexander for MMSD. 277: l. Barry Talesnick/Retna Ltd.; r. Conrad Collette/Shooting Star. 278: t.l. Courtesy of MCA Records; m. Pictorial Press; r. Barry Talesnick/Retna Ltd.; b.l. Bettmann Archive. 279: l. Balthazar Korab; r. Bettmann Archive. 280: Andy Sacks for MMSD. 281: Courtesy of Carl Owen. 284: l. Andy Sacks for MMSD; m. Messana Photos; r. Frank Cezus/TSW. 285: t.l. Jonathan Daniel/Allsport; t.r. UPI/Bettmann Newsphotos; b.l. Jerry Cooke/Sports Illustrated; b.r. Stephen Dunn/Allsport. 286: l. Mary Kate Denny/Photo Edit; m. Lawrence Migdale; r. Bob Daemmrich. 288: Andy Sacks for MMSD. 289: Matt Bradley. **Almanac:** 306: Andy Sacks for MMSD. 313: t.l. Michigan State University Archives & Historical Collection; t.m. William H. Gordon; t.r. William Bailey/Auto Foto; m.r. Courtesy of Chrysler/AMC; b.l. William Bailey/Auto Foto; b.r. Courtesy of Ford Motor Company. 320: t.l. Henry Mattison; t.r. UPI/Bettmann; m. Mark Sennet/Onyx. 320-321: b.r. Mark Hanauer/Onyx. 321: t.l. Michael Putland/Retna Ltd.; t.r. Ira Margolin/LGI; m.l. Reuters/Bettmann Newsphotos; m.r. Fotex/Jens Meyer/Shooting Star; b. Stephen Harvey/LGI.

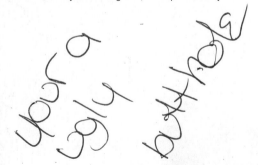